Rubens *Drawing on Italy*

SPONSORED BY

BAILLIE GIFFORD

INVESTMENT MANAGERS

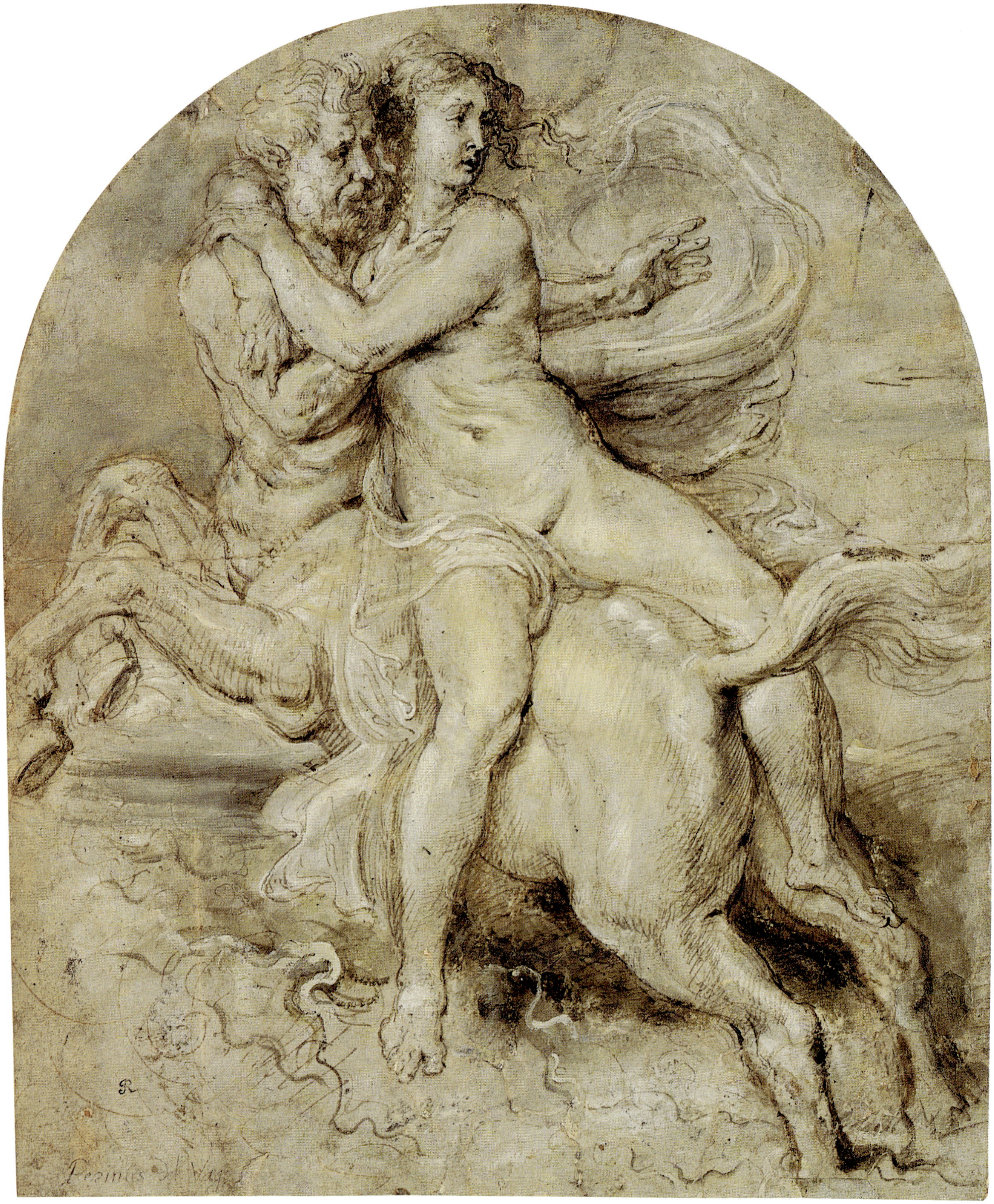

Jeremy Wood

RUBENS
DRAWING ON ITALY

National Gallery of Scotland
Edinburgh · 2002

Published by the Trustees of the National Galleries of Scotland to accompany the exhibition *Rubens Drawing on Italy* held at the National Gallery of Scotland, Edinburgh from 14 June to 1 September 2002 and the Djanogly Art Gallery, Nottingham from 20 September to 8 December 2002.

The exhibition has been organised by the National Gallery of Scotland, Edinburgh, in conjunction with the Djanogly Art Gallery, Nottingham, and with the collaboration of the British Museum, London.

ISBN 1 903278 31 7

Designed by Dalrymple
Typeset in Dante by Brian Young
Printed by Snoeck-Ducaju & Zoon, Belgium

Front cover illustration:
Anonymous Sixteenth-Century Italian Artist after Polidoro da Caravaggio, retouched by Rubens
A Man Leading a Horse [cat.no.33]
The British Museum, London

Back cover illustration:
Rubens after Michelangelo
Leda and the Swan [cat.no.8]
Stephen Mazoh, New York

Frontispiece:
Anonymous Draughtsman after Perino del Vaga, retouched by Rubens
Nessus and Deianeira [cat.no.41]
The British Museum, London

CONTENTS

SPONSOR'S FOREWORD

Baillie Gifford takes an active interest in sponsorship of the arts and has been closely associated with the National Galleries of Scotland for a number of years.

This year, we are delighted to be supporting the National Gallery of Scotland's summer exhibition, *Rubens Drawing on Italy*. This is an intriguing show which looks at the visual sources for Rubens's career in greater depth than ever before.

Over the years, we have been proud to sponsor many of the leading exhibitions which the National Galleries attracts from around the world.

Baillie Gifford also has a global reach and manages investment portfolios for clients in North America, Japan and Europe, as well as a large business in the UK. We are a private partnership employing over 400 staff and remain committed to our Scottish base.

We look forward to extending our relationship with the National Galleries of Scotland for many years to come.

SARAH WHITLEY
Partner, Baillie Gifford

FOREWORD

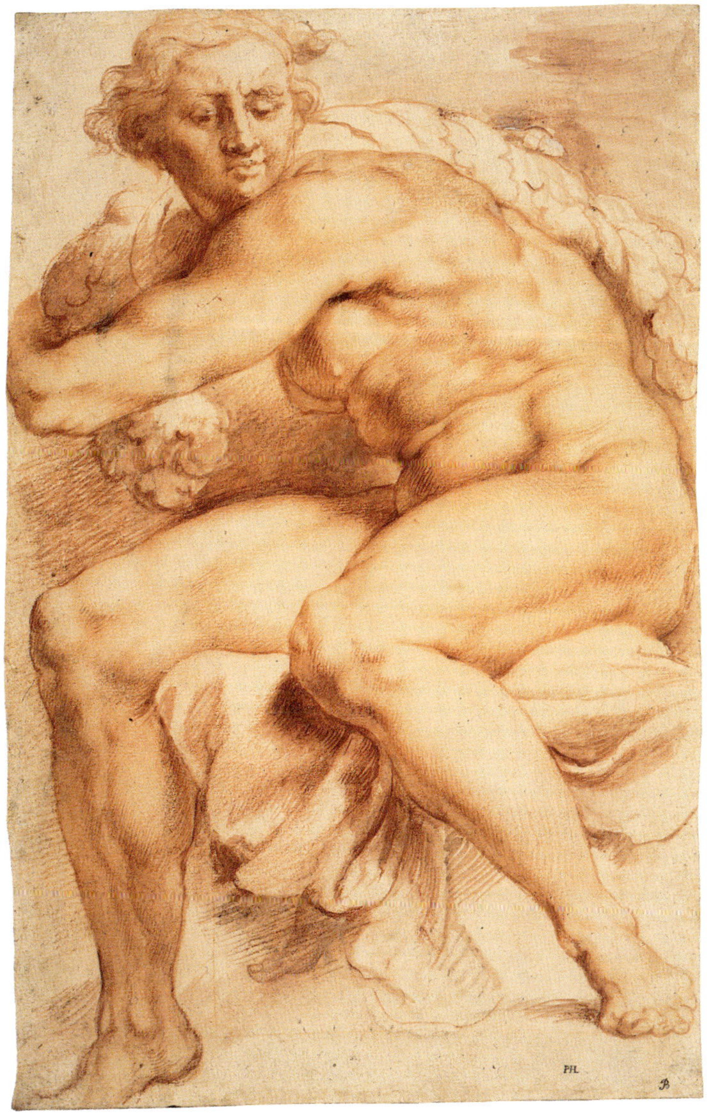

Rubens after Michelangelo
A Nude Youth Turning to the Left [cat.no.13]
The British Museum, London

Peter Paul Rubens (1577–1640) was the most learned, inventive and prolific artist of the Northern Baroque. The range of his work was prodigious, encompassing portraiture, allegory, religious painting, landscapes, and designs for ornament, tapestry, books and prints. A diplomat and scholar, his intelligent use of iconography was never rivalled. He was a *pictor doctus* – a learned artist – and had a gift for devising imagery that was perfectly matched to his patrons' aspirations, while his emotive religious works were actively intended to provoke empathy and devotion as part of the Catholic Church's Counter Reformation armoury against the onslaught of Protestantism.

Knighted twice and acquainted with most of the crowned heads of Europe (many of whom were his patrons), Rubens travelled extensively and frequently, visiting Italy, Spain, France, Britain and the Northern Netherlands. But it is his links with Italy which this exhibition celebrates, already by Rubens's time the prime destination of young ambitious artists passionate about their profession. Italy provided a museum indoors, outdoors and underground: on display were the works of classical antiquity that were being discovered and the wonders of Renaissance painting and architecture that could be repeatedly plundered for visual inspiration.

Rubens spent enormously formative and influential periods in Italy between 1600 and 1608. This exhibition, the first of its kind to be held in Britain, explores how he copied, studied and adapted the work of Italian artists, not just in his early years but throughout his life, both in painting and in drawing. Apart from making relatively faithful copies after Renaissance and later masters, Rubens also intervened on originals and copies by other artists and had no compunction in 'improving' their work, occasionally taking scissors and paste to a motif, and drawing new sections. At the core of the exhibition is a large group of drawings by Italian artists, many owned by Rubens and extensively transformed by him. The exhibits show that Rubens did not simply imitate Italian art but conducted a dialogue with it through an extensive process of reworking and adaptation. His copies attracted the attention of scholars and collectors even during his lifetime. The painted copies were never sold by him and the drawings formed part of his study collection, showing that Rubens, remarkable for his vitality, variety and invention, considered this intriguing and continuing dialogue with Italian art to be crucial to his own creativity.

Our personal guide to this fascinating 'detective' work is Jeremy Wood, lecturer in the History of Art at the University of Nottingham, whose idea this exhibition was and whose impressive scholarship and undoubted enthusiasm have brought that idea to fruition. We are enormously grateful to him for his hard work and attention to detail. We should also like to thank the Djanogly Art Gallery, Lakeside Arts Centre, University of Nottingham, for approaching us to organise the show in conjunction with them, in particular Joanne Wright, and also Neil Walker, Neil Bennison and Tracey Isgar.

The exhibition has been drawn primarily from British collections, both public and private but also some from abroad. We should sincerely like to thank all those who have so kindly lent to the show, and also to add our appreciation to those mentioned by Jeremy Wood in his acknowledgements. A couple of lenders stand out for special mention for the sheer scale of their generosity. The Department of Prints and Drawings at the British Museum has lent so many prime works to both venues that this exhibition can very truly be said to be organised with its collaboration and we are most grateful to Antony Griffiths and Martin Royalton-Kisch for making this possible. We are also hugely indebted to the département des Arts graphiques, Musée du Louvre, Paris, for their kindness in lending, and extend our thanks to Françoise Viatte and Catherine Loisel for all their help.

Any such show depends on the dedication and expertise of our own staff in all departments at the National Galleries of Scotland. Our thanks go to Janis Adams who, with the help of Christine Thompson, has so efficiently produced the catalogue, elegantly designed by Robert Dalrymple. We should also like to thank colleagues in the Conservation Department and those working in the Registrar's Department, in particular the registrar for exhibitions, Agnes Valenčak-Krüger as well as our fine art technicians who installed the show and colleagues in the Development and Marketing Departments. We are also grateful to William Anderson and Dallas Arnold for their help in administration of the exhibition at the National Gallery of Scotland.

For financial support, the Gallery is indebted to the beneficence of our sponsors, once again, the investment management firm Baillie Gifford whose primary offices are in Edinburgh. Having previously sponsored a number of shows at our sister institution the Scottish National Portrait Gallery, they have recently funded an exhibition a year at the National Gallery of Scotland: *Turner and Scott* (1999–2000), *Andrew Geddes* (2001) and this show, *Rubens Drawing on Italy*. Such stalwart support is heart-warming – we are most grateful, and, of course, hope it may long continue.

MICHAEL CLARKE
Acting Director-General, National Galleries of Scotland

JULIA LLOYD WILLIAMS
Acting Director, National Gallery of Scotland

LENDERS TO THE EXHIBITION

Cambridge, Fitzwilliam Museum, cat.no.61

Chatsworth, Devonshire Collection, cat.nos.7, 58, 64, 73

The Right Hon. the Earl of Derby, cat.no.53

Knole, The National Trust, cat.no.54

Liverpool, Walker Art Gallery, cat.nos.11, 70

London, British Museum, cat.nos.3, 4, 5, 6, 12, 13, 17, 18, 22, 26, 29, 33, 37, 38, 39, 40, 41, 43, 49, 50, 55, 56, 57, 60, 71, 74

London, The Courtauld Institute Gallery, cat.nos.47, 51

London, Victoria and Albert Museum, cat.nos. 68, 76

Stephen Mazoh, cat.no.8

Oxford, Ashmolean Museum, cat.no.28

Oxford, Christ Church, cat.nos.24, 67

Paris, Département des Arts graphiques, Musée du Louvre, cat.nos.1, 2, 9, 10, 15, 16, 20, 21, 23, 25, 27, 30, 31, 34, 35, 42, 44, 45, 46, 63, 65, 72, 75

Paris, Collection Frits Lugt, Institut Néerlandais, cat.nos.14, 59

Collection of the Earl of Pembroke, cat.no.66

Lenders who prefer to remain anonymous, cat.nos.32, 36, 48

ACKNOWLEDGEMENTS

This exhibition has been made possible through the generosity of many lenders, in particular, the Louvre and the British Museum, who possess the largest surviving groups of drawings related to Rubens's study of Italian art. My warm thanks go to Françoise Viatte, conservateur général of the département des Arts graphiques, and Antony Griffiths, Keeper in the Department of Prints and Drawings, who have been prepared to lend exceptionally large groups of works from the collections in their care. In France, the basis for all study of Rubens's drawings after Italian models was laid in the late seventeenth century by Everhard Jabach. No fewer than thirteen sheets from his first collection (bought by Louis XIV in 1671) are present in this exhibition. In Britain, a number of eighteenth- and nineteenth- century connoisseurs, including Jonathan Richardson and Sir Thomas Lawrence, studied the Italian drawings which Rubens owned and retouched. Their expertise fed into the great public collections from which this exhibition is largely drawn, and all subsequent understanding of the material has been shaped by their labours.

Despite this pioneering British interest in Rubens's study of Italian art, no exhibition on the topic has been held here before now. Further afield in Cologne, Justus Müller Hofstede organised an important survey devoted to Rubens's Italian period (*Rubens in Italien*, 1977), and, in Canberra, David Jaffé brought together a stimulating mix of Italian sixteenth-century paintings and works by the Flemish artist (*Rubens and the Italian Renaissance*, 1992). Rubens's copies after Titian's *Bacchanals* were shown together in Madrid and Stockholm in 1987, and his copy of Titian's *Rape of Europa* was put alongside the original at the Isabella Stewart Gardner Museum, Boston in 1998. But the present exhibition – although overlapping these earlier shows – is different in focus from them, not least because it combines copies entirely from Rubens's hand with drawings by Italian artists that he retouched.

My work on this topic began longer ago than I care to recall when I was asked by the Board of the Nationaal Centrum voor de Plastische Kunsten van de 16de en de 17de eeuw in Antwerp to write Volume xxv, part 2, of the *Corpus Rubenianum Ludwig Burchard* devoted to Rubens's adaptations and copies from Italian art. Arnout Balis, my patient editor, has been a model of encouragement over the years. In 2001/2 I was awarded research leave by the Arts and Humanities Research Board to write up the Corpus volume, and this enabled me to complete a large part of the manuscript, at the same time providing a basis for the more abbreviated entries to be found in the present catalogue.

Over the years I have incurred a great debt to three friends, Kristin Belkin, Anne-Marie Logan, and Elizabeth McGrath who have generously shared their understanding of Rubens's work with me. At the Louvre I have benefited from stimulating discussions with Varena Forcione, Catherine Loisel Legrand, Catherine Monbeig Goguel and Bernadette Py. At the British Museum, Hugo Chapman and Martin Royalton-Kisch have been invariably generous with their time and help. Clare Tilbury read a draft of the introduction and her comments did much to improve it, although its faults remain my own. Invaluable help with a number of loans has been provided by Amanda Askari, Christopher Baker, Màrìa van Berge-Gerbaud, Brenda Brod, Christopher Brown, Peter Day, Ivan Gaskell, Cécile Kruyfhooft, Stephen Mazoh, John Murdoch, Charles Noble, Duncan Robinson, and Julian Treuherz. Many other people have given me information, ideas, corrections, and the occasional valuable hint, among them Ulrich Haussmann, Julius Held, Nico Van Hout, Charles Hope, David Howarth, David Jaffé, Marianne Joannides, Paul Joannides, Jo Kirby, Alastair Laing, Gregory Martin, Gabriele Neher, Clare Robertson, Gregory Rubinstein, Richard Schofield, David Scrase, Donatella Sparti, Ernst Vegelin van Claerbergen, Hans Vlieghe, Catherine Whistler, Lucy Whitaker, Zahira Veliz, and Alejandro Vergara. My apologies to many others who should also be listed but have not been forgotten.

It has been my good fortune that the idea for this exhibition was received enthusiastically by Michael Clarke, Director of the National Gallery of Scotland and Joanne Wright, Director of the Djanogly Art Gallery at the University of Nottingham. My greatest debt, however, has been to Julia Lloyd Williams, Curator of Dutch and Flemish Art at Edinburgh, who has been unfailingly supportive throughout and with whom it has been a pleasure to work. Much of the administration of this exhibition has fallen to the Registrar's Department in Edinburgh, and, in particular, into the capable hands of Agnes Valenčak-Krüger. Neil Walker, Exhibitions Officer at Nottingham, has worked hard to reinvent the exhibition in its second venue. I owe a very large debt to these and many other colleagues in both institutions and hope that everyone involved will think the results worthwhile.

JEREMY WOOD

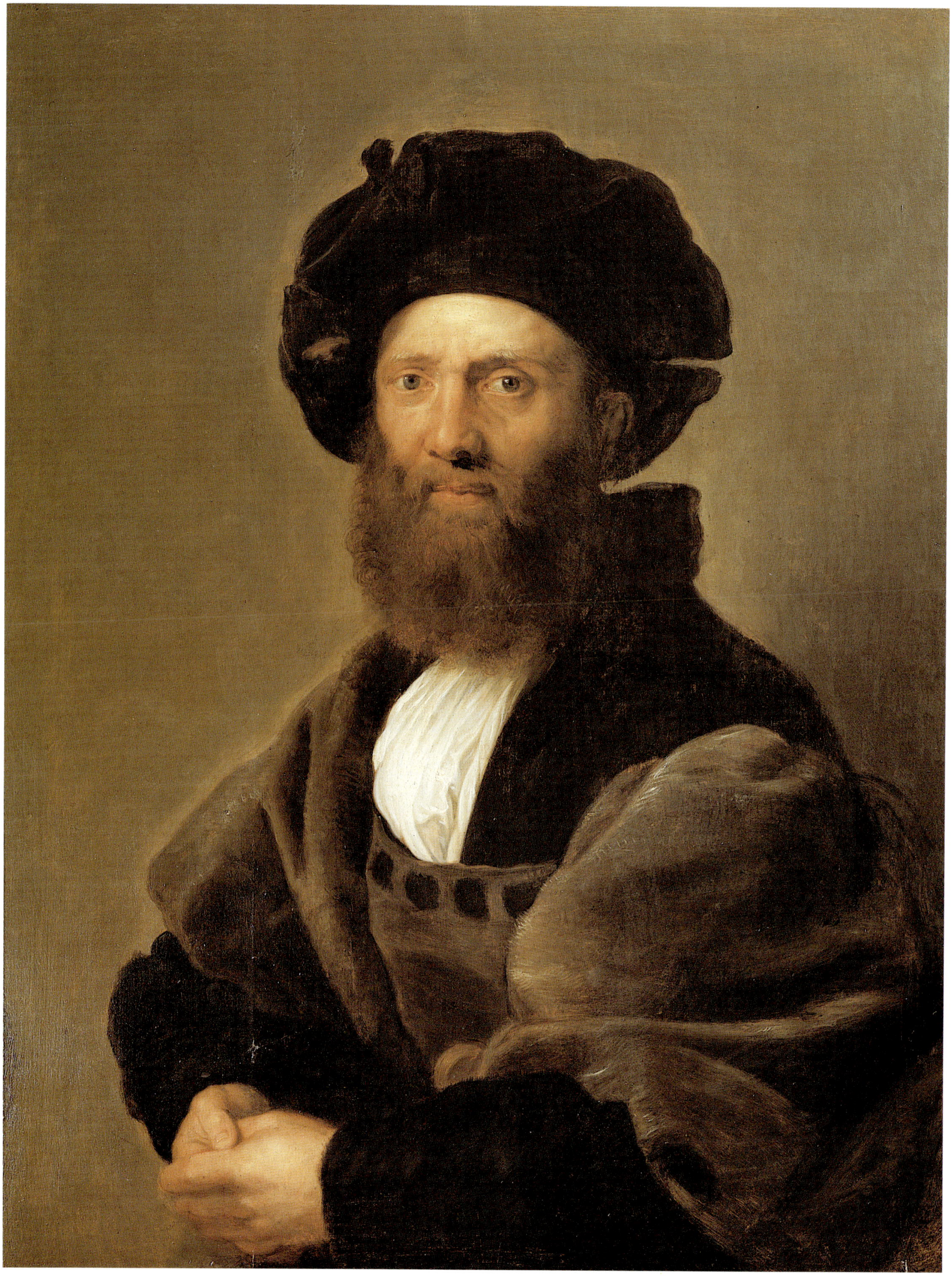

RUBENS AND ITALIAN ART

Rubens has sometimes been called an Italian artist, particularly by Italophiles,[1] and it was Giovanni Baglione, author of the first life of the artist to appear in print (1642), who said that he had adopted 'a good Italian style'.[2] It is hard to think of an assertion that could be more irritating to Rubens's fellow countrymen, since, despite spending eight years in Italy, he decided to return to the southern Netherlands in 1608 in the full knowledge that he could have pursued a successful career in Rome, had he so chosen. Nevertheless, there is something about Rubens's cosmopolitanism (which included a preference for writing in Italian), his regular travels abroad, and his absorbtion in the literature of classical antiquity, that point to an impatience with any restriction on his artistic or intellectual life. This exhibition brings together a mass of material that seems to confirm Rubens's Italianism, but it needs to be remembered that he never repudiated his Netherlandish background and that he also made copies and adaptations from northern art throughout his life.

There were two main areas in the art of the past that interested Rubens: the art of antiquity and that of the European sixteenth century. When studying the former, particularly in Rome, he did not think much of the available drawn and engraved reproductions, preferring to make copies for himself. But, when dealing with more recent art, he adopted a different approach. It is the argument of this exhibition that Rubens bought quantities of sixteenth-century Italian drawings which he took to Antwerp, and that, during the remainder of his life, he returned to this material from time to time and retouched individual sheets, sometimes very extensively. This urge to rework was very different from the business of making a direct copy because it involved improvisation and a degree of distance from the original. Indeed, his approach to these drawings amounted to destroying another artist's handiwork. The literature on Rubens's attitude to Italian art has tended to make him appear subservient, fawning with admiration over a canon of excellence,[3] but the evidence suggests something closer to a sense of personal competition, which is absent from his study of the art of antiquity.

According to Giovanni Pietro Bellori, the seventeenth-century critic and historian, Rubens carried 'good Venetian colour' back to Antwerp,[4] and most of the artist's early critics and biographers described him as more of a Venetian than Flemish artist.[5] Rubens was certainly influenced by the workshop practice of Titian (*c.*1490–1576) and Jacopo Tintoretto (1518–1594), but he never used canvas texture to the extent that they did, and he had no taste for allowing colour to remain visible in the grain of the canvas so as to be modified by what is brushed across it. As has often been observed, Rubens treated the canvas as a smooth surface rather than a rough one and remained at heart a panel painter in the northern tradition.

Opposite
Rubens after Raphael
Portrait of Baldassare Castiglione
The Courtauld Institute Gallery, London

RUBENS'S ITINERARY IN ITALY AND SPAIN, 1600–8

There was nothing unusual about Rubens's decision to travel to Italy in 1600. For the previous hundred years innumerable artists from the Netherlands had made this journey. But what they wanted from this experience, and the use they made of it, varied considerably. A great deal depended on the specialism of the individual. For example, a landscape painter would travel knowing that he could offer something different from his Italian rivals, and might not change his work much whilst abroad. By comparison, painters of subjects from history and literature found themselves up against stiff competition, but knew that what they could learn in Italy would stand them in good stead for the rest of their career. Rubens fits into the second category, but he was unusual as he obtained commissions to paint altarpieces in Italian churches, particularly in Rome where the competition could not have been more tough.

Rubens's understanding of Italian art was transformed during the years that he spent in Italy. Although much is known about his movements at this time, his visits to picture collections are less well documented, and, unlike Anthony van Dyck (1599–1641), he left no sketchbook recording what he saw as he moved from place to place. It has been assumed that many drawings after Italian works were made directly by Rubens during his travels, but if, as I think, these are mostly copies by other artists that he simply retouched, they cannot be used as evidence that he had seen the originals. Indeed, the inaccessibility of a particular work could be the reason why he wanted a copy of it in the first place. However, his period as court artist in Mantua certainly meant that he knew the work of Andrea Mantegna (1430?–1506), Giulio Romano (*c.*1499–1546), Antonio da Correggio (*c.*1490–1534), and Titian at first hand, and his position as a servant of the Gonzaga must have helped open doors elsewhere.

Rubens left Antwerp to travel to Italy on 9 May 1600. His nephew wrote later that he went first to Venice.[6] To my mind no copies entirely by Rubens survive from this visit, although, as will be shown later, he stopped and made some in Treviso. Within a year of arriving in Italy, Rubens entered the service of Duke Vincenzo I Gonzaga (1562–1612) of Mantua. Exactly when this happened is unknown,[7] and, although it may have occurred before the end of 1600,[8] there is no firm evidence to confirm it before 1601. At any rate, once Rubens had secured a job in Mantua he did not stay there long. He had obtained an income and social status, but knew that he needed to travel further afield. In late July 1601, Rubens persuaded his employer to let him go to Rome, where he arrived with a letter of introduction to Cardinal Montalto, nephew of Pope Sixtus V.[9] He was back in Mantua before July 1602 when he made a brief visit to Verona in order to meet his brother.[10]

Rubens's time in Italy was split into two separate periods by a visit to Spain between 1603 and 1604. Duke Vincenzo decided to send some costly presents to Philip III (1578–1621) and Francisco Sandoval y Rojas, Duke of Lerma (1552–1625), the powerful royal favourite, and Rubens was chosen to deliver them, which suggests he had risen faster through the ranks as a courtier than as a painter. The visit did not interrupt Rubens's studies because it gave him a glimpse of the many Italian pictures that had been sent to Spain during the sixteenth century on the orders of Charles V and Philip II. Indeed, Venetian secular art was then (as now) better represented in Madrid than in Venice itself. As early as 24 May 1603, Rubens wrote to Annibale Chieppio, Duke Vincenzo's secretary of state, about the 'many splendid works of Titian, of Raphael and others, which have astonished me, both by their quality and quantity, in the king's palace, in the Escorial, and elsewhere'.[11] Since this was written only eleven days after arriving in Valladolid, Rubens must have been fast on his feet. At this point he would have seen a number of portraits and religious works by Titian, but it is unlikely that he gained access to the king's private apartments in the Alcázar at Madrid where the mythological paintings were kept,[12] and this was not achieved until his second visit to Madrid in 1628–9.[13]

The exact date of Rubens departure from Spain and return to Italy is unknown, but it is usually placed early in 1604.[14] On 2 June Rubens was documented as receiving his court salary at Mantua, backdated to 24 May,[15] which suggests that he sailed from Spain in March. Back in Italy, Rubens returned to Mantua where, among other duties, he was documented in 1605 painting two copies for presentation to the Emperor Rudolf II in Prague after works by Correggio in the ducal collection.[16]

In 1606 Rubens went back to Rome from where he wrote to Chieppio that he had 'devoted all summer to the study of art',[17] and this city became his base until departing for Antwerp on 28 October 1608. He would never return (although he wanted to do so in 1629),[18] but, during the eight years of his travels in Italy and Spain, Rubens had not only given himself a visual education but had assembled a 'paper museum' to take home with him. This contained copies of works he had seen, and preparatory studies by earlier artists and records of works that had been lost or exported from Italy, ranging in date from the 1480s to the time of his visit.

RUBENS AND LATE FIFTEENTH-CENTURY ITALIAN ART

Most artists of Rubens's generation were entirely indifferent to Italian art of the fifteenth century, but Rubens was not. One of the earliest Italian drawings which he obtained and retouched (or at least one of the earliest that can be dated with some confidence) is a copy after Giovanni Bellini's *Saints Benedict and Mark* [fig.1, cat.no.3] from the *Frari Triptych*, painted in 1488, and this is among the first drawings catalogued in the exhibition. It must be admitted though that Rubens's interest in Quattrocento art was limited and he may have agreed with Vasari that it looked dry, hard, and sharp,[19] something which could also explain his aversion to the work of Albrecht Dürer.

The exceptions are Rubens's copies and adaptations based on Andrea Mantegna's *Triumphs of Caesar*, now at Hampton Court, the great series of canvases painted for Francesco Gonzaga in the late 1480s and completed in the 1490s.[20] Rubens not only studied these works when he was in Mantua, but returned to their compositions in the 1620s when he painted a free version incorporating two of them [see fig.11], discussed below, and made the drawing of *Three Men with Staves* [cat.no.2]. If there is any coherance in Rubens's occasional study of the Quattrocento it is that he chose work by artists with an evident response to classical antiquity.

RUBENS AND SIXTEENTH-CENTURY ITALIAN ART

The largest numbers of drawn copies by Rubens, or retouched by him, are after the work of Michelangelo (1475–1564), Raphael (1483–1520), Giulio Romano, and Polidoro da Caravaggio (1490/1500–1543?), which suggests a bias towards central Italian art of the first half of the sixteenth century. There is less evidence of Rubens's study of Leonardo (1452–1519) but *The Battle of Anghiari* [represented here by Gerard Edelinck's engraving after Rubens's copy, cat.no.4] had a lasting influence on his battles and hunts, and the impact of this composition was obvious, soon after arriving in Italy, in one of his most important early drawings, a large and ambitious composition showing warriors fighting fiercely for possession of a standard [cat.no.5].

By comparison, he possessed very few drawings after Venetian pictures or by Venetian artists (which makes his ownership of a sheet by Domenico Campagnola [fig.2, cat.no.56] all the more unusual and interesting). This lacuna was counter-balanced by the large number of full-sized painted copies he made from the work of Titian, which will be discussed later in this essay. Perhaps surprisingly, the majority of these recorded portraits, a field which Rubens generally avoided in his own work, unless painting friends or the sort of people who could not be refused. For Rubens, it seemed there was little point attempting to reproduce the colour and texture of Venetian art in anything other than pigment on canvas.

Fig.1 · Anonymous Fifteenth-Century Draughtsman after Giovanni Bellini, retouched by Rubens
Saints Benedict and Mark [cat.no.3]
The British Museum, London

Fig.2 *opposite* · Domenico Campagnola, retouched by Rubens
The Assumption of the Virgin [cat.no.56]
The British Museum, London

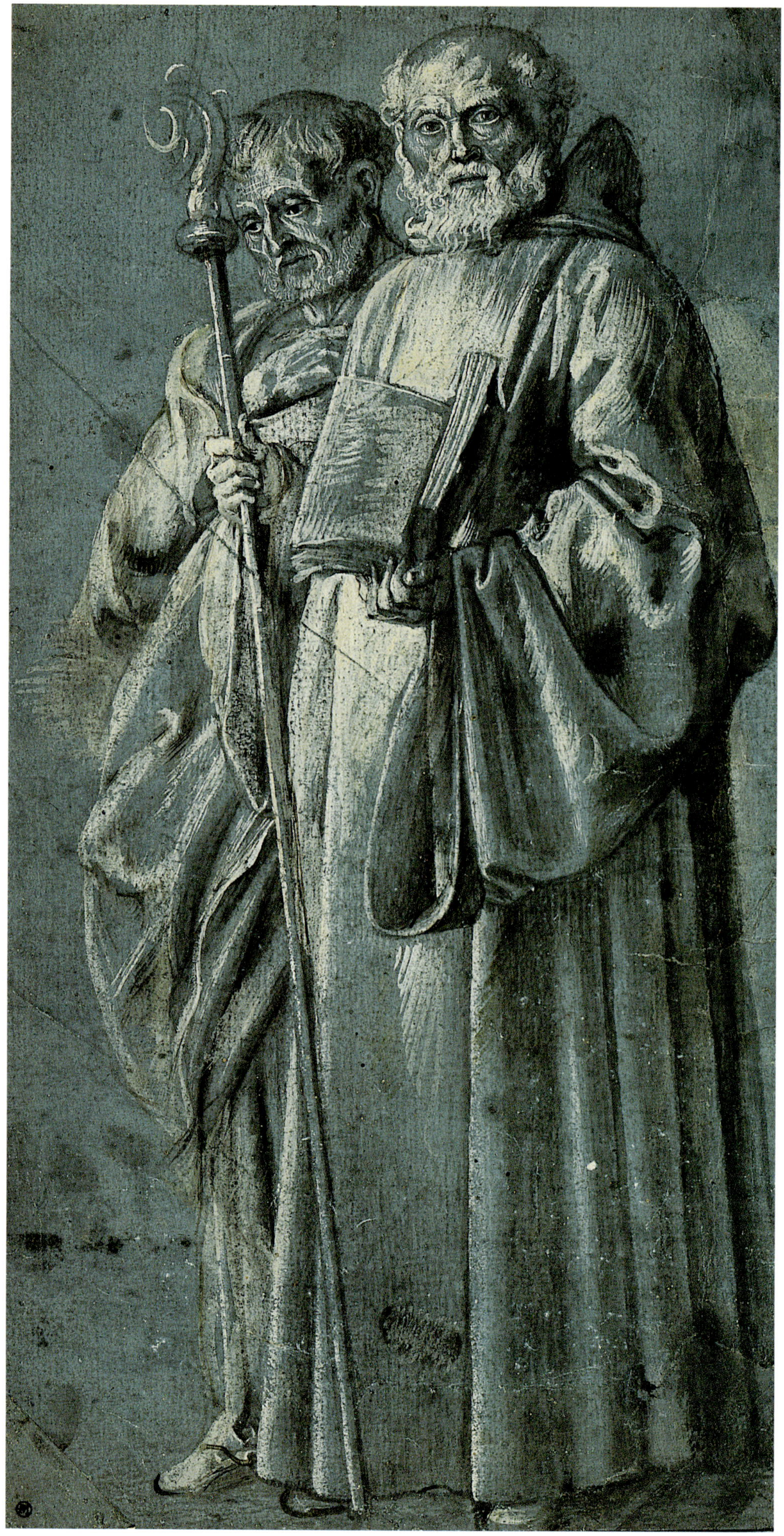

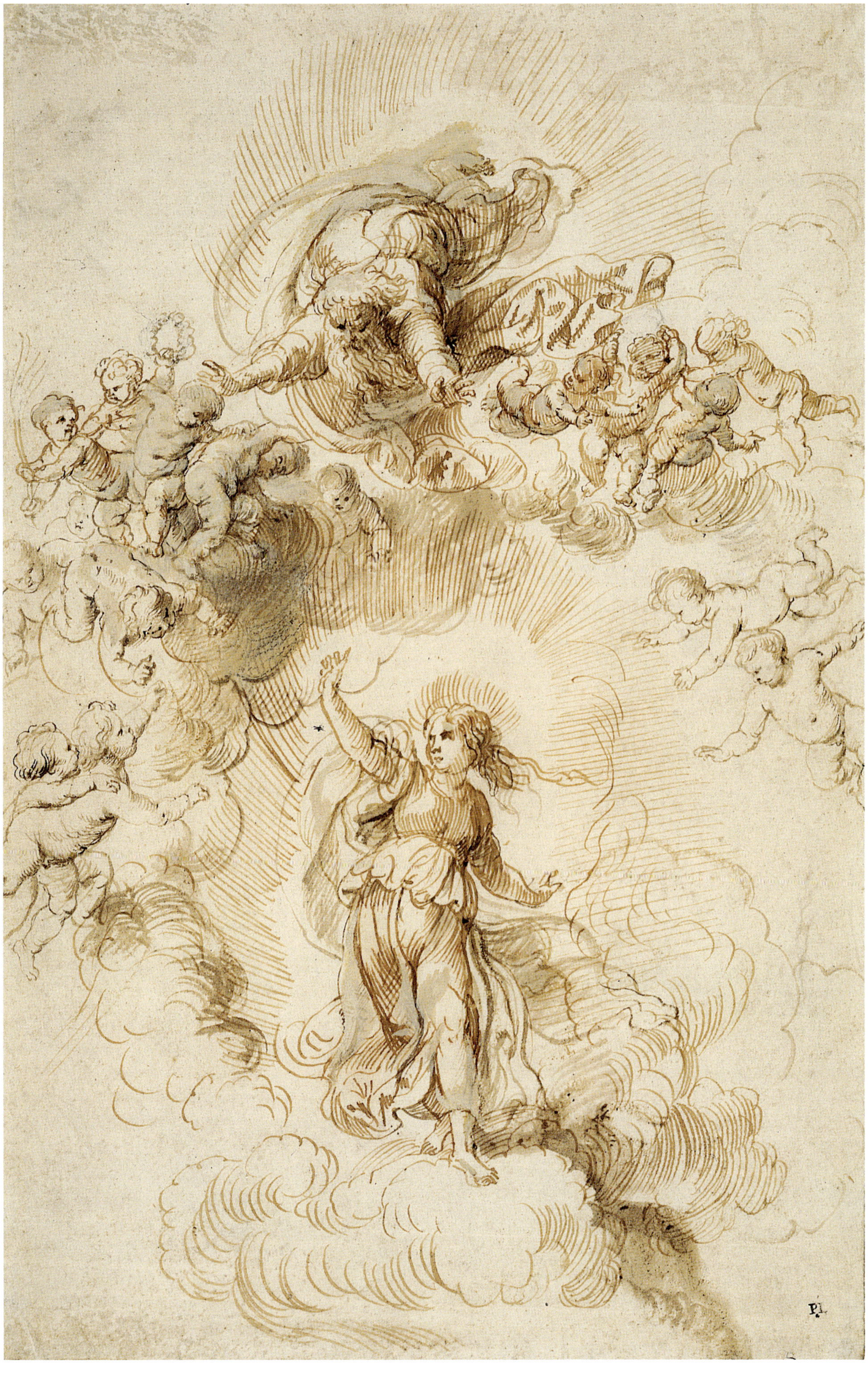

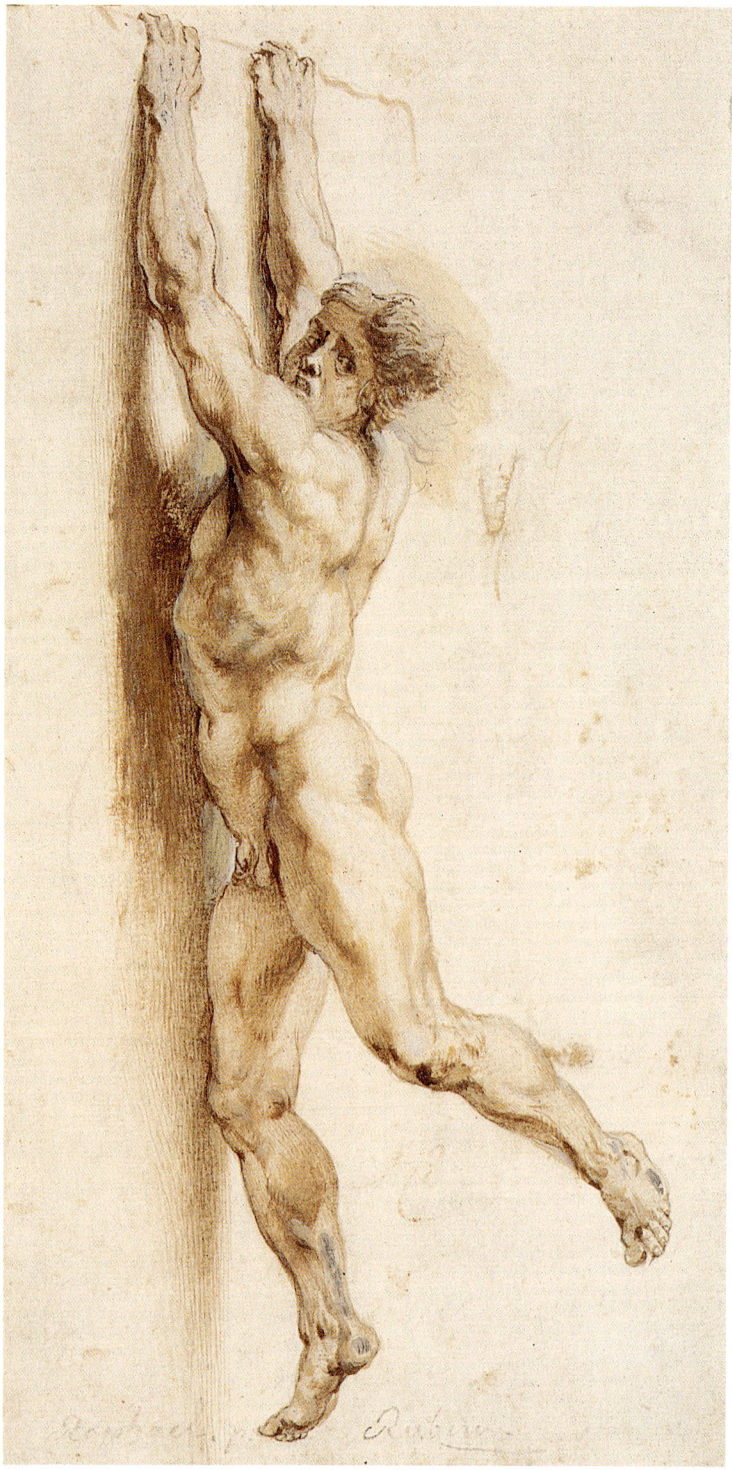

Fig.3 · Anonymous Sixteenth-Century Draughtsman after Raphael, retouched by Rubens *A Naked Man Clinging to a Wall* [cat.no.22]

The British Museum, London

Rubens's interest in Michelangelo's work was stimulated by his visit to the Sistine Chapel soon after arriving in Rome in 1601 when he made eight drawings after the prophets and sibyls on the ceiling [see cat.nos.9, 10] and several more after the *Last Judgement* on the altar wall. In this Rubens was out of step with many contemporary artists in Rome, who, whatever their stylistic allegiance, tended to view Michelangelo's work with caution and even distaste, a shift in taste that became increasingly obvious as the century progressed.

Rubens owned a diverse group of drawings after Raphael, including a number recording individual figures or small groups taken from larger works, rather than complete compositions. One outstanding example is an early copy from Raphael's studio, retouched by Rubens, which depicts *A Naked Man Clinging to a Wall* [fig.3, cat.no.22], one of the figures in the famous fresco of the *Fire in the Borgo* from the Stanza dell'Incendio in the Vatican. Perhaps surprisingly, the frescoes in the Stanze were less absorbing to Rubens than Raphael's designs for the Acts of the Apostles. Despite what is usually said, he probably knew these better from the tapestries in the Sistine Chapel than from the cartoons because the latter (which he may have seen in Genoa) had been cut into strips to help the weavers.

Rubens bought quantities of drawings after Giulio Romano's designs, probably from his studio in Mantua. The largest subgroups were twenty-one large copies (which have been very little studied), now in the Louvre,[21] after the triumph of a Roman emperor from the Sala degli Stucchi at Palazzo Te in Mantua, and three after the small cartoons (known as the *petits patrons*) for the great series of tapestries on the life of Scipio Africanus that were woven for François I of France. The most brilliantly and extensively retouched sheet from the latter group, depicts *Scipio Welcomed Outside the Gates of Rome* [fig.4, cat.no.36]. Rubens also owned red chalk counterproofs from at least two of the remaining compositions in this series, which appear to have been retouched in his studio at a later date [see cat.no.39]. Although Rubens studied a range of Giulio's designs, these two groups suggest a parallel with Mantegna's similarly imperial *Triumphs*, which had also been made in Mantua. Aretino's famous (and untranslatable) characterisation of Giulio's work as *anticamente moderni e modernamente antichi* could as well be applied to Rubens.[22]

Rubens was also interested in the work of another Raphael pupil, Polidoro da Caravaggio, but, rather than buying drawings from his studio, he had to make do with the work of journeyman copyists dating from the mid-sixteenth century, when reproductions were virtually mass-produced after the much-admired façades that Polidoro had decorated in Rome during the 1520s. However, Rubens did obtain an original drawing by Polidoro, a Saint Paul [cat.no.27], which he also retouched. Of all Polidoro's palace façades, the one painted for Giovanni Antonio Milesi was perhaps the most admired, and Rubens owned and retouched no fewer than nine drawings after it, five of which are present in this exhibition [cat.nos.30–4], among them *The Castration of Uranus by Cronus* [fig.5, cat.no.32] from the frieze between the first and second floors. Rubens's collecting and reworking of this material reflected the taste of his time since Polidoro's reputation remained very high during the seventeenth century.

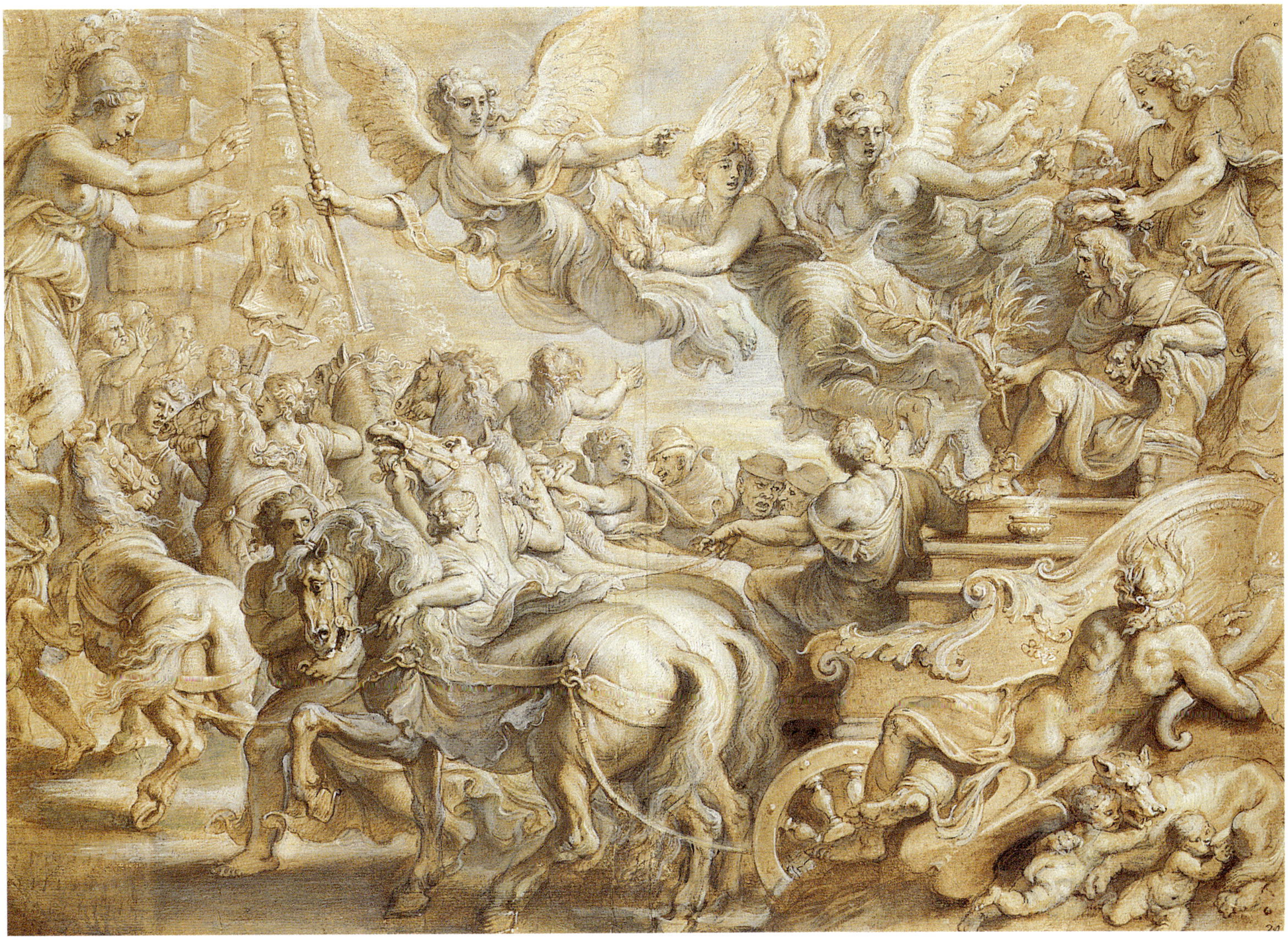

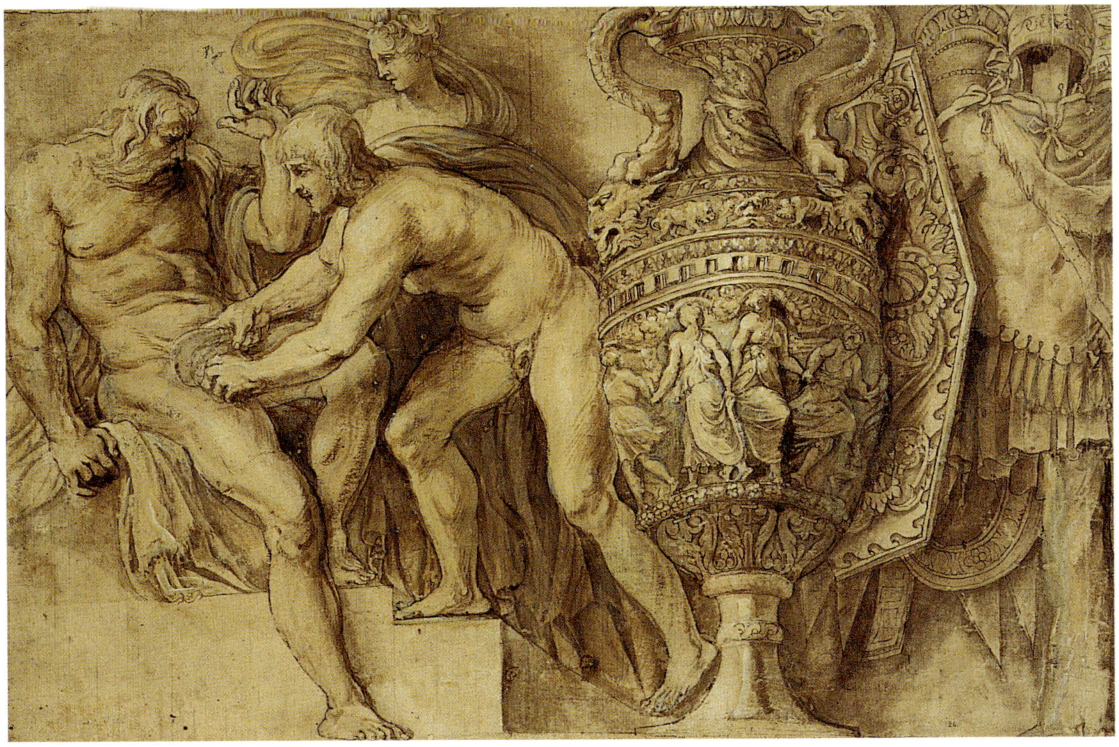

Fig.4 · Rubens
after Giulio Romano
The Life of Scipio Africanus: Scipio Welcomed Outside the Gates of Rome [cat.no.36]
Private Collection

Fig.5 · Anonymous Sixteenth-Century Draughtsman after Polidoro da Caravaggio, retouched by Rubens
The Castration of Uranus by Cronus [cat.no.32]
Private Collection

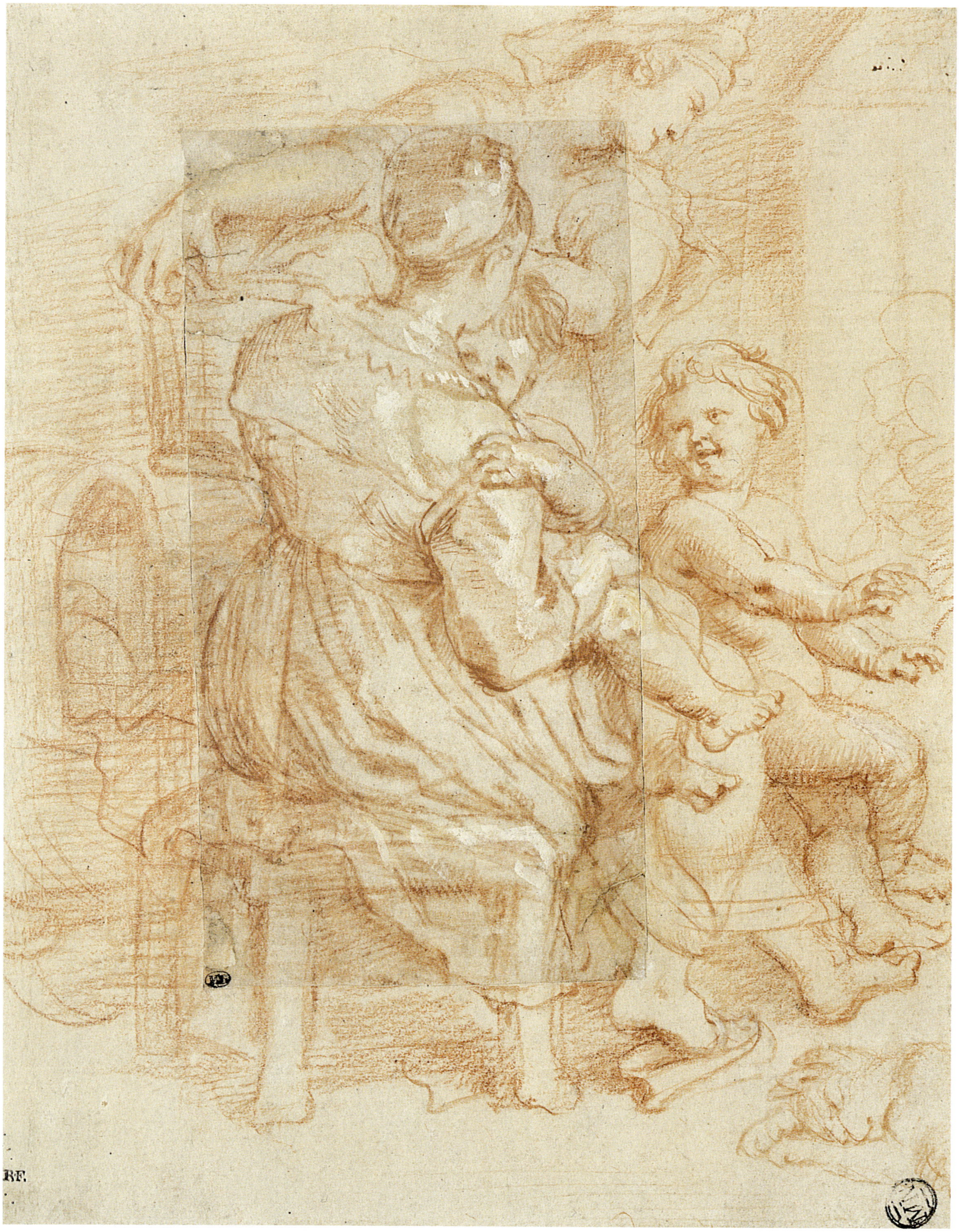

In February 1607 Rubens recommended the purchase of Caravaggio's *Death of the Virgin*, now in the Louvre, Paris, to Duke Vincenzo.[23] It was perhaps his most generous acknowledgement of a living artist's work. Among other contemporaries, he probably met the very elderly Federico Zuccaro (1540/41–1609) in Rome in 1602 or Mantua in 1605, and obtained some drawings that dated from earlier in Federico's career [see cat.nos.67, 68, 70]. He also knew something of another artist of mature years, Federico Barocci (1535?–1612), whose work was to be seen near that of Rubens in the Chiesa Nuova in Rome, and whose significance for his working methods will be discussed later. By contrast, when Rubens was in Spain, he dismissed the work of his contemporaries there (both native-born and Italians in exile) as showing 'incredible incompetence and carelessness', adding 'God preserve me from resembling them in any way'.[24] But Rubens was not that keen on the work of modern artists in Italy either, whom he may reasonably have viewed as rivals unless they specialised in fresco, like Federico Zuccaro. The mass of visual evidence suggests he kept his eyes firmly fixed on the example of the early sixteenth century.

The exception was Annibale Carracci (1560–1609). Rubens's knowledge of his work can be studied from a fragmentary sheet by this artist which Rubens enlarged into an intimate and tender family group at a fireside [fig.6, cat.no.75], as well as the only drawing that documents his knowledge of any of Annibale's Roman works, which is a copy after a section of the vault in the Galleria Farnese [cat.no.76]. But, perhaps surprisingly, the latter was not made by Rubens from the original when in Rome but is a pedestrian copy by another artist which he reworked vigorously in the 1630s. At times Rubens may have been less well informed than might be expected. For example, he owned three red chalk figure studies that Annibale had made when in Bologna before he travelled to Rome [cat.nos.71, 72, 73], but all were incorrectly inscribed by Rubens as the work of the early sixteenth-century artist Antonio da Correggio,[25] even though he almost certainly met Annibale when in Rome.

Fig.6 · Annibale Carracci, retouched by Rubens
A Woman with Two Children in Front of the Fire, Accompanied by a Woman Carrying a Basket
[cat.no.75]
Département des Arts graphiques,
Musée du Louvre, Paris

THE PAINTED COPIES

Rubens differed from his contemporaries as he made painted copies on the same size as the originals at almost every stage of his career, even though this was normally something that an artist would only do when at the beginning of his training. It is all the more surprising because Rubens was a shrewd businessman who did not waste his time and energies unnecessarily; he was used to delegating a great deal of work to his assistants (who included many proficient copyists), and the painted replicas were not made for sale, but were almost invariably kept in his own collection. In the past there have been differences of opinion over the attribution and dating of both the painted and drawn copies.[26] This makes it crucial to establish a secure chronology within which to place the more controversial works.

It seems that Rubens started making large painted adaptations from Italian art before he left Antwerp for Italy, but, for obvious reasons, he had to use intermediary copies as models, not the originals. His earliest efforts were not helped by being painted on panel which provided an un-Italian hardness of surface. These pre-1600 copies are not documented in any way, so their attribution is something of an act of faith. They are also different from most of Rubens's later painted copies because they were made on a larger scale than the models. The most plausible attribution is a version of Michelangelo's lost *Leda and the Swan*, now in the Gemäldegalerie, Dresden, which is represented in this exhibition by a second, smaller, but almost certainly autograph version [cat.no.8 and back cover].

When Rubens reached Italy he switched to painting on canvas and started making full-size facsimiles of works that interested him. In my opinion, the earliest surviving example is a copy in the Kunsthistorisches Museum, Vienna, after Titian's *Isabella d'Este, in Red* [fig.7],[27] the original of which was then in Mantua but is now lost. The copy looks like the work of a Flemish artist and has an exaggerated attention to surface at the expense of the volume and texture found in Titian's portraits. The relative tightness of this copy suggests it was painted in 1600–1, soon after Rubens's arrival in Italy, because it does not have the confident paint handling found in his work after 1603, which he learned from Tintoretto as much as from Titian.

The two copies which can be dated to Rubens's first visit to Spain are included in this exhibition [cat.nos.47, 48]. Rubens usually preferred to make a complete record of a work which interested him, but, in one case, he copied only the head from Titian's *Charles V on Horseback*, then hanging in the Madrid Alcázar, although he did so on the same scale as the original. His record of Titian's *Charles V in Armour with a Drawn Sword* [fig.8] was not made in Madrid – as usually assumed – but at the fortress of Simancas, conveniently near Valladolid. It has been assumed that Rubens was bowled over by the splendour of these Habsburg portraits, but he may have been just as interested in them as likenesses of famous figures from history, which he guessed – quite rightly as it transpired – could be turned to profitable use in his own work.

The painted copies were usually the product of his travels, made so that he could take home a record of a work that was only briefly available to him, and, as a result, he made fewer copies after he had returned to Antwerp. An exception is the *Cupid Shaping*

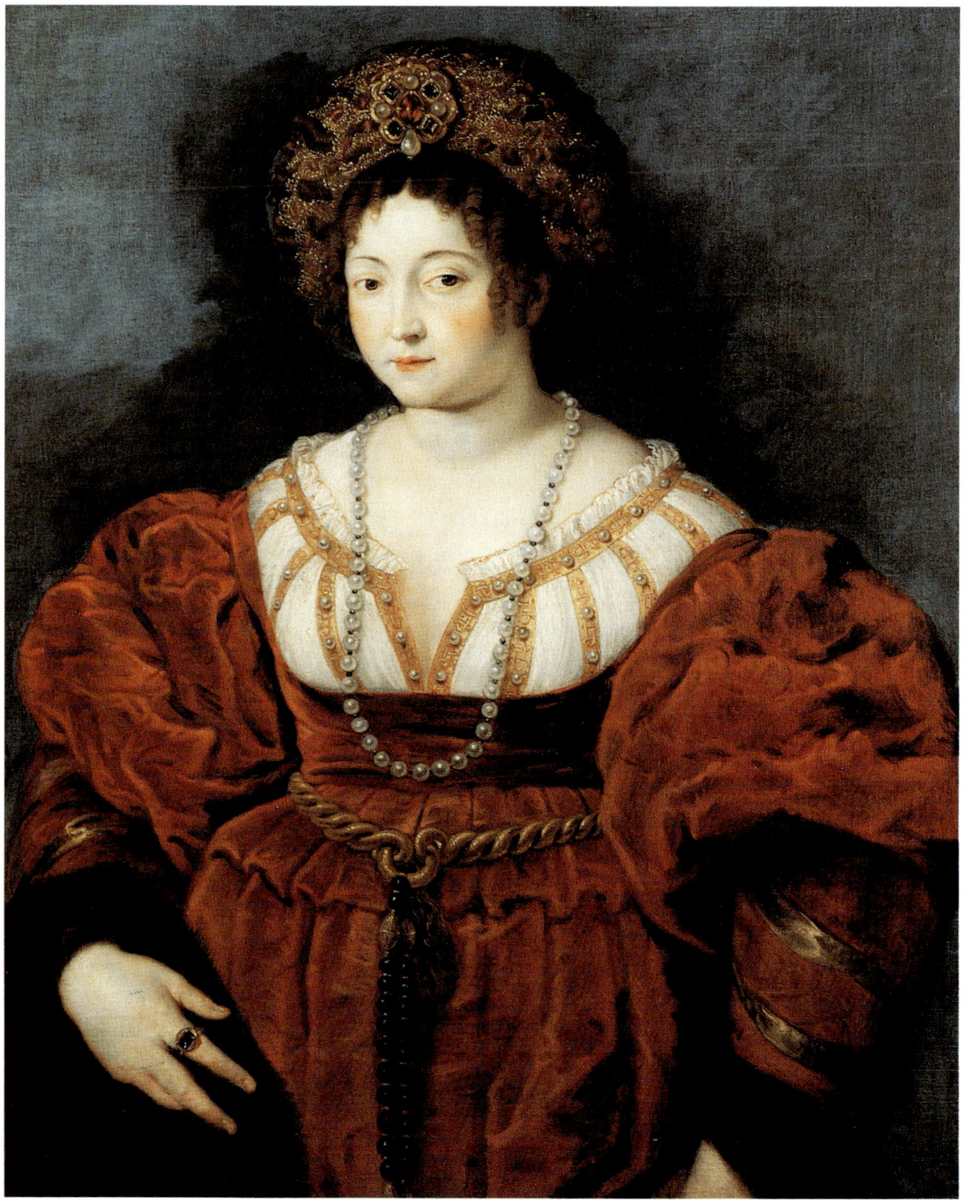

Fig.7 · Rubens after Titian
Isabella d'Este in Red
Kunsthistorisches Museum, Vienna

Fig.8 *opposite* · Rubens after Titian
Charles V in Armour with a Drawn Sword
[cat.no.48]
Private Collection

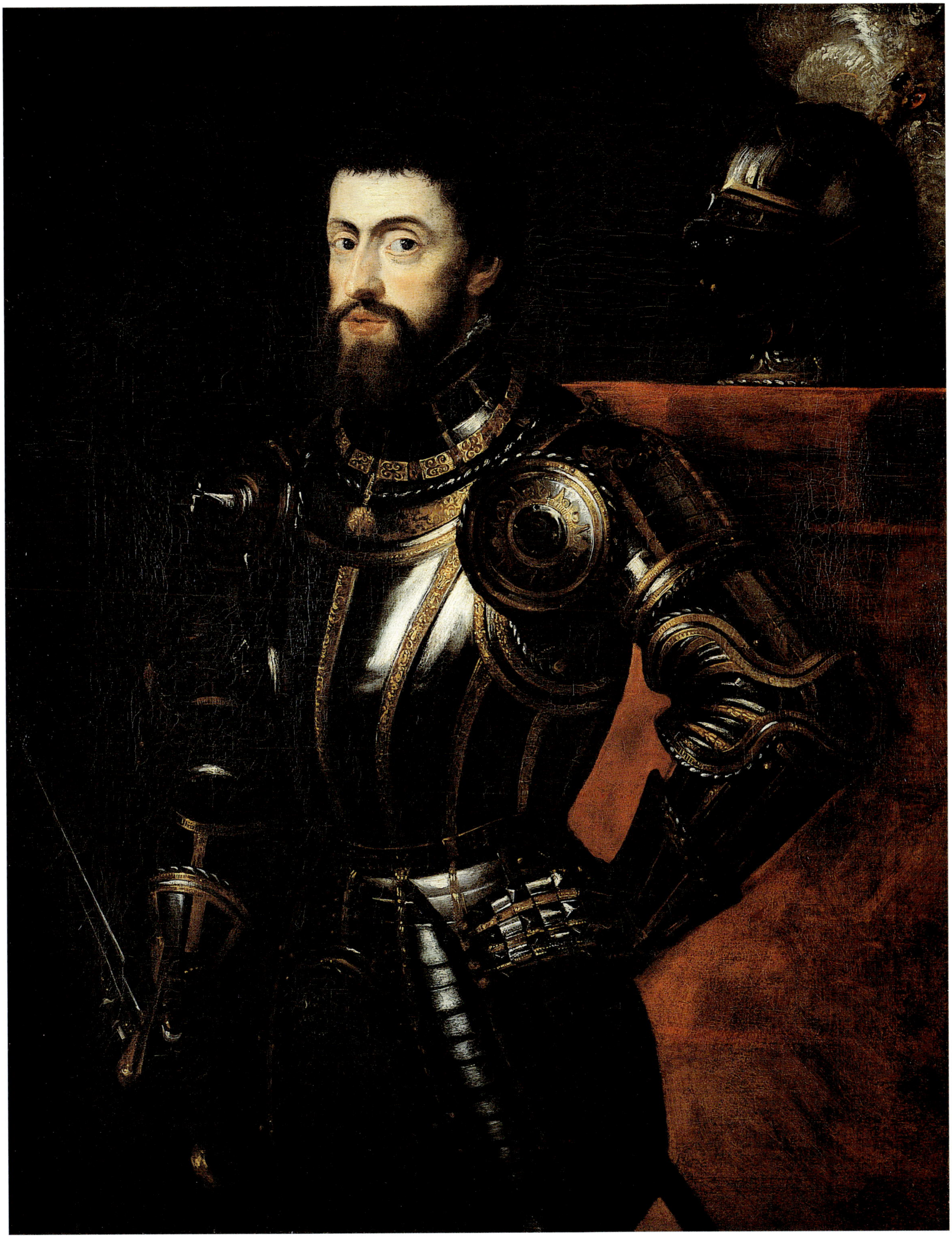

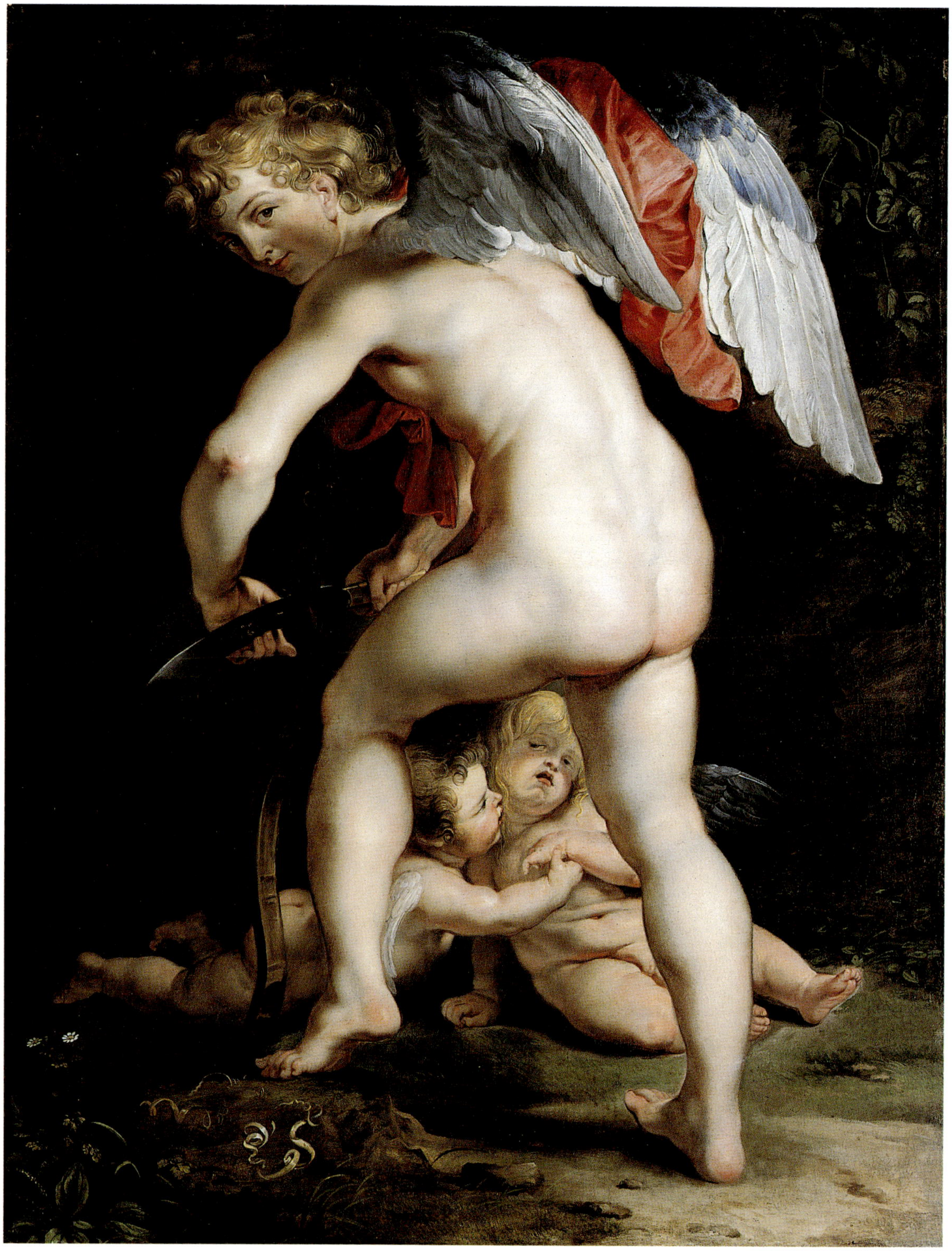

Fig.9 · Rubens after Francesco Parmigianino
Cupid Shaping his Bow
Alte Pinakothek, Munich

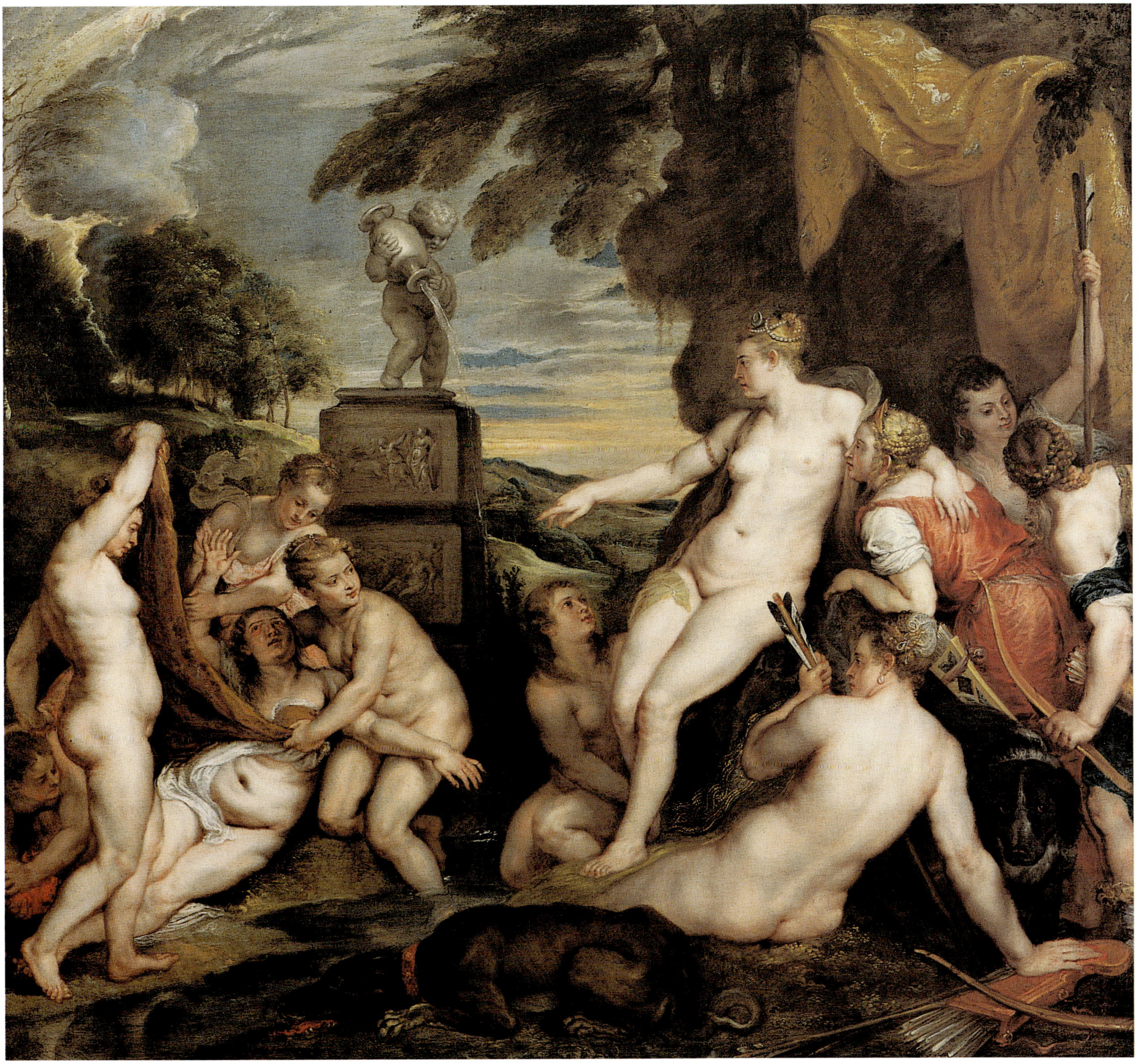

Fig.10 · Rubens after Titian
Diana and Callisto [cat.no.53]
The Right Hon. the Earl of Derby

his Bow [fig.9], now in Munich, based on a work by Parmigianino (1503–1540), which, exceptionally for Rubens, was dated as 1614, at which time the original had been taken to Vienna. Rubens could have seen it when he was in Spain in 1603–4, but this was a return to his practice before going to Italy when he had made adaptations from Italian art using intermediary copies. Parmigianino's invention seems against the grain of Rubens's temperament,[28] and he made the Cupid more masculine, stripping the figure of most of what makes it provocative and unsettling.

Rubens set out for his second journey to Spain in late August 1628 and he arrived in Madrid by 15 September.[29] It was this visit that precipitated the most sustained and remarkable series of painted copies in his entire career. Rubens was not in Madrid for long (he left on 29 April 1629), but, in addition to his duties as a diplomat, he painted a number of works for the king and leading courtiers, as well as full-size replicas of many of the works by Titian in the royal collection. All of this was achieved without the help of the large workshop that he was used to having at his beck and call in Antwerp, and must have been made at extraordinary speed. An authoritative list of the copies was provided by Francisco Pacheco in his *El Arte de la Pintura* of 1649,[30] who had obtained his information from Diego Velázquez, his son-in-law and Rubens's frequent companion at this time. Pacheco's information is confirmed by the inventory of Rubens's collection drawn up after his death in 1640. One of the largest and most impressive of these copies, *Diana and Callisto* [fig.10, cat.no.53], can be seen in this exhibition alongside Titian's original [cat.no.52] for the first time since Rubens painted his version in the Alcázar.

He continued painting full-scale copies during the 1630s. It must have been relatively early in the decade that Rubens made his version, now in the Courtauld Institute Gallery, after Raphael's portrait of *Baldassare Castiglione* [illustrated on p.10], the original of which is now in the Louvre. The banker Lucas van Uffelen bought the Raphael in 1631 and took it to Amsterdam straight away,[31] quite possibly stopping in Antwerp, en route, and it is hard to explain how Rubens saw the original otherwise. Although the prototype was on canvas, Rubens painted his copy on panel, thereby making the soft and tactile surfaces of Raphael's work look more hard and more resilient. In doing this, Rubens returned yet again to one of the features of his earliest painted copies.

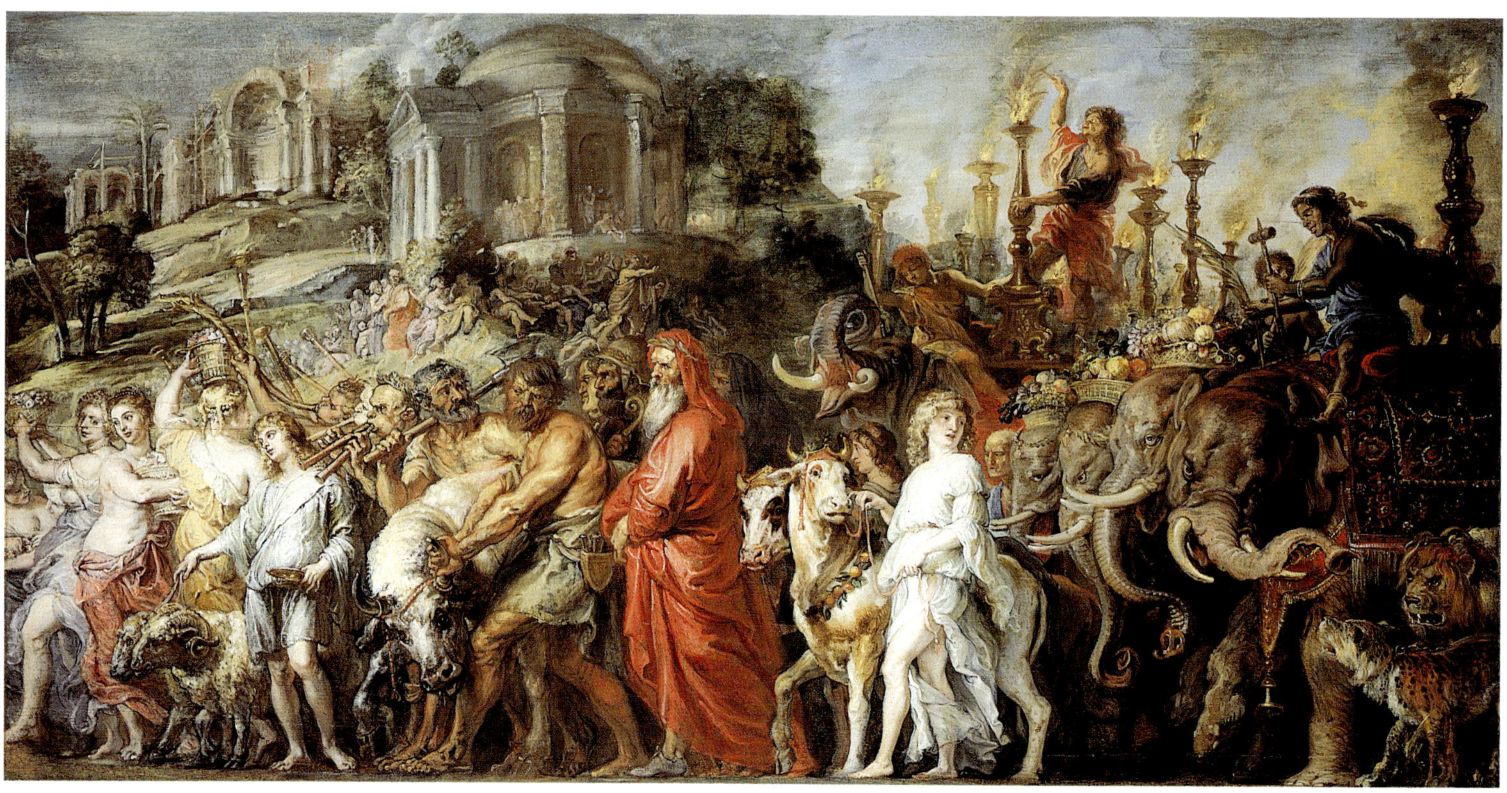

Fig.11 · Rubens
A Roman Triumph
National Gallery, London

THE RETOUCHED AND RESTORED PAINTINGS

Seventeenth-century sources make it clear that Rubens occasionally retouched paintings by earlier artists, and two examples, after compositions by the Netherlandish artist Marten van Cleve (1527–1581), survive in private collections.[32] When Rubens arrived in Valladolid in 1603 he brought with him gifts of eight large copies that had been painted by a contemporary Italian artist, Pietro Fachetti, after scenes designed by Raphael and Francesco Salviati (1510–1564). Fachetti's canvases became 'rotted and spoiled' during the journey and Rubens was forced to give them a very rapid restoration in order to save the day.[33] Again, when Rubens visited England in 1629 he was not too grand to 'mend' a portrait by Giulio Romano in the collection of Charles I.[34] These may seem like humdrum jobs, but, as will be shown later by looking at Rubens's retouched drawings, he found these interventions congenial.

The restorations already mentioned were clearly meant to be as discreet as possible, but there is a rather different and far more extreme example of Rubens reworking some earlier painted copies. *A Roman Triumph* [fig.11] in the National Gallery, London, usually dated to the 1620s, has for long been recognised as a free version of two different scenes from Andrea Mantegna's *Triumphs of Caesar*, now at Hampton Court. But, in order to create it, Rubens did not start afresh but took two small painted copies on canvas from a series after Mantegna's cycle and stuck them down onto a panel.[35] He made use of a complete copy of *The Elephants* which occupies the right-hand side of the new work,[36] and he cut down a copy of *The Vase Bearers*, keeping only the right-hand portion, which he fixed to the left-hand side of the panel. The strip which joins these down the middle was an entirely new piece of canvas added by Rubens. He then proceeded to work all over the surface so as to unify the appearance of this patchwork, adding a new landscape with classical buildings and completely obliterating many figures, but also leaving some visible, such as the youth leading the sacrificial bulls. Three of the remaining copies from the set after Mantegna, which Rubens had owned but did not cannibalise to make new compositions, have survived, and are now in the Národní Galerie, Prague.[37]

In short, the method found in *A Roman Triumph* was exceptional among Rubens's painted copies, but it is not unlike the way he treated some of his own works by adding strips of wood or canvas to their edges before reworking. It is even closer to the way he intervened on earlier drawings which he liked to cut up, stick onto new pieces of paper, and retouch.

DRAWN COPIES BY RUBENS AND THEIR CHRONOLOGY

The drawn copies entirely from Rubens's hand form a tiny group in comparison to the huge mass of retouched material. As a young artist in Antwerp, Rubens made small pen and ink copies after sixteenth-century northern printmakers which reproduced the calligraphy of the originals very carefully, and it seems that before 1600 his bias was towards northern art. Soon after arriving in Italy, Rubens made two exceptionally large watercolour copies after frescoes by Giovanni Antonio da Pordenone (1483/4?–1539) in the Malchiostro or Annunciation Chapel in the Duomo, Treviso, one of which, *The Emperor Augustus and the Tibertine Sibyl* [fig.12, cat.no.46], shows that he had completely changed his way of working when faced with large images in a different medium. Both drawings were made using black chalk for the underdrawing with some red reserved for areas of flesh. The figures were made to look weighty and massive through the crisp delineation of their outlines which were filled with flattish areas of coloured wash, a technique which Rubens adopted as a response to Pordenone's broad handling of fresco.

A similarly large scale was adopted in the series of chalk copies of Michelangelo's prophets and sibyls [fig.13] which Rubens made not long afterwards in Rome in 1601.

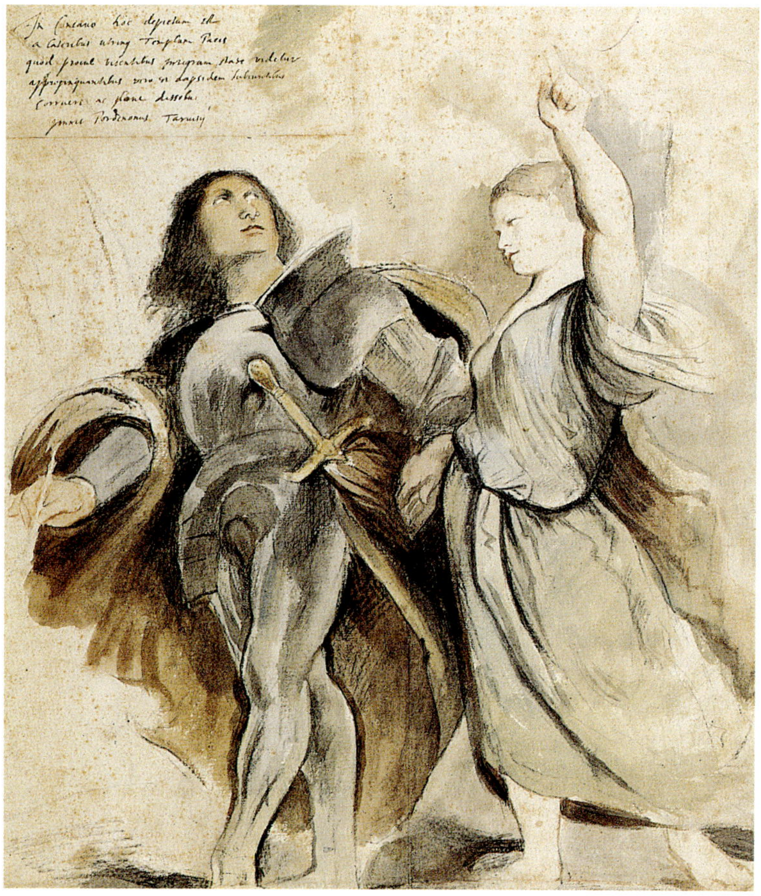

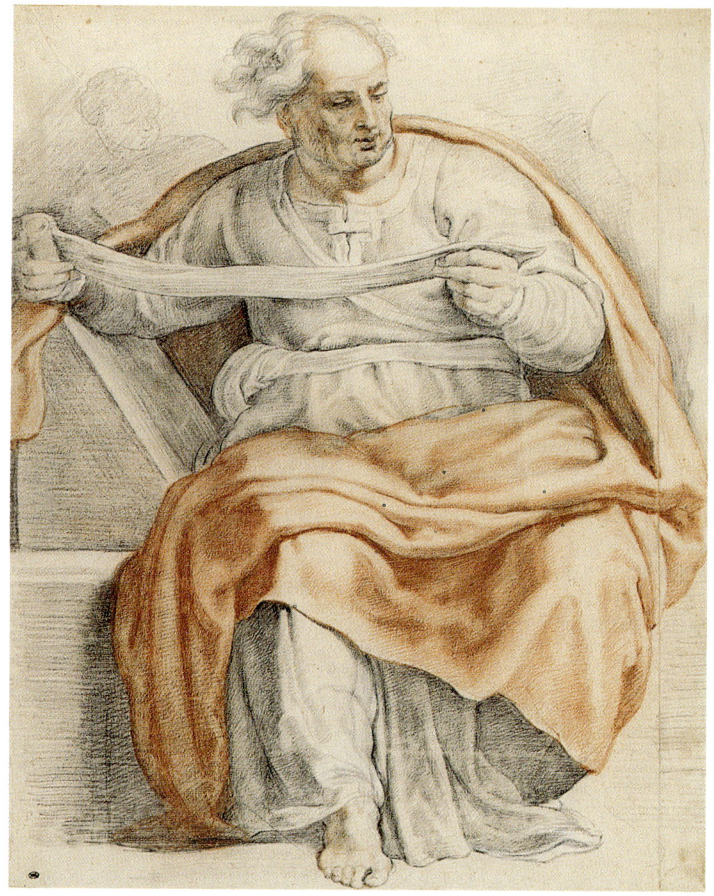

Fig.12 · Rubens after Giovanni Antonio da Pordenone *The Emperor Augustus and the Tibertine Sibyl* [cat.no.46]
Département des Art graphiques, Musée du Louvre, Paris

Fig.13 · Rubens after Michelangelo *The Prophet Joel* [cat.no.10]
Département des Arts graphiques, Musée du Louvre, Paris

Fig.14 *opposite* · Rubens after Titian *A Naked Woman Bending Forward, and Five Women's Heads*
The J. Paul Getty Museum, Los Angeles

Rubens drew the earlier sheets in the series entirely in black chalk and added red almost as an afterthought, but, as work proceeded, he became more assured in separating different areas which were to be drawn either in red or black. This combination of different coloured chalks to describe particular areas of the draperies can only have been based on direct study of the colour in the frescoes themselves.

These large copies are sometimes a little angular and stiff, but are certainly by Rubens, not least because *The Emperor Augustus and the Tibertine Sibyl* has a lengthy inscription in his hand. He soon turned to making smaller and less laborious copies, preferring black chalk for sculptures and red chalk for paintings. Two examples of the latter, in this exhibition, were made from works by Michelangelo: a copy of one of the nude youths on the ceiling of the Sistine Chapel [cat.no.12] and another of God the Father [cat.no.11] from the *Creation of Adam*. A similar gain in concision and assurance can be seen in his studies from ancient sculpture.

Whilst Rubens's travels of the late 1620s stimulated a spate of full-size painted copies mostly after Titian, already discussed, only a couple of drawings after earlier works of art can be securely dated to this period. One, now in the J. Paul Getty Museum, Los Angeles [fig.14], was drawn in red and black chalks and extracted several studies of women from Titian's *Venus and Adonis*, *Diana and Actaeon* and *Diana and Callisto*, which were all then hanging in the first of Philip IV's private apartments in the Alcázar at Madrid.[38] Rubens used the chalk in a very north Italian way, but he organised this sheet along the lines of the Netherlandish model books that had influenced his youthful copies in Antwerp, creating a miniature anthology of women's heads with elaborately braided hairstyles.

Almost immediately after visiting Madrid, Rubens arrived in London where the picture collections were no less impressive. A sheet, now in the Boijmans van Beuningen Museum, Rotterdam, [39] has on one side a copy of some figures [fig.15] from Titian's famous *Christ Presented to the People*, now in Vienna, but then in the

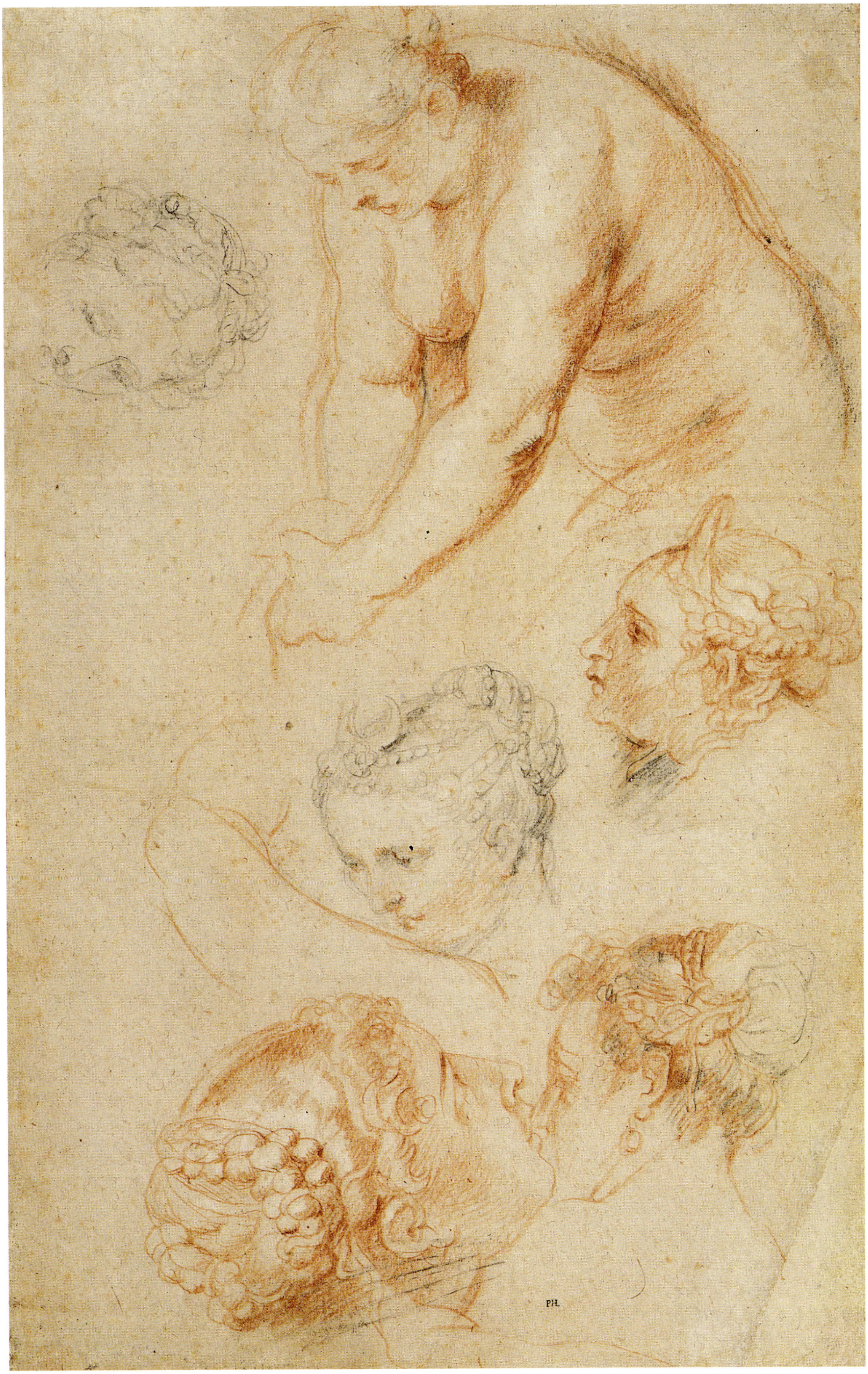
PH.

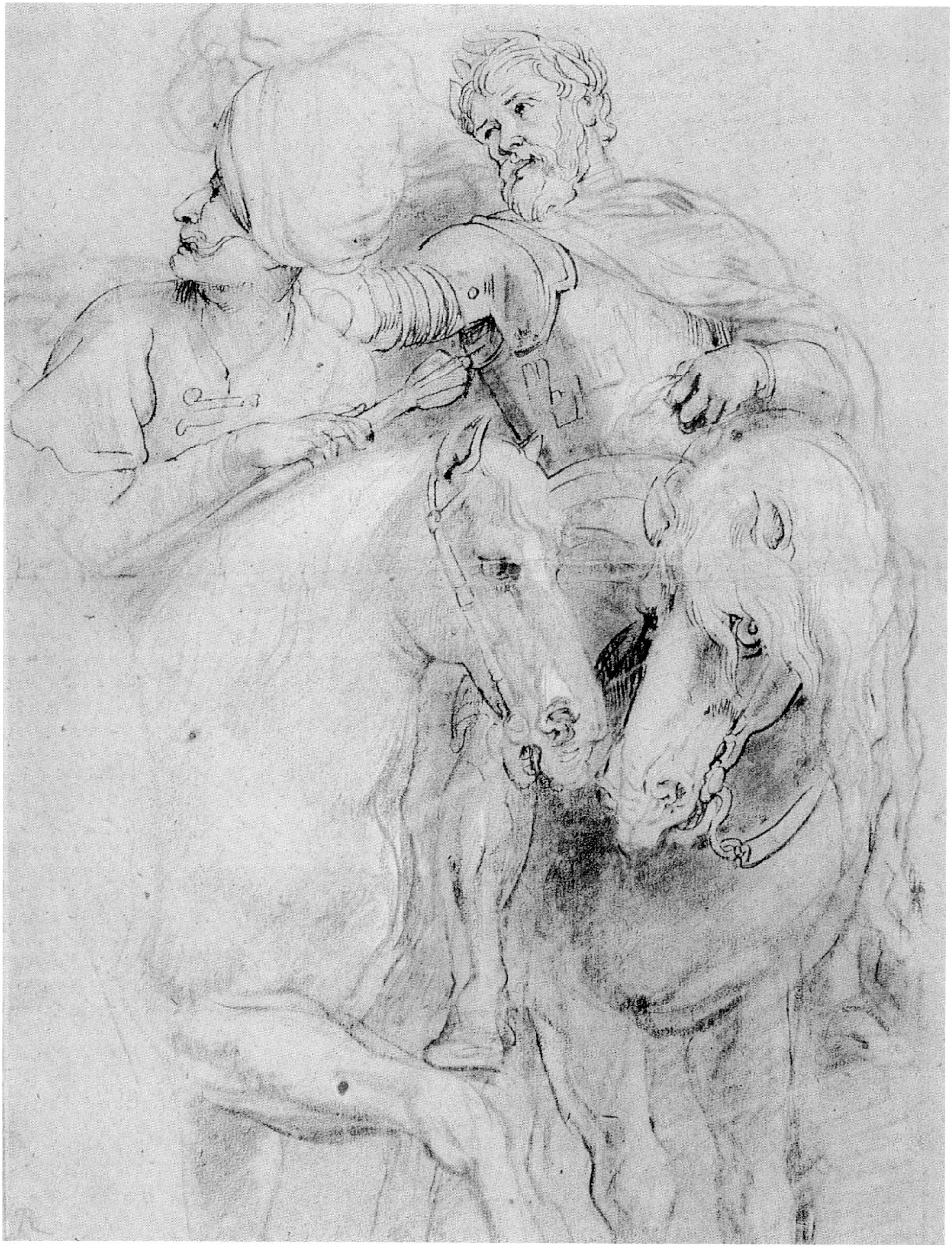

possession of George Villiers, Duke of Buckingham (1592–1628), recently deceased, whose collection Rubens singled out for praise in a letter dated 9 August 1629.[40] On the verso is a study for a painting that he made for Charles I, during the visit, which makes the dating of the copy reasonably secure. By comparison with the Getty drawing, made in Madrid, Rubens changed his use of materials, employing chalk to make rough guidelines over which he drew fluently in pen and ink, making some changes of detail and transforming Titian's two horsemen into Süleyman the Magnificent and the Emperor Charles V,[41] following an identification current at the time although not stated in print until 1648.[42]

The last broadly dateable group of drawn copies in Rubens's career was adapted from frescoes by Francesco Primaticcio (1504–1570). He must have seen them at Fontainebleau in the early 1620s, but the way in which the drawings were made with the brush (not unlike an oil sketch) with soft tonalities and slightly acidic colours, points to a later dating in the 1630s.[43] Two of Rubens's pupils, Abraham van Diepenbeeck (1596–1675) and Theodoor van Thulden (1606–1669) visited Paris in the early 1630s and were busy as copyists. Van Thulden issued a series of etchings of the Galerie d'Ulysse in 1633, and there are many more detailed and accurate black chalk copies in the Albertina, Vienna, and elsewhere after Primaticcio's frescoes, which are sometimes given to Van Thulden but have more recently been attributed to Van Diepenbeeck.[44] A number of correspondences of detail with Rubens's copies prove that he had access to these chalk copies and that the coloured drawings were made in the mid-1630s. Some of the coloured adaptations were based on complete compositions by Primaticcio, as in the very rich but transparently handled *Ulysses Sacrificing to Pluto* [fig.16] in the Kunstsammlungen at Weimar,[45] while others combined figures taken from a number of sources to make new compositions with different subjects.

Fig.15 *opposite* · Rubens after Titian
Süleyman the Magnificent and the Emperor Charles V on Horseback
Museum Boijmans van Beuningen, Rotterdam

Fig.16 · Rubens after Francesco Primaticcio
Ulysses Sacrificing to Pluto
Kunstsammlungen, Weimar

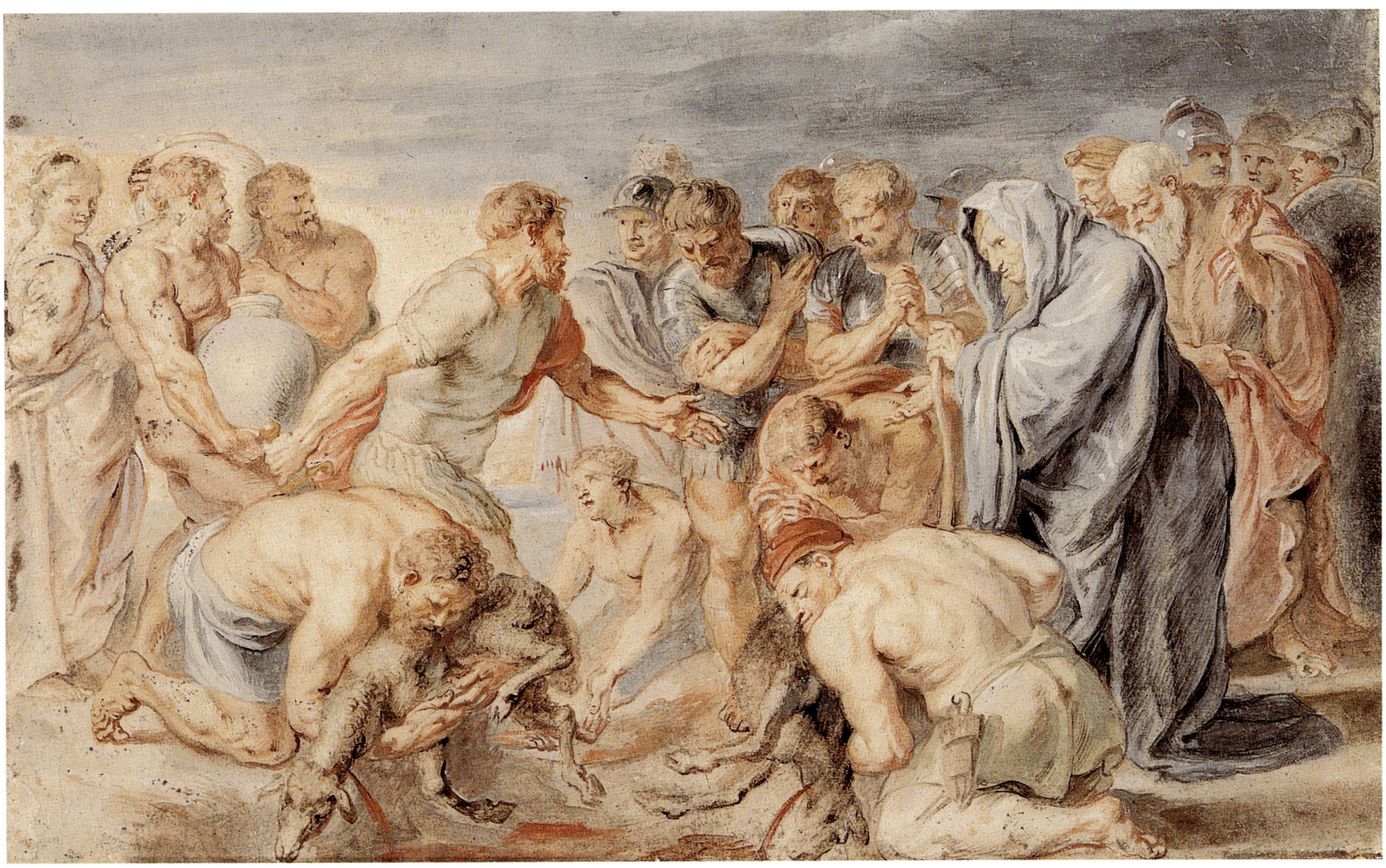

RUBENS'S RETOUCHED DRAWINGS

One may wonder what historical evidence exists to prove that Rubens retouched so many drawings in the manner claimed. He left no convenient explanation for posterity, and this was clearly a private activity that he did not need to discuss with others. But it should be remembered that he frequently retouched *modelli* (finished sketches for works of art) which had been drawn by assistants in his workshop after his own compositions, which were to be engraved. In addition, there is evidence that Rubens sent drawings made by his assistants of antiquities (or pseudo-antiquities) to his friend Nicolas-Claude Fabri de Peiresc (1580–1637), which he both inscribed and retouched in pen and ink.[46] It would have been entirely consistent if he treated the drawings in his collection in the same way.

From the early eighteenth century onwards there was no doubt among those people who studied and collected drawings that Rubens had retouched many earlier sheets. The key figures in this were Jonathan Richardson (1667–1745) and Pierre-Jean Mariette (1694–1774), who, between them, more or less created the modern study of old master drawings. Their information must often have come from artists themselves, whose knowledge had been handed down within the workshop system. In Richardson's *Essay on the Art of Criticism* of 1719, he wrote that he owned several drawings, both originals and copies, that had been reworked by Rubens.[47] Richardson distinguished between two different kinds of retouched drawing, and, in both Rubens's intervention was viewed as an original contribution not a copy. In one case he was working on top of what were seen as essentially mechanical reproductions by journeymen copyists, and, in the other, he used original designs by earlier artists, which, in Richardson's opinion, provided the best of both worlds.

Rubens reworked earlier drawings in a number of different ways, at one extreme only adding a few small touches of emphasis, and, at the other, almost completely obliterating the prototype. (Detailed discussions of many works of this kind are to be found in the catalogue entries that follow this introduction). He used a wide range of materials, but had a preference for working with the brush in bodycolour which was thick enough to mask the underdrawing. Despite the diversity of this material, two main groups can be discerned: drawings that were simply retouched and drawings that were enlarged or had sections of paper cut away and replaced before being reworked.

One of the most extreme examples of Rubens enlarging and reworking an earlier

Fig.17 *below left* · Bartolommeo Passarotti, retouched by Rubens *Saint Bartholomew and Saint Mary Magdalene with Two Other Figures*
Staedelsches Kunstinstitut, Frankfurt

Fig.18 *below right* · Rubens after Michelangelo *Night* [cat.no.14]
Collection Frits Lugt, Institut Néerlandais, Paris

Fig.19 *opposite* · Anonymous artist after Federico Barocci, retouched by Rubens *The Martyrdom of Saint Vitalis* [cat.no.66]
The Collection of the Earl of Pembroke

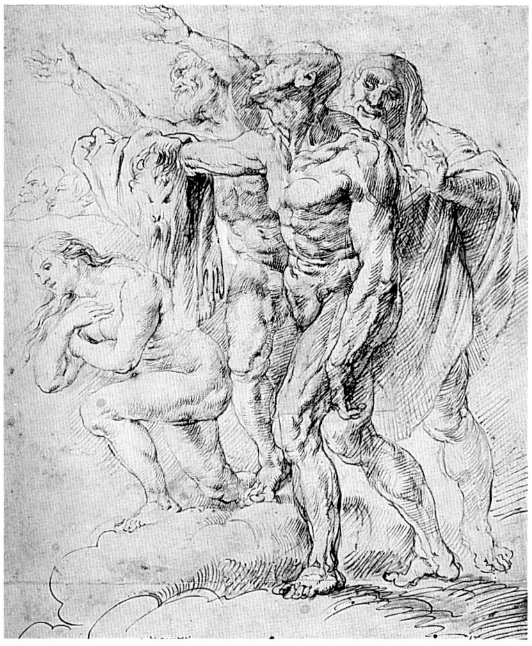

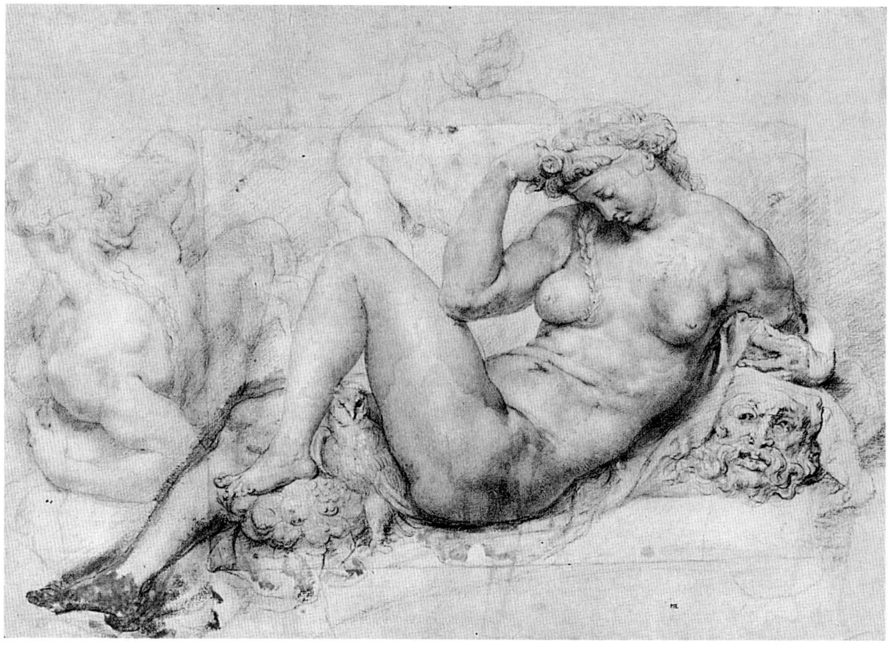

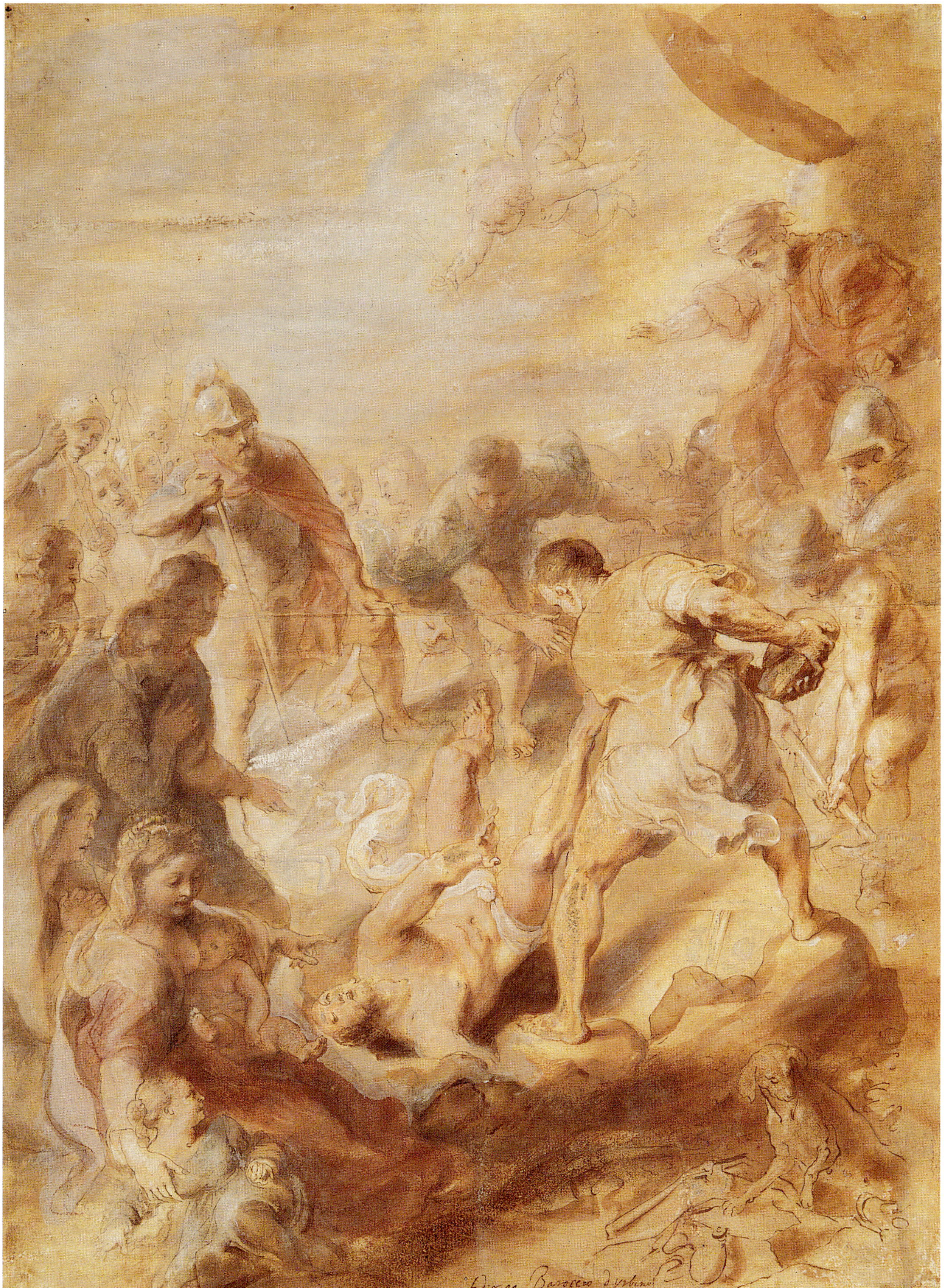
fedirigo Baroccio d'urbino
PHL

drawing is a sheet depicting *Saint Bartholomew and Saint Mary Magdalene with Two Other Figures* [fig.17] in the Städelsches Kunstinstitut, Frankfurt am Main.[48] The nucleus is a small fragment of an Italian drawing, executed in a hard and fluent pen style by the same artist who was responsible for three drawings in the present exhibition: *Hercules* [cat.no.16], and *The Punishment of Haman* after Michelangelo [cat.no.15], and a drawing of *Two Robed Men* [cat.no.61], all of which are here attributed to Bartolomeo Passarotti (1529–1592) or his school. Rubens's first step was to take the Italian drawing and attach it to a bigger sheet so as to expand the composition. He then cut this sheet vertically along the outline of a standing male nude so as to get rid of his outstretched right arm. The left-hand side was discarded and a new piece of paper added, so that he could turn the standing man into Saint Bartholomew holding his flayed skin and add the kneeling figure of the Magdalene. The core fragment is perhaps an eighth of the entire sheet and the remainder entirely by Rubens.

On other occasions Rubens took drawings which had previously been trimmed and stuck them down onto larger sheets or attached them to new margins, expanding the composition on all or some of the edges. Several of these enlarged works are in the exhibition. One is after the figure of *Night* [fig.18, cat.no.14] from the tomb of Giuliano de'Medici in the New Sacristy at San Lorenzo, Florence. This is an unusual example of Rubens taking one of his own copies and reworking it at a later date. The other is a red chalk study, here attributed to Annibale Carracci, which depicts *A Woman with Two Children in Front of the Fire* [fig.6, cat.no.75]. The difference between these works is that in the first case Rubens used the new margins to make further studies of the sculpture as if turning it around in space, while in the other he took a small drawing of a seated woman seen from the back and expanded it into a completely new family group. Both indicate what a creative and thoughtful activity this was for Rubens.

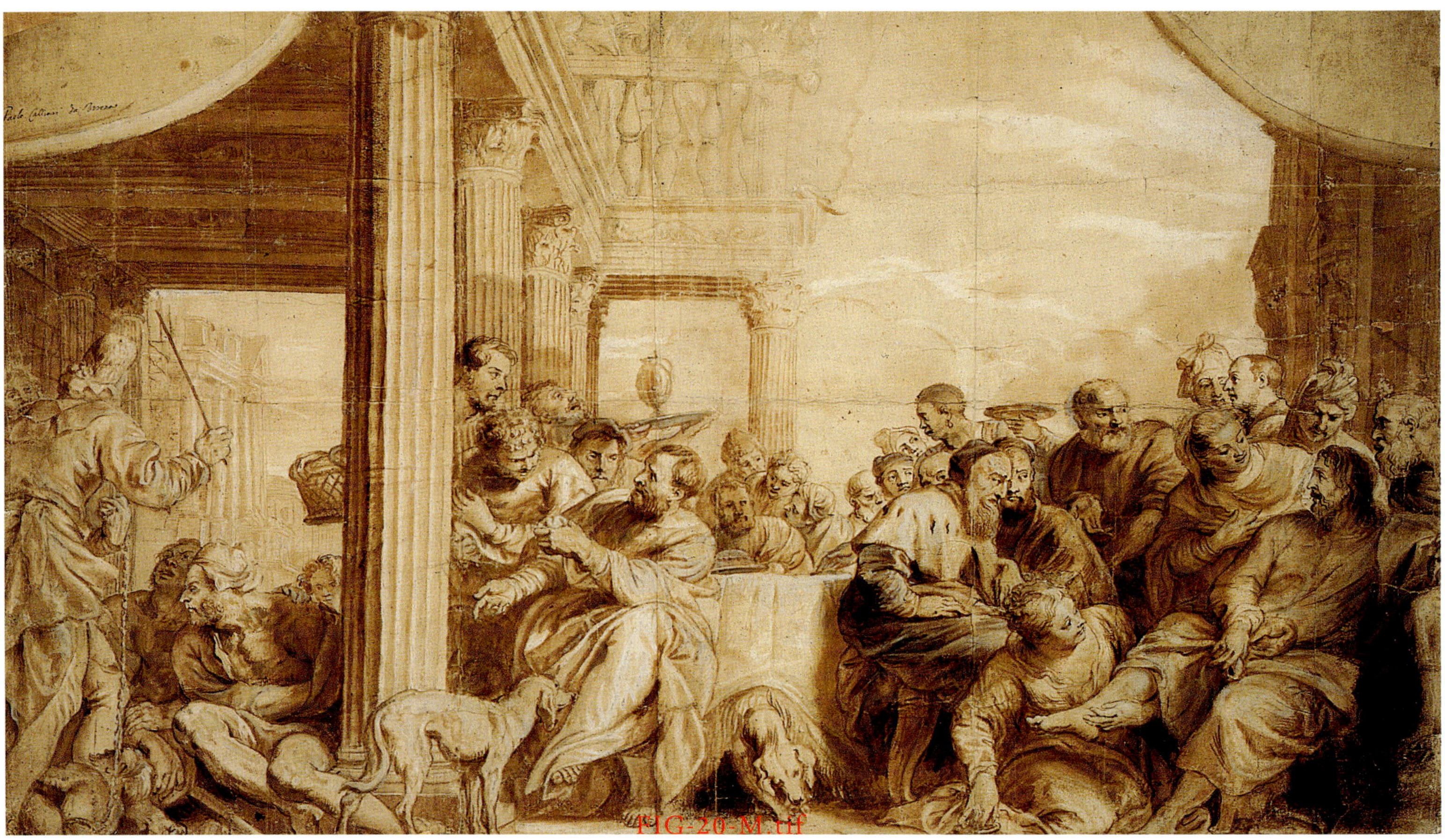

Fig.20 · Anonymous Draughtsman after Paolo Veronese, retouched by Rubens *Christ in the House of Simon* [cat.no.60] The British Museum, London

RUBENS AND ITALIAN WORKING METHODS

Rubens had been trained in one pictorial tradition in Antwerp, but, while in Italy, had to compete in another, and he returned to the Netherlands with an exceptional mastery of two very different approaches to art. No doubt his own work looked like that of a foreigner to his Italian contemporaries, since there were purely technical aspects of the way that he painted flesh, for example, that revealed his Netherlandish training. But he was remarkably successful in Rome and his work remained in demand among Italian patrons, particularly in Genoa. Rubens equipped himself to beat the Italians at their own game and he did so before returning to find even greater success in his homeland.

In Italy, Rubens had learnt how to run a workshop and how to design large works that could be prepared fast and efficiently by a team of assistants. One of the most important steps in this process for the Italians was the preparation of a detailed compositional drawing or painting (a *modello*), which could be made in a range of media (including oil paint), but generally on paper. But Rubens preferred to make oil sketches on canvas whilst in Italy, using a rust-brown ground,[49] not unlike the one he would adopt in the final work. This was very different from the streaky *imprimatura* which became such a feature of his later oil sketches,[50] only possible if working on panel. Rubens's oil sketches show the grafting of Italian working methods on to a preference for northern materials.

He was particularly interested in the systematic way some Italian artists prepared their works, and he owned and retouched copies of two of Raphael's *modelli* for his famous altarpiece of the *Transfiguration* in San Pietro in Montorio, Rome, one of which is included in the present exhibition [cat.no.20]. Rubens found that this practice had been developed much further in Urbino by Federico Barocci, who was reaching the end of his life at the time Rubens arrived in Italy. Surprisingly, there is only one surviving copy after a work by Barocci that can be convincingly attributed to Rubens [fig.19, cat.no.66] and it is a retouched sheet after a finished altarpiece, not a preparatory study.

Barocci had become famous for making both monochrome oil sketches and ones in colour on paper.[51] These show how carefully he prepared his work, since these could only be made after the entire composition had been resolved. Rubens was not always as thorough as this and his way of working was more flexible, allowing a greater degree of improvisation. Many Italian artists, including Raphael and Barocci, also made full-size cartoons on paper, but Rubens probably thought this method too laborious and worked straight onto the canvas in a north Italian manner. When he painted his *Transfiguration* of 1604–5 for the Santissima Trinita in Mantua, a work now in the Musée des Beaux-Arts, Nancy, Rubens used ideas taken from Raphael's altarpiece of the same subject. But Rubens did not follow his elaborate preparatory methods, adopting instead a broad and quick way of painting, closer to that of Tintoretto, placing outlines on the figures in red or deep pink, leaving areas of the reddish-brown ground exposed, and creating vivid effects of light with white lead.[52] Rubens adopted a canonical Roman model in this work, but his own treatment was unconventional in terms of recent Roman painting.

After returning to Antwerp, Rubens generally started work by making a quick pen sketch on paper, but, in some cases, he replaced this with a concise monochrome study on panel, followed by a larger oil sketch in colour (following in Barocci's footsteps), as when preparing the ceiling panels of the Antwerp Jesuit church in 1620–1.[53] He must have realised that the only way to produce this huge commission in a short time was to adopt Italian workshop practices.

CONCLUSION

Rubens's visit to Italy had a curious impact on Flemish art of the early seventeenth century. Many of the next generation of artists passed through the large and very successful workshop that he established on returning to Antwerp, but it is striking how few of these pupils and assistants bothered to go to Italy, with the important exception of Van Dyck. Rubens's teaching and his study collection of drawings and painted copies were sufficient to make young artists think twice about undertaking the long, expensive, and sometimes dangerous journey.

It has been usual to think of Rubens's retouched drawings as the activity of a young man learning fast, and to date them during his visit to Italy.[54] But the variety of approach found in them reflects the range and development of his draughtsmanship throughout his career and should be spread accordingly. A chronological yardstick is provided by the *modelli* for engravings which Rubens had made by assistants in his studio and then retouched. These run from the mid-1610s to the end of his career, and can be dated with some accuracy from the prints which were based upon them. They show a distinctive development from the restrained use of pen and ink in the earliest examples to a vigorous and impatient application of wash and bodycolour in those from the 1630s.

Rubens was not the only artist to retouch earlier drawings. This complicates matters since his celebrity has led to any reasonably competent retouched drawing being attributed to him. The aim of this exhibition has been to select only drawings that have been plausibly reworked by Rubens, but some borderline cases are identified here [see cat.nos.39, 67]. Enough drawings were retouched in Rubens's manner to suggest that Flemish artists found this a good way to make old and tired copies saleable. But, in some cases, there may have been more creditable motives for imitating Rubens's practice. It has been suggested that Jan Erasmus Quellinus (1634–1715) made drawings in Italy in 1660 that were retouched on his return to Antwerp by his father, Erasmus Quellinus II (1607–1678).[55] Quellinus's distinctive manner can be seen from his copy after Titian's *Pentecost*,[56] formerly attributed to Rubens,[57] and currently in a private collection. A drawing often said to be by Rubens, the *Perseus Disarming and the Origin of Coral* after Giulio Romano [cat.no.38], is here argued as retouched by Quellinus. On the other hand, the recent suggestion that a large copy after Paolo Veronese's *Christ in the House of Simon* [fig.20, cat.no.60] was copied by Jan Erasmus and retouched by his father, is unconvincing because it is broadly handled in Rubens's late manner and also inscribed by him. The attribution has been based on a comparison with Quellinus's paintings, which are largely irrelevant in determining the niceties of graphic style.

This exhibition and its catalogue have attempted to show that Rubens's engagement with the work of other artists was an activity sustained throughout his life, involving a variety of approaches which stretch the word 'copy' to its limits. A careful study of this material reveals what he admired unconditionally, what he found useful or instructive, what fed his imagination, and what he revised or developed. These activities suggests a man sufficiently confident of himself to learn something new from artists of a different time and tradition, sometimes of inferior abilities.

NOTES

1. See Bernard Berenson as cited by Jaffé 1977, p.7.
2. Baglione 1642, p.362: 'una maniera buona Italiana'.
3. For example, see Jaffé 1977.
4. Bellori 1672, p.248: 'il buon colorito veneziano'.
5. See Wood 2000, pp.154–5, with further references.
6. See Lind 1946, p.38.
7. See Baschet 1886–7, I, pp.406–13.
8. The statement that Rubens had entered the duke's service by October 1600, made by Jaffé 1977, p.9, has no documentary basis.
9. For the text, see Rooses/Ruelens 1887–1909, I, p.28, no.IV.
10. See Philip Rubens's letter to Jan Woverius of 26 June 1602 in Rooses/Ruelens 1887–1909, I, pp.51–2, no.XI.
11. See Rooses/Ruelens 1887–1909, I, pp.145–6, no.XXXI: 'tante cose bellissime del Titiano e Raphaello et altri che mi hanno fatto stupire in qualità e in quantità, in casa del Re et in Escuriale et altrove'.
12. The statement in Jaffé 1977, p.33, that Rubens saw Titian's *poesie* in Madrid in 1603 is unsupported by any evidence.
13. See Volk 1983, p.142; M. Díaz Padrón, 'Tiziano y Rubens en los preceptistas y viajeros Españoles: Adan y Eva y el Rapto de Europa' in Madrid 1987, pp.47–8.
14. See the comments on this problem in Rooses/Ruelens 1887–1909, I, p.240.
15. For this document, see Rooses/Ruelens 1887–1909, I, p.242, no.LX; and Mantua 1977, p.60.
16. For the documents, see Rooses/Ruelens 1887–1909, I, pp.276–9, nos.LXV–LXVIII.
17. See the letter of 2 December 1606 in Rooses/Ruelens 1887–1909, I, pp.354–5, no.XIC: 'haver impiegato tutta l'estate nei studij dell'arte'.
18. See the letters from Rubens to Peiresc of 2 December 1628 in Rooses/Ruelens 1887–1909, V, pp.10–11, no.DLXIV; Gevartius to Peiresc of 15 January 1629 (V, pp.21–2, no.DLXVII), and Rubens to Peiresc of 9 August 1629 (V, pp.152–4, no.DCXVI).
19. Vasari 1568, II, sig. *****, 3v: 'secca, & cruda, & tagliente'.
20. The dating is controversial, see Lightbown 1986, pp.428–9, under no.28.
21. Inv.nos.3732–3742, 3744, 3746–3749, 3751, 3753–3756.
22. Aretino 1957–60, I, pp.214–15, no.CXLII. The phrase was borrowed by Vasari in his 1550 edition of the *Vite* (II, p.883), but dropped from the edition of 1568.
23. See the letter from Giovanni Magno to Annibale Chieppio, dated 17 February 1607, in Rooses/Ruelens 1887–1909, I, p.362, no.XCI.
24. See Rubens's letter of 24 May 1603 to Annibale Chieppio, Rooses/Ruelens 1887–1909, I, p.145, no.XXXI, referring to 'l'incredibil insufficienza e dapocagine de questi pittori'; 'Idio men guarda di rassomigliari in niente'.
25. See Wood 1994, pp.342–6.
26. The corpus of works discussed in Jaffé 1977, was challenged by Freedberg 1978, pp.82–5, and Vlieghe 1978, pp.471–3. New criteria for the attribution of the drawn copies were established in Logan/Haverkamp-Begemann 1978, pp.93–6; and developed further in an important series of reviews by Logan (Logan 1977, pp.403–17; Logan 1978, pp.419–50; Logan 1987, pp.63–82, amongst others).
27. See K. Schütz in Vienna, 1977, p.55, no.5, repr., with further references. The consensus has been a date of *c.*1605. Müller Hofstede 1967, p.91, note 127, suggested 1620–5, and Muller 1989, p.107, under no.56, proposed 1629–30.
28. By contrast, the thorough discussion by M.E. Wieseman in Boston/Toledo, 1993, pp.242–4, no.11, treats it as self-evident that Rubens would admire this work.
29. See Vergara 1999, p.58.
30. Pacheco 1649, bk.I, chap.VIII, p.100.
31. See Eiche 1981, pp.134–5.
32. See Wood 1995, pp.18–21, and Vlieghe 2000, pp.681–6.
33. See the letter from Rubens to Chieppio of 14 May 1603 in Rooses/Ruelens 1887–1909, I, p.144, no.XXXI ('putrefatte e marzze').
34. See Millar 1958–60, pp.40, no.16; 201; Millar 1970–2, p.263, no.113.
35. As proposed by Balis 1994, p.106.
36. As first observed by Martin 1970, p.167.
37. See Slavíček 1991, pp.114–19.
38. For the location of the pictures, see Volk 1981, pp.519, 526.
39. See Meij 2001, pp.124–6, no.23.
40. For this letter to Peiresc, see Rooses/Ruelens 1887–1909, V, p.152, no.DCXVI.
41. See Müller Hofstede 1962, p.105.
42. See Ridolfi 1914–24, I, p.172.
43. A dating of around 1630 for the group of coloured copies after Primaticcio was proposed by Burchard/d'Hulst 1956, p.95 (under no.111); and Burchard/d'Hulst 1963, text vol., pp.252–3 (under no.163). This was accepted by Jaffé, 1956, p.314, and Held 1986, p.138 (under no.176), but, as argued here, is still too early. The attribution of this entire group was questioned by Logan 1978, pp.434–5.
44. For the attribution to Van Diepenbeeck, see Wood 1990, pp.3–53.
45. Now known to have been attributed to Rubens as early as 1695, see Py 2001, p.146, no.581, identifying this drawing in the collection of Everhard Jabach.
46. For example, see the drawing of a *Parade Burgonet in the Shape of a Dolphin* in the Bibliothèque Nationale, Paris; Van der Meulen 1994, I, pp.29–30, note 12; 124–5; repr. text illus. 76; and Karcheski 2001, pp.29–33, repr. fig.4.
47. Richardson 1719, pp.175–6.
48. See Logan 1976–8, p.107, repr. fig.2. Formerly owned by Mariette, see Basan, Mariette 1775, p.155, no.1005.
49. See, for example, Held 1980, I, p.458, under no.331.
50. See Von Sonnenburg 1979, I, pp.89–92.
51. Bellori 1672, pp.195–6, described Barocci making colour *modelli* (in his terminology, *cartoncini*) after the full-size cartoon, in order to get the right balance between tone and hue. See also Von Sonnenburg 1979, I, p.94.
52. See J.-P. Rioux and F. Dijoud in Nancy 1990, pp.94–5.
53. The relevant oil sketches for *Saint Barbara Pursued by her Father* survive in the Ashmolean, Oxford, and Dulwich Picture Gallery, London, see Held, I, pp.55–7, nos.29–30, repr. II, pls.29, 31. See also Von Sonnenburg 1979, I, p.95.
54. See, for example, Logan 1978, p.430.
55. See Vlieghe 1994, pp.217–20, and B.W. Meijer, 'On drawings and Flemish-Venetian relations in the seventeenth century' in Meij 2001, pp.35–6.
56. See Vlieghe 1994, p.218, repr. fig.4.
57. Jaffé 1977, p.35, repr. pl.81 (as Rubens, *c.*1605).

CATALOGUE

The catalogue is divided into three sections, corresponding with the fifteenth, sixteenth and seventeenth centuries. The sixteenth century is further sub-divided into:

- *Artists working in Florence and Rome*
- *Artists working in North Italy*
- *Italian artists working in France*

The sequence is chronological, by date of birth of each artist. Within the groups for each artist the entries are arranged according to the likely date when copied or retouched by Rubens.

The information at the start of each catalogue entry for a drawing is presented as follows:

- *(When appropriate) medium is described in terms of the underdrawing first and differentiated from Rubens's retouching.*
- *Inscriptions are only provided if written by Rubens himself. All others are ignored.*
- *The cutting, repair, and replacing of parts of drawings is described briefly, if by Rubens, but no later physical changes to the drawings are mentioned.*

I · RUBENS AND FIFTEENTH-CENTURY ITALIAN ART

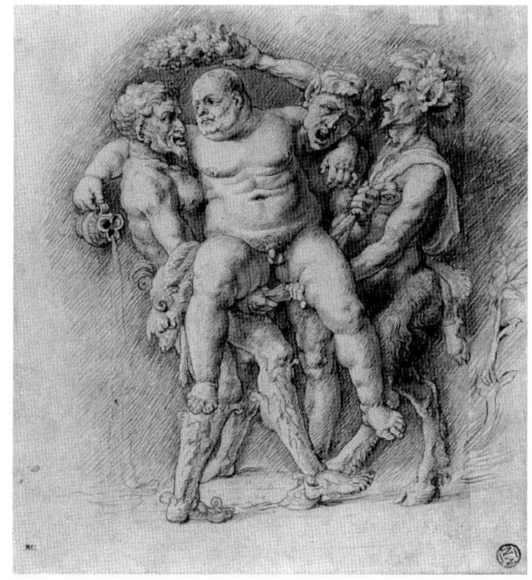
1

ANDREA MANTEGNA

1 · Anonymous Fifteenth-Century Draughtsman after Andrea Mantegna (*c*.1431–1506), retouched by Rubens *Silenus Carried by a Satyr and Two Fawns*

Pen and ink, retouched with dark brown wash, greenish and grey bodycolour; 24.5 × 21.9 cm. Extended by a strip of paper (2.5 cm at top, 2.4 cm at bottom) along the right-hand edge.
Département des Arts graphiques, Musée du Louvre, Paris, inv.no.20178
Exhibited in Edinburgh only

REFERENCES: Lugt 1949, II, p.27, no.1075; Burchard/d'Hulst 1956, pp.61–2, no.57; Burchard/d'Hulst 1963, text vol., pp.112–13, no.67; Jaffé 1977, p.42; Logan 1978, p.433; Sérullaz 1978, pp.84–5, no.80; Alpers 1995, pp.106, 118, 126, 167, note 2.

The drawing in the Louvre extracts the central group from Mantegna's famous engraving of the *Bacchanal with Silenus*, sometimes dated to the early 1470s. The print shows the obese figure of Silenus, one of the gods of the countryside, who is so intoxicated that he cannot walk.

The Louvre drawing was for a long time attributed solely to Rubens, but it is an early copy that he retouched.[1] Rubens extended the drawing by adding a vertical strip of paper along its right edge, and the crisp underdrawing in brown ink, which imitates Mantegna's drawing style, is found only on the larger piece of paper. Rubens thickened the back of the fawn on the left, and reinforced the outline of his arm in ink. The satyr had greyish wash added to areas of shadow and bold lines in yellowish pigment applied to his goat's legs. Silenus's head was made smaller, thus emphasising his corpulence.

Rubens's interest in depicting Silenus was at its most concentrated in the period from 1614 to 1620, when he painted a number of bacchanalian subjects, but these do not follow Mantegna and show the god standing, crowned with vine leaves and bearded, as found in an antique statue that was owned by Cardinal Flavio Chigi in the later seventeenth century, and which Rubens copied twice.[2]

The first time that Rubens made use of Mantegna's Silenus was in his *Drunken Hercules* in Dresden, dateable to 1613–14.[3] Although Hercules is here shown standing, there is a similarity in the way that he is supported by his companions, draping his right arm around the neck of a faun and with a wine jug dangling from his hand.

The most exact use that Rubens made of Mantegna's Silenus was as a relatively minor figure, hurtling through the air with legs widespread in the *Fall of the Damned* in Munich, dateable to *c*.1618–21. This grotesque and obese man is grasped by ferocious demons who pull him down, their talons and teeth clawing at his flesh as if trying to eat him alive. In the same picture Rubens also used another figure from Mantegna's print – the grossly fat woman who is found on the left-hand side of the engraving.[4]

It is reasonable to date Rubens's retouchings on the Louvre drawing to the period of these adaptations, and therefore after 1613 and before 1621. The restraint of these changes suggests a restoration rather than a complete revision, and Rubens's technique, in particular the way he strengthened outlines in dark wash, is comparable to his interventions on *modelli* for prints around 1615.

1. As proposed by Logan 1978, p.433.
2. See Van der Meulen 1994, II, pp.50–1, nos.28–9, repr. III, figs.58, 61.
3. As noted in Burchard/d'Hulst 1963, text vol., p.112, under no.67.
4. Kauffmann 1976, p.24; see also Freedberg 1984, p.225, under no.52.

2 · Rubens after Andrea Mantegna *Three Men with Staves*

Brown wash over red chalk; 17.9 × 31.2 cm
Département des Arts graphiques, Musée du Louvre, Paris, inv.no.22179
Exhibited in Nottingham only

REFERENCES: Lugt 1949, II, p.58, no.1259; Burchard 1956, p.415; Jaffé 1956, p.318; Burchard/d'Hulst 1963, text vol., p.41, under no.21, p.228, under no.146; Jaffé 1977, p.42; Logan 1978, p.433; Sérullaz 1978, p.85, no.81.

The Louvre drawing contains copies of two figures (one drawn twice) from the sixth canvas of Mantegna's *Triumphs of Caesar*: the *Bearers of Golden Vessels, Trophies, and Crowns* (also known as the *Corselet Bearers*), now at Hampton Court. In the original, each man is shown carrying a cuirasse on a pole, but this is barely indicated in the drawing.

All traces of Mantegna's style and many significant details are absent from the Louvre drawing. The man on the left, who has lost the brooch on his cloak and the sword at his side, is shown bare-footed instead of wearing boots. His stance is changed so that he stoops forward, unlike the upright figure in the original. The crisp folds of Mantegna's draperies are turned into dough. In both figures, the faces appear sullen, so that the men seem to be dragging their burdens resentfully rather than marching in triumph.

This is an unusually awkward drawing for Rubens, but there is no reason to doubt the attribution. It belongs among a group of stylistically similar sheets from the period 1628 to 1630. These are distinctive in being drawn with brush over chalk, using fluid outlines to give the figures a soft and malleable appearance. Most were made in preparation for documented paintings, one of the earliest being a study in Stockholm,[1] for the *Virgin and Child Adored by Saints*, painted for the Sint-Augustinuskerk in Antwerp, and dateable

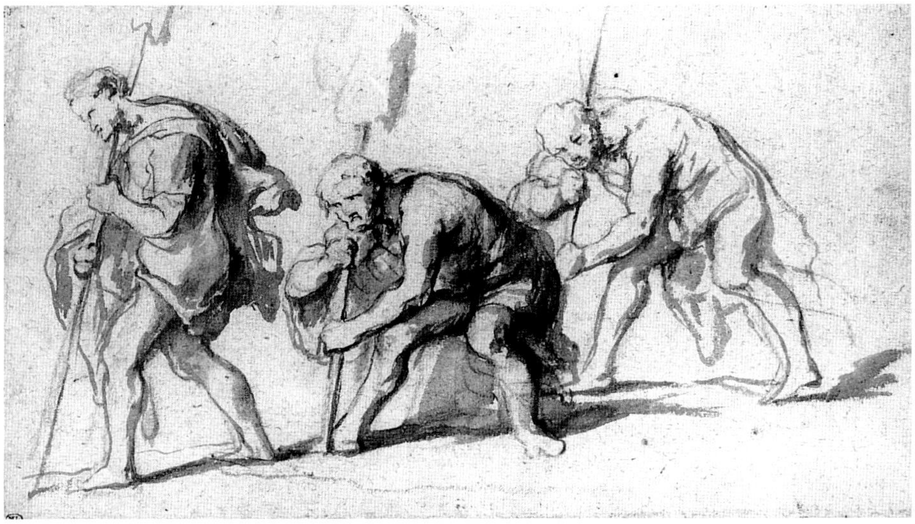

2

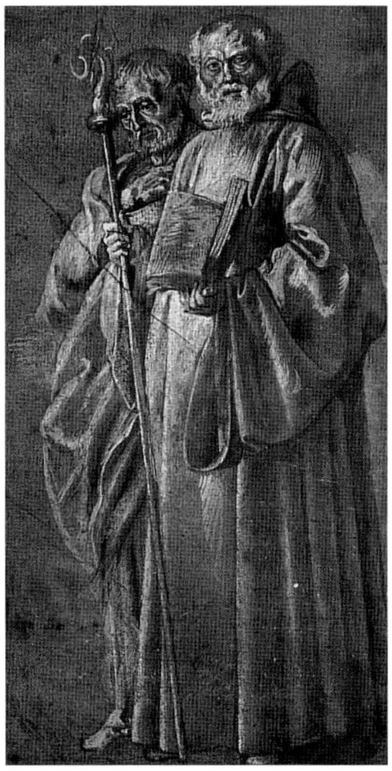

3

before Rubens's departure for Madrid in 1628. In addition, several comparable studies were made for the *Glorification of the Eucharist* on the high altar of the Carmelite Church in Antwerp, now destroyed, which was designed by Rubens around 1630 but not painted until 1637–8 by Gerard Seghers (1591–1651) from Rubens's oil sketches.[2] The Louvre drawing is so close to these sheets – although different in function – that it must be similar in date. Some scholars have found the last mentioned group unusually distorted,[3] but they have the characteristics of preparatory works with numerous changes of mind and they make no sense as imitations.

It has been said that the Louvre drawing was made in London in 1629–30 when Mantegna's *Triumphs* may have arrived from Venice,[4] but it is very different from copies that Rubens based directly on originals. It could just as well have been taken from an intermediary record, perhaps one of the painted versions of the *Triumphs* that Rubens owned,[5] or even made from memory. Alternatively, he could have used a well-known early fifteenth-century engraving by Giovanni Antonio da Brescia which shows the crouching man with a mop of hair, not bald as in the original, which could explain this change in Rubens's copy.

1. Inv.no.1966–1863, recto. See Held 1959, I, p.117, no.53r., repr. II, pl.59; Burchard/d'Hulst 1963, text vol., pp.225–7, no.145, repr.
2. See Held 1980, I, pp.530–1, under no.392; for two drawings in the Albertina, see Mitsch 1977, pp.110–14, nos.47–8, repr.
3. See Held 1980, I, p.531, under no.392; Logan 1983, p.415.
4. Burchard 1956, p.415.
5. See Muller 1989, p.144.

GIOVANNI BELLINI

3 · Anonymous Fifteenth-Century Draughtsman after Giovanni Bellini (*c*.1434?–1516), retouched by Rubens *Saints Benedict and Mark*

COLOUR ILLUSTRATION ON PAGE 14

Brush with black wash and white heightening on dark blue prepared paper, retouched with cream and white bodycolour; 28.1 × 14.2 cm
The British Museum, London, inv.no.Oo.–9–31

REFERENCES: Popham 1927, p.47; Tietze/Tietze-Conrat 1944, p.92, no.344; Popham/Pouncey 1950, cat. vol., p.13, no.20; Jaffé 1977, p.42; Rowlands 1977, p.53, no.45; Freedberg 1978, pp.83, 90, note 19.

The British Museum drawing corresponds with the right-hand panel from Giovanni Bellini's triptych of the *Virgin and Child with Saints Peter, Benedict, Nicholas and Mark* in Santa Maria Gloriosa dei Frari, Venice, usually referred to as the *Frari Triptych*, signed and dated in 1488. The chapel for which it was painted had been endowed in 1478 by Niccolò Benedetto, and Marco Pesaro, the sons of Pietro Pesaro and Franceschina Tron. The central section containing the enthroned figures of the Virgin and Child is flanked by two smaller panels, each containing two figures, who are identifiable as the name saints of the Pesaro brothers and their father.

It is uncertain whether the drawing was originally a preparatory study by Giovanni, a record of a lost preparatory study from the Bellini workshop, or a copy after the *Frari Triptych* itself. It was originally made with a brush and black wash, applied with blended parallel strokes and some delicate white heightening. This is easiest to see on Saint Mark's head, where the curls of his beard are described with extremely fine lines, far more fussy in handling than would be the case in Rubens's work. At this stage, Mark was almost entirely pushed into the background by the figure of Benedict, as in the finished painting, with little more than his head and hand visible.

In the eighteenth century the British Museum drawing belonged to the distinguished collector Pierre-Jean Mariette (1694–1774), whose inscription on the mount shows that he recognised it as a work retouched by Rubens. Although Mariette was not infallible, there are good grounds for accepting his identification. The drawing was retouched in cream and white bodycolour in order to enrich its tonality. Benedict's robe was made more three dimensional by adding brilliant highlights which come into play against the dark wash of the under-drawing and the deep blue prepared ground of the paper. The most noticeable change, entirely characteristic of Rubens, was to add bulk to Mark's figure by enlarging his robes on the left side.

In terms of dating, this retouching fits with Rubens's taste for using bodycolour in the 1620s, at which time he liked to give greater volume to figures, intensifying the play of light on surfaces, and adding a silken texture to fabrics and skin. Unlike some of his other retouched drawings where Rubens left his intervention legible, here he seems to have tried to integrate his contribution as smoothly as possible. However, it could be argued that this went against the grain of Bellini's design, imposing opulent effects of texture and light onto a more reticent model.

II · RUBENS AND SIXTEENTH-CENTURY ITALIAN ART

Artists Working in Florence and Rome

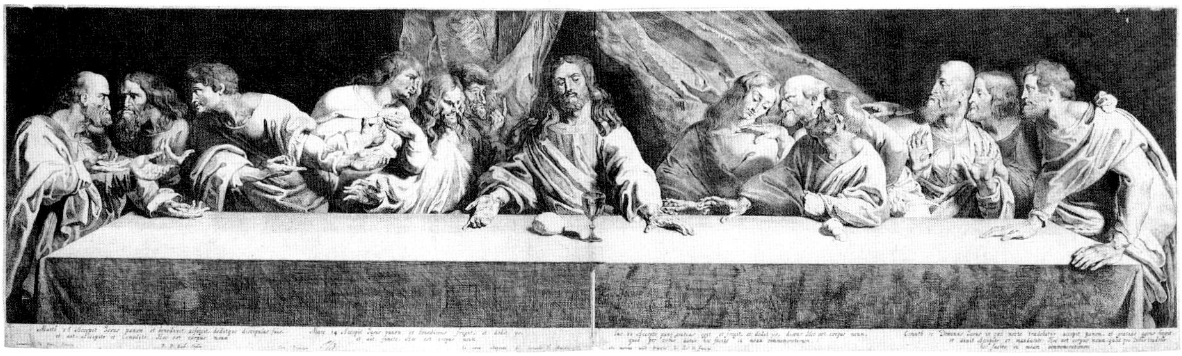

6

LEONARDO DA VINCI

4 · Gerard Edelinck (1640–1707) after Rubens, after Leonardo da Vinci (1452–1519) *The Battle of Anghiari*

Engraving, inscribed *L. da finse pinx* and *G. Edelinck sc*; 44.9 × 60 cm
The British Museum, London, inv.no. Cracherode V-1-88

REFERENCES: Voorhelm Schneevoogt 1873, p.152, no.130; Van den Wijngaert 1940, p.44, no.170; Alberici 1984, p.167, no.254; Zöllner 1991, pp.180–2; Zöllner 1998, p.38, no.XXIII.

Gerard Edelinck's engraving of Leonardo's *Battle of Anghiari*, dateable to *c*.1660,[1] helped spread the fame of this destroyed wall painting, but the printmaker did not identify his immediate source. This was a drawing now in the Louvre,[2] often said to be entirely by Rubens, but, more plausibly, a sixteenth-century copy retouched by him.[3]

Leonardo agreed to make a wall painting in the Sala del Gran Consiglio of the Palazzo Vecchio, Florence, in 1503. Work was not far advanced by 1506 when he abandoned the commission. In so far as Leonardo achieved his ideas for this work, he did so in the cartoon and a fragment painted on the wall, but neither survived for long. The subject was the battle at Anghiari (29 June 1440) where the Florentines defeated the forces of Filippo Maria Visconti, Duke of Milan. Leonardo may have planned a large, multi-figure composition, but only realised the section known as the *Fight for the Standard*, which depicted four horsemen struggling for possession of the Milanese flag, with three additional soldiers in combat on the ground.

Rubens's Louvre drawing is made up of two sections of paper: a large core and an extension around all four edges. The nucleus is an earlier copy in black chalk. This can be established by comparison with two other sheets now in the Koninklijk Huisarchiv, The Hague,[4] and the Armand Hammer Museum of Art and Cultural Center, Los Angeles.[5] These are similar in size to each other and to the core section of the Louvre drawing. Both correspond closely with the underdrawing in that work, but do not contain the later changes made in bodycolour and white heightening, and so must record its appearance before retouching and enlargement. These copies are all derived from Leonardo's cartoon, not the wall painting. Some differences between Edelinck's print and the Louvre drawing help to identify a later intervention in the early nineteenth century when that sheet was rebacked and restored.

Leonardo's *Battle of Anghiari* provided a powerful model for Rubens's depiction of violent conflict, notably in his hunting and battle scenes. Rubens understood how Leonardo had given his horses 'human' emotions and made them participants in the drama, as Vasari had observed.[6] However, the influence of the *Battle of Anghiari* went further and Rubens deliberately intensified its savagery. This is evident in his oil sketch for a *Lion Hunt* in the National Gallery, London,[7] dated around 1615. Here three horsemen collide as a lion leaps onto the rear of one of the horses, and the way in which it sinks its teeth into the man's shoulder recalls the manner in which one of Leonardo's horses bites another; the animals' ferocity echoing that of the warriors.

1. This dating, before Edelinck left Antwerp for Paris, has been based on the Flemish spelling used in the inscription.
2. Inv.no.20271. Lugt 1949, II, pp.29–30, no.1084, repr. pl.L.
3. Logan 1977, pp.408–9; Logan 1978, p.433; Logan 1987, p.70–1; Zöllner 1991, pp.177–90; Zöllner 1998, pp.13–14, 33–4, no.IX.
4. See Zöllner 1998, pp.13, 33, no.VIII, repr.
5. See Zöllner 1998, p.38, no.XXI, repr.
6. Vasari 1568, II, p.9.
7. As noted by Martin 1970, p.184.

5 · Rubens *The Fight for the Standard*

Black and red chalk, with grey and brown wash; 41.5 × 52.2 cm. Indistinctly inscribed in lead or black chalk in Rubens's hand at upper left: *...sara Medesima*[.] *far si che colui / il corpo si alsi su piedi sopra le staffe / per avvicinare gli nemici*.
The British Museum, London, inv.no.1895-9-15-1044

REFERENCES: Hind 1923, p.12, no.21; Glück/Haberditzl 1928, pp.11, 29, no.8; Müller Hofstede 1964, p.105; J. Müller Hofstede in Cologne 1977, I, p.194, no.28; Jaffé 1977, pp.30, 71; Rowlands 1977, p.33, under no.21, p.34, no.22.

This aggressive and densely-organised drawing was freely derived from Leonardo's lost wall painting of the *Battle of Anghiari*. Echoes of this composition can be found in the ferocious struggle to possess a standard; the group of men in combat on the ground; the animated horses' heads which suggest vivid emotions, and, in particular, those animals at the upper right who bite each other savagely. Rubens went one step further than Leonardo and showed a warrior sinking his teeth into the standard as though it were alive.

The drawing has an inserted section of paper at the lower left containing the men on the ground who are fighting to the death. The Leonardoesque character of this group can be seen from the grotesque head of the man with furrowed brow and jutting jaw. This area is more densely worked in black chalk than the remainder of the drawing and may have been cut by Rubens from another dismembered sheet.

The drawing was begun in hard black chalk and the areas where this is visible show numerous changes of outline. Next, some pale grey wash was added to give solidity to the forms. Red chalk was used sparingly to define the tail and mane of two of the horses. Lastly, brown wash was added on the head of the horse on the left and on the ferocious and

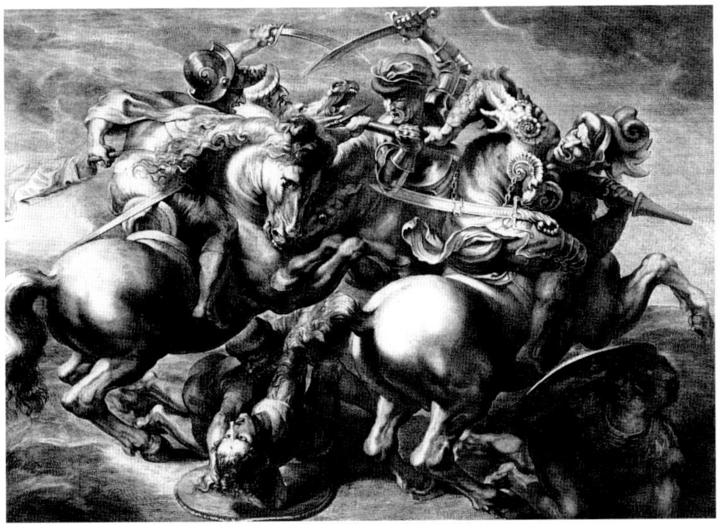

4

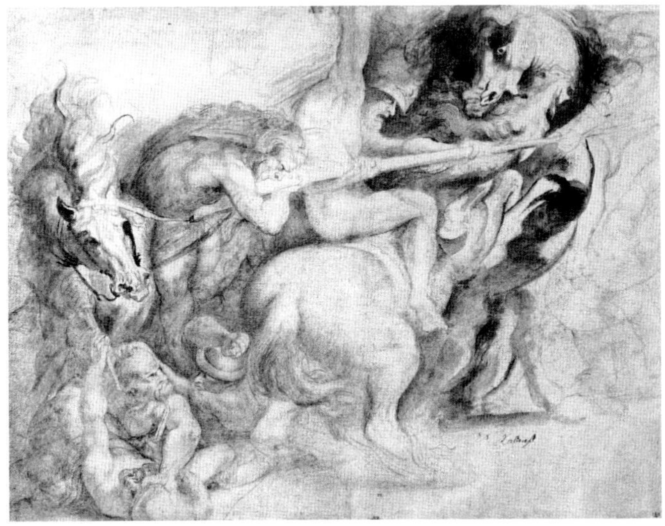

5

alarmed animal that rears up on the right.

Rubens added a black chalk inscription at the upper left which is abraded and has proved difficult to interpret.[1] It can be translated as: 'make it so that he who raises his body up on his feet in the stirrups ... to get closer to the enemies'. Leonardo depicted one of the horsemen in the *Battle of Anghiari* as rising up in his saddle and pressing his knees against his horse's neck to preserve his equilibrium.[2] The annotation suggests Rubens had observed this demonstration of balance in motion.

There can be little doubt this work dates from soon after Rubens's arrival in Italy. Like some other large drawings of this period, it does not appear to have been made in preparation for any other work. The inscription described above is similar in function and placing to several others from this period, including one on a copy after Pordenone [cat.no.46], securely dateable to 1600.

Rubens reused the warrior who raises his right arm to strike a fierce blow, seated on a horse that twists round violently to bite another one, in his *Battle of the Amazons* which is in Munich, dateable around 1615. This literal return to a drawing made about fifteen years earlier is characteristic of Rubens, who was often economical in reusing his own work.

1. See Hind 1923, p.12, under no.21; Glück/Haberditzl 1928, p.29, under no.8, and Müller Hofstede 1964, p.105.
2. See Zöllner 1991, p.188.

6 · Pieter Claesz. Soutman (*c*.1580–1657) after Rubens, after Leonardo da Vinci

The Last Supper

Etching on two plates; 29.8 × 100 cm
The British Museum, London, inv.no.1868-6-12-371

REFERENCES: Bottari/Ticozzi 1822–5, II, pp.241–2, 283, 284; V, pp.432; 440; Voorhelm Schneevoogt 1873, p.38, no.231; Van den Wijngaert 1940, p.92, no.631; Bodart 1977, pp.28–9, no.24; Alberici 1984, p.62, no.41; Steinberg 2001, pp.258–60, no.41.

Leonardo's famous wall painting of the *Last Supper* in the Dominican church and friary of Santa Maria delle Grazie, Milan, dates from between 1494 and late 1497 or early 1498. The composition was well-known in Rubens's circle. One of the earliest painted copies, attributed to Andrea Solario (*c*.1465–1524), was bought by Abbot Arnout Streyters in 1545 for the Norbertijnenabdij at Tongerlo,[1] where it has remained. But the etching by Pieter Claesz. Soutman must have been based on a drawing by Rubens, now lost, because the second state was inscribed *P.P. Rub[ens] Delin*. Soutman worked in Antwerp from around 1615 until he returned to Haarlem in 1628, and this seems the likely period when the etching of the *Last Supper* was made.

Soutman's etching includes all the figures from Leonardo's composition but adopts a broad horizontal format that cuts off everything above the Apostles's heads and below the edge of the tablecloth. Soutman also stripped the table and added a chalice and loaf of bread. This Eucharistic emphasis was reinforced by inscribing the texts from the Gospels in which Christ is described as breaking bread and drinking wine, saying, 'This is my body and this is my blood; do this in remembrance of me' (Matthew 26: 26–8; Mark 14: 22–4; Luke 22: 19–20). This fits with the Counter-Reformation emphasis on the Sacraments in which Eucharist was given prominence.

A drawing after the *Last Supper* in Dijon has sometimes been wrongly attributed to Rubens.[2] Soutman's etching has a number of differences of detail from this model and is unlikely to have been based upon it. The drawing shows a strap around Bartholomew's upper right arm and a purse in Judas's hand, as in the wall painting, but Soutman treated the sleeve differently and placed the bag of money near Judas's right hand on the table. The etching is far more refined and detailed than the Dijon drawing, but, interestingly, on several points the print is less close to Leonardo's wall painting.

One of the few recorded statements by Rubens on Italian sixteenth-century art concerned the *Last Supper*. His Latin text was transcribed and translated by Roger de Piles from a pocket-book that was subsequently destroyed.[3] This reveals Rubens admiration for the way that Leonardo had varied the psychological response of each Apostle through pose and gesture. On the other hand, Rubens adopted a vertical rather than a horizontal format in his own depictions of this subject where he grouped the Apostles closely together, and it seems the great fame of Leonardo's composition forced him to find different ways of treating the subject.

1. See Marijnissen 1959, p.13.
2. Jaffé 1965a, pp.26, 32, note 15; Jaffé 1965b, p.380; Jaffé 1966b, I, pp.32–3, 64–5, 88, note 37; Jaffé 1977, pp.24, 29.
3. Piles 1699, pp.166–8.

7
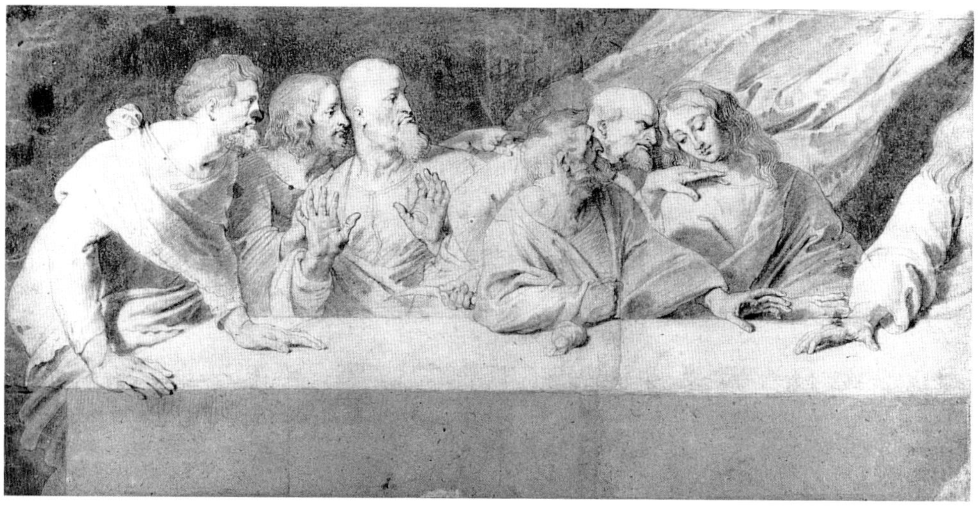

8
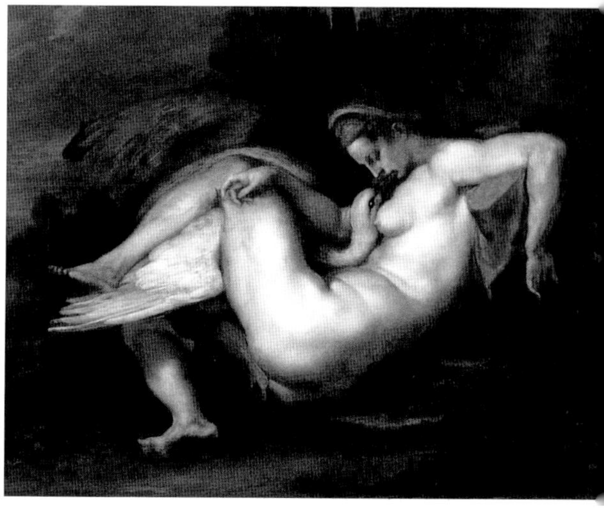

7 · Pieter Claesz. Soutman after Rubens, after Leonardo da Vinci *Six Apostles*

Red and black chalk, 20.2 × 51.5 cm
Devonshire Collection, Chatsworth, inv.no.677

REFERENCES: Jaffé 1965a, p.32, note 15; Jaffé 1966b, I, pp.32, 88, note 37; A.K. Wheelock in Washington 1983–4, unpaginated, under no.13.

Pieter Soutman did not travel to Italy, so he never saw Leonardo's *Last Supper*, but this did not prevent him from making one of its most famous reproductions. His etching [cat.no.6] was made from a drawing by Rubens, now lost, but, perhaps, the very large copy sold from the Nijman collection in 1807. Soutman did not work directly onto the plate from this work, however, because he made an elaborate preparatory drawing, the left-hand section of which survives at Chatsworth and provides some idea of what Rubens's drawing must have looked like.

Soutman's etching did not only make Leonardo's wall painting famous, but Rubens's drawing as well. The absence of the latter's name from the first state led to some confusion in the eighteenth century, although it became widely accepted that the etching was made under his supervision, as noted in a letter from Pierre-Jean Mariette to Giovanni Bottari of 1765.[1] In 1771, Jean François Marie Michel stated in print that Rubens had made a large drawing from the original when in Italy, which he had brought back to Antwerp where it had been etched.[2] The print was the subject of much critical correspondence at that time between Mariette, the Comte de Caylus (1692–1765), and Franceso Maria Niccolò Gaburri (1676–1742),[3] who seem to have disliked its tainted Flemish character and would clearly have preferred a reproduction that was more Italianate.

The way in which Leonardo showed the Apostles seated on one side of a long table, so that each one is visible to the spectator, followed earlier precedents, but their arrangement in groups of two or three was new. Reading from Christ's right the figures seen in the Chatsworth copy (and in the original wall painting) are John, Peter, and Judas who leans backwards between them; Andrew and James the Greater who form a group that is linked to Peter because they were witnesses to the Transfiguration and companions of Christ in the Garden of Gethsemane; and Bartholomew, the steward, who stands leaning against the table at its end.

Rubens's notes on Leonardo's *Last Supper* show that he understood how and why Leonardo had varied the psychological response of each Apostle.[4] This understanding was developed out of something said by Vasari, who wrote that Leonardo had succeeded in expressing the range of conflicting emotions felt by the Apostles on learning that one of them would betray Christ, as well as their confusion at being unable to understand his meaning.[5] It is clear that this work was crucial for Rubens's depiction of emotion.

1. See the letter dated 30 December 1765 in Bottari/Ticozzi 1822–5, V, p.440, no.CLXII (wrongly dated as 1766).
2. Michel 1771, p.38.
3. See Bottari/Ticozzi 1822–5, II, pp.283–4, no.XCII; V, p.432, no.CLIX; and also note 1 above.
4. Piles 1699, pp.166–8.
5. Vasari 1568, II, p.6.

MICHELANGELO

8 · Rubens after Michelangelo (1475–1564) *Leda and the Swan*

COLOUR ILLUSTRATION ON BACK COVER

Oil on panel; 64.5 × 80.5 cm
Stephen Mazoh, New York

REFERENCES: Jaffé 1968, pp.180–3; Knauer 1969, pp.5–8, 10–13; Jaffé 1977, pp.64–5; Held 1983, p.19; Jaffé 1989, p.147, no.9; J. Wood in Canberra/Melbourne 1992, pp.114–16, no.32.

Michelangelo painted a *Leda and the Swan* for Alfonso d'Este between November 1529 and October 1530, but never handed it over. It passed to François I in 1532, and remained at Fontainebleau until its destruction as obscene at some time between 1638 and 1643. It has been claimed that a large painted copy by Rubens now in the Gemäldegalerie, Dresden, as well as this smaller (and possibly unfinished) version in New York, were made after visiting Fontainebleau on his way south to Italy.[1] But an unknown Flemish artist would not have gained access to a notorious work kept in one of the more private rooms at the chateau.

Alternatively, it has been said that the Dresden panel was painted in Antwerp before Rubens left for Italy in 1600, using a reversed engraving of the painting by Cornelis Bos (*c.*1510–1556).[2] While this early dating for both versions is persuasive, Rubens worked from a copy of Michelangelo's lost cartoon,[3] a work which can be reconstructed from a full-size drawing in black chalk attributed to Rosso and now in the Royal Academy, London. Rubens cannot have used Bos's print because the angle of Leda's left arm is exactly as found in all the copies that derive from the cartoon.

The New York version gives the figure of Leda more space to breathe than the Dresden panel. Although the former is constructed from a core with added strips of wood on all sides, this does not mean it started out looking like the Dresden version, and X-radiographs have revealed an oval painted frame underneath overlapping the inner and outer sections.[4] This once contained a portrait (or at least a head) since part of a face, an eye and a nose are visible. Similar frames appear in a series of larger, life-sized heads of emperors painted by several Antwerp artists, including Otto van Veen (1556–1629) and the young Rubens, now known largely from copies.

Visible alterations to Leda's left hand, waist, and right knee in the New York version establish that it was never a copy of the Dresden panel. In short, while the former was not a conventional preparatory sketch for the latter, it was also not a straightforward copy from it, and they may have been made concurrently, the Dresden work being brought to completion and the New York panel being abandoned at an advanced stage.

Pietro Aretino eulogised Michelangelo's *Leda* in 1542 by saying that 'one cannot look on without envying the swan'.[5] Rubens responded to this carnal image without prudishness, and, after returning to Antwerp, he interpreted the subject for himself in a version, now lost, which was recorded in 1618.[6] The importance of Michelangelo's *Leda* for him at this time is shown by its echo in his *Rape of the Daughters of Leucippus*, now in Munich, of about 1616.

1. Jaffé 1968, pp.180–3; Jaffé 1977, pp.64–5; and Jaffé 1989, p.147, no.9.
2. J. Müller Hofstede in Cologne 1977, I, pp.46–7. For the print, see Schéle 1965, pp.134–8, no.59a, repr. pl.21.
3. As established by Wilde 1957, p.278, and Carroll 1987, pp.320, 326, note 2.
4. See Jaffé 1968, repr. fig.18.
5. Aretino 1608–9, II, pp.2–3; Aretino 1957–60, I, p.247, no.CLXVII: 'non si può mirar senza invidiare il cigno'.
6. See Rooses / Ruelens 1887–1909, II, p.137.

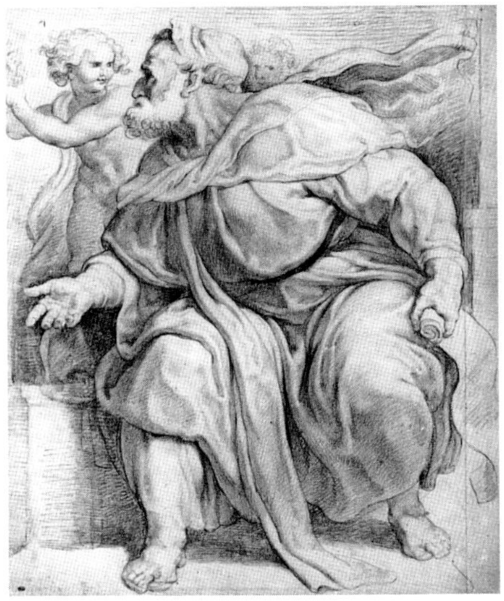
9

9 · Rubens after Michelangelo
The Prophet Ezekiel

Black and red chalk with faint white heightening;
46 × 38 cm
Département des Arts graphiques, Musée du Louvre, Paris, inv.no.20231
Exhibited in Edinburgh only

REFERENCES: Reiset 1866, p.321, no.572; Rooses 1886–92, V, p.195, no.1369; Glück / Haberditzl 1928, pp.10, 30, no.16; Lugt 1949, II, p.22, no.1042; Jaffé 1977, p.21; Logan 1978, pp.432, 433–4; Sérullaz 1978, p.90, no.89.

The prophet Ezekiel is depicted on the third pendentive on the right from the entrance to the Sistine Chapel, part of the ceiling painted by Michelangelo for Julius II between 1508 and 1512. Ezekiel twists sideways with a violent movement that contradicts his enthroned pose. There is an intense dialogue between the prophet and the infant genii in which their eyes meet and he gestures emphatically with his hands. The hot colours of Ezekiel's robes in the fresco add to the impact of his aggressive pose and formidable size.

Michelangelo's conception of Ezekiel was based on hints found in the Bible where he is described as dressed as a priest (Ezekiel 1: 3) and sent a scroll of lamentations (Ezekiel 2: 9–10). But the prophet disregards the scroll in his hand and is depicted less as someone who reads and more as one who sees visions: 'The Heavens were opened, and I saw visions of God' (Ezekiel 1: 1). He may be shown at the moment when he saw 'the likeness of four living creatures' (Ezekiel 1: 5), the Tetramorph, from which come the symbols of the Four Evangelists.

This is one of eight surviving drawings in black and red chalk after the prophets and sibyls that are now in the Louvre and were probably once part of a complete series. Black chalk was used to establish the main design with red added on top to describe areas of flesh and Ezekiel's robe. Red chalk was applied lightly to describe this robe and to give a sheen to its surface, which was intensified by the use of faint white heightening on the knee. The cooler areas in the fresco, notably the prophet's cloak (which is coloured pale grey) and shawl (pale blue) were copied in black with further white heightening, and this helped create a subtle differentiation of tone and hue between the cloak and the robe. This respect for differences of colour in the fresco makes it certain that the copy was made from the original.

The laborious nature of these drawings in the Louvre, as well as their large scale, make it likely that they date from very early in Rubens's Italian period and specifically from his first visit to Rome in 1601. However, the relative boldness of this drawing suggests that – like the powerful and well-preserved sheet of *Joel* [cat.no.10] – it was one of the last in the series to have been executed.

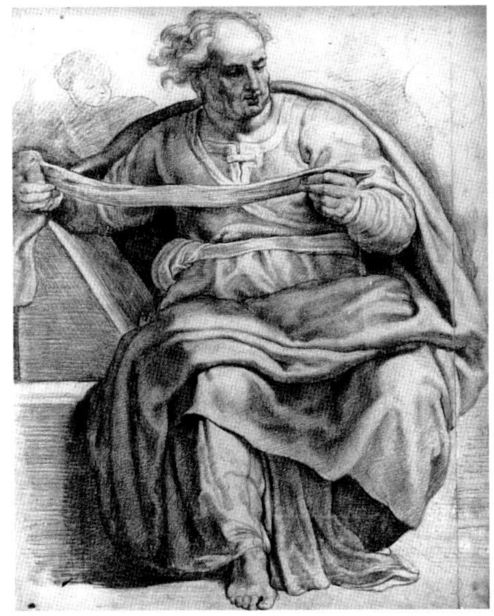
10

10 · Rubens after Michelangelo
The Prophet Joel

COLOUR ILLUSTRATION ON PAGE 26

Black and red chalk; 47 × 37 cm
Département des Arts graphiques, Musée du Louvre, Paris, inv.no.20230
Exhibited in Nottingham only

REFERENCES: Reiset 1866, p.321, no.571; Rooses 1886–92, V, pp.194–5, no.1368; Glück / Haberditzl 1928, pp.10, 30, no.18; Lugt 1949, II, p.22, no.1041; Jaffé 1977, p.21; Logan 1978, pp.432, 433–4; Sérullaz 1978, p.90, no.90.

Michelangelo's Joel is located at the entrance end of the Sistine Chapel, on the first pendentive to the right when looking towards the altar. This prophet was painted early in the first campaign of work on the ceiling between 1508 and 1510.[1] As with most of the other prophets and sibyls, it is not obvious why he was included, and his book in the Old Testament is largely concerned with the triumph of the Jewish people.

This is amongst the most massive and frontally-posed of all the prophets and sibyls. Michelangelo suggested Joel's inner turmoil by making the locks of his hair blow sideways as if in a fierce wind, and he conveyed his mental concentration through the intense way he scans his scroll, as Vasari noted.[2] This emphasis on reading continues in the figures of the two infant genii, one of whom (only lightly outlined by Rubens) holds a book while the other looks over Joel's shoulder at the text he is studying.

This copy is the best preserved of the series of eight that survive in the Louvre after the prophets and sibyls, and it is striking for its confident handling of chalk on a large scale. A dating to Rubens's first visit to Rome in 1601 is argued in the introduction above and in relation to the copy of *Ezekiel* [cat.no.9]. As elsewhere in this series, red chalk was used for those areas that are warm in hue in the frescoes, and this suggests that the copy was made in front of the original. Rubens applied red chalk with some force on Joel's cloak which is a terracotta colour in the fresco, while his robe, which was painted pale lilac, was left in black. Red chalk was also used more faintly to describe the flesh of Joel's face, hands, and right foot. The infant genii were only very lightly indicated, drawn only in black chalk, and do not seem to have interested Rubens.

None of the other copies in the series quite matches this one for accuracy, and, while some simplify the priestly robes worn by the prophets, here the edging and the tab at the neck which ties it together are legible, though the border is made more round than square, and the circular motifs are omitted. Joel's face is perhaps made softer, more fleshy, and less intense than in the fresco, and this hints at the way Rubens changed Michelangelo's work in accordance with seventeenth-century taste.

1. Hartt 1991, I, p.234.
2. Vasari 1568, III, pp.734–5.

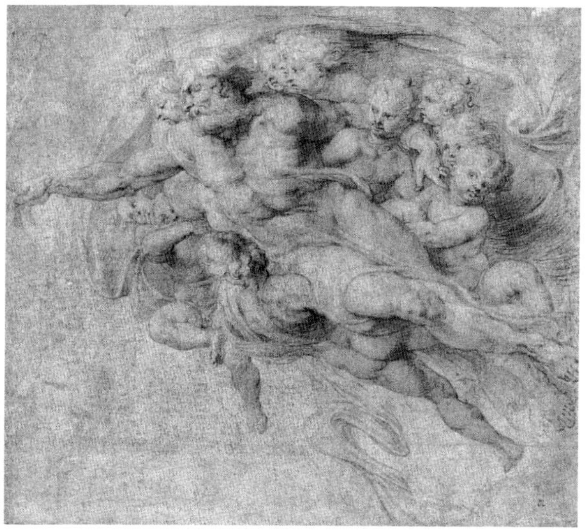

11

11 · Rubens after Michelangelo

God the Father Supported by Angels

Red chalk with red wash and cream bodycolour; 25.5 × 28.6 cm. A substantial section cut away at the lower left and replaced.
Walker Art Gallery, Liverpool, inv.no.WAG 1995.083

REFERENCES: Richardson 1747, p.40, no.54; Rooses 1886–92, V, pp.193–4, no.1, 365; Jaffé 1957, p.376; Burchard/d'Hulst 1963, text vol., p.45, under no.24; Jaffé 1977, pp.21, 60; Brooke 1998, pp.139–40, no.77.

The Liverpool drawing records the figure of God supported by a mass of child angels from Michelangelo's famous fresco of *God Creating Adam* on the Sistine Ceiling, painted during the second phase of work between September 1510 and October 1512.

In art, God has sometimes been shown giving Adam the breath of life (*spiraculum vitae*) as described in Genesis, or standing in profile and blessing him, as depicted in Jacopo della Quercia's relief on the main portal at San Petronio, Bologna. Michelangelo, however, showed God in movement, carried by the mass of child angels, and appearing to fly horizontally, as if swimming through the heavens. His upper body is shown twisted slightly so that his left arm rests on the shoulders of an angel, 'as if to support himself' as Vasari observed,[1] and with his right arm stretched forward so as to transmit life to Adam.

Red chalk was used with precision in the Liverpool drawing and some strengthening in red wash was added with the tip of the brush, particularly to enliven locks of hair, to define the torso of God, and to animate his face and those of the angels. These heads were made to look different from Michelangelo's originals, since Rubens gave them more rounded cheeks and almost impish expressions, quite unlike the pensive heads seen in the fresco. Finally, fluent touches of cream bodycolour were added on God's flowing beard and hair and to the eyes of the angels. The Liverpool drawing is close in handling to a copy by Rubens after one of Michelangelo's *ignudi* [cat.no.12], also in red chalk. Both are more refined than the large and laborious copies after the prophets and sibyls [cat.nos.9, 10] of 1601, and, a dating of shortly after Rubens's return to Rome in 1606 is likely.

It has been suggested that the pose of God was adapted by Rubens for the figure of Christ in his *Raising of the Cross*, painted for S. Croce in Gerusalemme, Rome,[2] in 1601–2, now only known from a copy in the cathedral at Grasse.[3] This may seem strange but there is a parallel in the way the right leg is stretched out and the left one crossed behind. The pose does not suit the crucified Christ since his upper body is pinned down and his legs are made to kick out wildly. This link could be used to date the Liverpool drawing to 1601, but, as argued above, its visual character is very different from the other Michelangelo copies dated to this year.

1. Vasari 1568, III, p.733.
2. Evers 1944, p.100.
3. See Vlieghe 1972–3, II, pp.65–8, no.112.

12

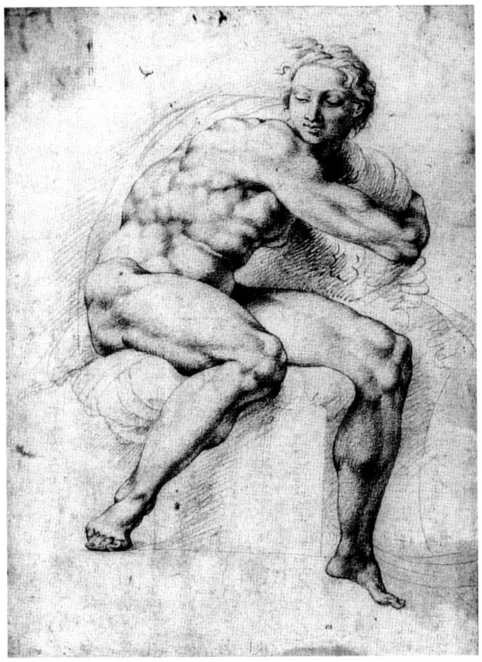

13

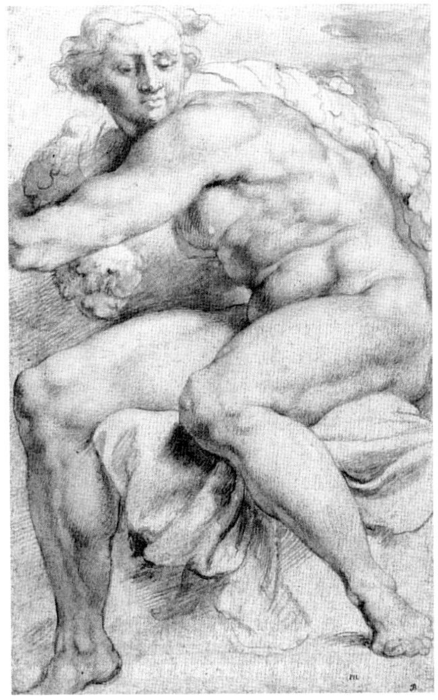

12 · Rubens after Michelangelo

A Nude Youth Turning to the Right

Red chalk, with red wash applied with the tip of the brush; 38.9 × 27.8 cm
The British Museum, London, inv.no.1870–8–13–882

REFERENCES: Jaffé 1957, p.376; Held 1959, I, pp.52, 156, no.158; Burchard/d'Hulst 1963, text vol., pp.36–7, no.18; J. Müller Hofstede in Cologne 1977, I, p.274, no.67; Logan 1977, p.410; Rowlands 1977, p.44, no.37; Logan/Haverkamp-Begemann 1978, pp.93, 95.

This drawing in the British Museum is copied from one of the nude youths by Michelangelo on the Sistine Ceiling. These figures, who sit on blocks above the thrones of the prophets and sibyls, are known as *ignudi*, a term that derives from two of the artist's sixteenth-century biographers, Condivi,[1] and Vasari.[2] The youths hold ribbons which are threaded through slits in the marble frames of large bronze medallions. Unlike some of the other more austerely seated youths, this one sits on a cushion and so is human enough to feel discomfort.

Vasari commented on the variety of pose and temperament in the *ignudi*.[3] In general, they express either lethargy or alarm, sometimes contrasted in each pair of figures, and the youth in this drawing recoils as if surprised while his companion (not shown in the copy) stretches his limbs as if yawning.

Red chalk is used precisely in the drawing and with few revisions (although there is a small change to the right ankle). The sheet was strengthened in red wash, applied with the tip of the brush, as seen on the face and hair, as well as the chest and left foot. Rubens later made a counterproof of this drawing [cat.no.13], in the early 1630s, and he added these retouchings then as the chalk drawing may have lost some of its freshness and needed reviving.

The body of Michelangelo's *ignudo* is quite soft and simplified by comparison with some of his more muscular companions on the ceiling. Rubens, however, intensified the structure of bone and muscle, tilted the head slightly, and made his version more tense and active. He lit the head more evenly, also omitting the fillet, no doubt because it was not easy to see from the floor of the chapel. The overall result is that Rubens's figure looses the passivity of the original.

This drawing has been generally dated to Rubens's Italian period and is thought to have been made in Rome in front of the original.[4] But it is more assured than the laborious copies after the prophets and sibyls of 1601 [cat.nos.9, 10] and a dating to 1606 for this sheet and the *God the Father* [cat.no.11], also in red chalk and after Michelangelo, is likely.

1. Condivi 1553, fol.23v.
2. Vasari 1568, III, p.733.
3. Vasari 1568, III, p.733.
4. Held 1959, I, p.156, under no.158 (around 1601); Jaffé 1983, p.401, note 8 (*c*.1606); Held 1986, p.74, under no.22 ('1601–1605').

13 · Rubens after Michelangelo

A Nude Youth Turning to the Left

COLOUR ILLUSTRATION ON PAGE 7

Red chalk counterproof, with red wash and white bodycolour; 32.2 × 19.9 cm
The British Museum, London, inv.no.1870–8–13–883

REFERENCES: Held 1959, I, pp.52, 156, under no.158; Burchard/d'Hulst 1963, text vol., pp.37–9, no.19; Müller Hofstede 1965, p.265, note 14; Müller Hofstede 1966, p.440; Logan 1977, pp.410, 412; Rowlands 1977, pp.44–5, no.38; Logan/Haverkamp-Begemann 1978, p.95; D. Jaffé in Canberra/Melbourne 1992, pp.189–90, no.73.

This drawing is a counterproof made by Rubens from his own red chalk copy, discussed above [cat.no.12], which reproduces one of the nude youths, called *ignudi*, from Michelangelo's Sistine Ceiling. The figure became reversed in the process.

The counterproof was made on a smaller piece of paper than the drawing from which it derived, and, as a result, the right foot was cut off at the lower edge. This missing detail was drawn separately between the legs of the youth, before being partly covered with drapery and shading. Rubens used wash to soften and blend the red chalk, little of which remains visible, before adding bodycolour to suggest highlights and reflections. The reworking suggests subtle effects of light on skin and greatly strengthens the palpability of the flesh.

Three main areas were developed in the reworking: Firstly, the cushion on which Michelangelo's nude youth sits in the fresco was transformed into a much larger cloth which falls down between his legs. Secondly, the face was made more masculine and rounded by Rubens, with a hint of a frown. Thirdly, the earlier red chalk copy [cat.no.12] had only lightly indicated the festoon of oak leaves found in the fresco, but Rubens added this when retouching the counterproof, suggesting that he was thinking back to the original, possibly

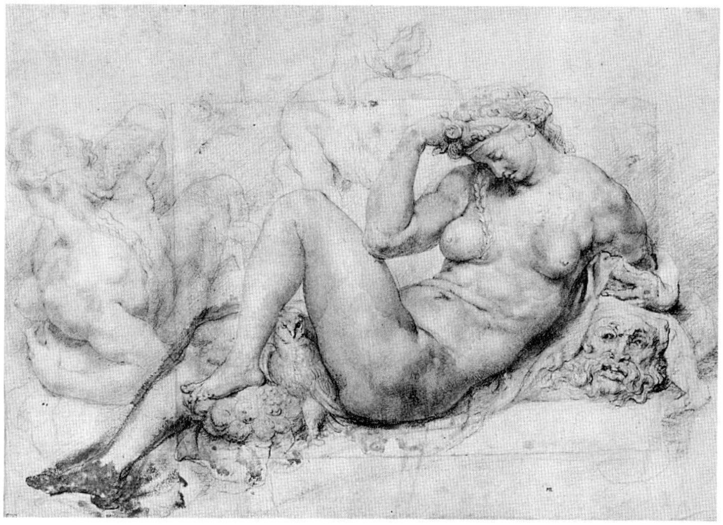

14

through Vasari's description.[1]

The counterproof was used in Rubens's Whitehall Ceiling,[2] completed in 1634, where *Royal Bounty* adopts the pose of the *ignudo* in reverse, exactly as in the drawing. This may seem to date the counterproof precisely, but scholars have suggested that it was made much earlier between 1600 and 1608 while Rubens was in Italy and reworked straight away.[3] This implies that it was made with no particular purpose in mind and was kept as study material. Two other views are possible. Firstly, that it was made during this period but not reworked until the early 1630s;[4] and, secondly, that it was made around 1632–3 (when Rubens needed to develop this figure for the Whitehall commission) and reworked at the same time.[5] The last mentioned view is the most likely in terms of the vigorous style of the revision and Rubens's known working methods.

Although the use to which Rubens put this counterproof is clear, it was never simply a preparatory drawing for *Royal Bounty* but an independent version, made more like Michelangelo's original by the restoration of the festoon of oak leaves. It shows Rubens returning to a red chalk drawing he had made around thirty years earlier, and the comparison demonstrates the difference between his copies over a wide time span.

1. Vasari 1568, III, p.733.
2. See Burchard/d'Hulst 1963, text vol., p.38. The point was discussed further in Held 1980, I, pp.214–15, under no.143.
3. Logan 1977, p.412; Logan/Haverkamp-Begemann 1978, p.95.
4. Müller Hofstede 1966, p.440.
5. Burchard/d'Hulst 1963, text vol., p.38.

14 · Rubens after Michelangelo
Night

COLOUR ILLUSTRATION ON PAGE 30

Black chalk, with brown wash and cream and white bodycolour; 36 × 49.5 cm. A smaller piece of paper, 24.5 × 33.2 cm, stuck down on to this sheet.
Collection Frits Lugt, Institut Néerlandais, Paris, inv.no.5251
Exhibited in Edinburgh only

REFERENCES: Glück/Haberditzl 1928, pp.10–11, 31, no.22; Goldscheider 1957, p.17; Burchard/d'Hulst 1963, text vol., pp.35–6, no.17; Müller Hofstede 1966, pp.439–40; C. van Hasselt in London/Paris/Bern/Brussels 1972, pp.99–101, no.76; Logan 1978, p.424.

This drawing records Michelangelo's *Night* from the tomb of Giuliano de'Medici in the New Sacristy at San Lorenzo, Florence. Vasari wrote that this figure represents 'the grief and melancholy of one who has lost a great and honoured possession',[1] that is, the dead prince. Of the four personifications in the chapel, *Night* is the most clearly identified through symbolic details: the crescent moon and star on her diadem, the bunch of poppies, the owl under her left leg, and the mask (of dreams).

The sheet was constructed by taking a refined black chalk copy of the sculpture and fixing it to a larger piece of paper which was then reworked in order to extend the missing parts of the figure, in particular the entire right leg. Rubens integrated these additions by working over the figure in brown wash with a fine brush and adding yellowish and white bodycolour to give it an almost silken sheen. Two subordinate views were then added showing the sculpture from the back and the side, their placing determined by the enlarged figure at the core of the sheet. This process of expansion fits Rubens's practice, but the key question is whether the nucleus was his own work, as generally assumed, or whether he reused another artist's copy.

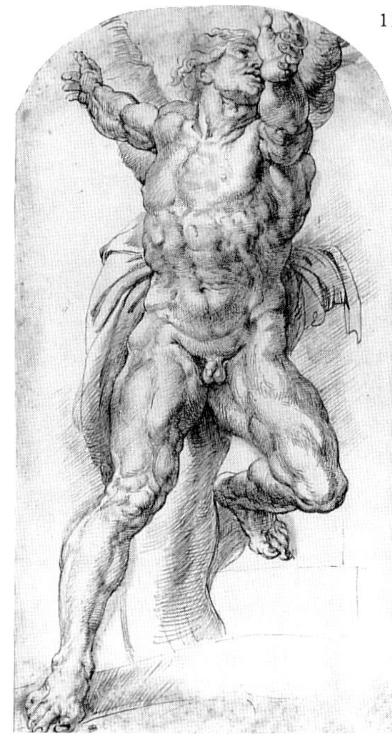

15

The genesis of this drawing can be analysed in several steps: Firstly, the core fragment recalls Rubens's early black chalk copies after classical sculpture and could have been made in Florence in 1600 or 1603. Secondly, the later reworking of the sheet may have dated from after Rubens's return to Antwerp, since it made use of another smaller version of the sculpture,[2] which included the missing left hand and made possible views from angles inaccessible in the chapel. Thirdly, the subordinate studies are different from the retouching in style and medium, and can be compared with two red chalk drawings, one in the Ashmolean Museum, Oxford,[3] the other present location unknown,[4] dateable to *c.*1616. These were made from a small sculpture of a naked reclining woman which has some affinity of pose, recording it from the side in order to examine foreshortening, exactly as in the present sheet.

The chilly eroticism of Michelangelo's *Night* has been traced in a number of Rubens's own works, and the pose was used for the reclining figure of Pan in the *Council of the Gods* from the Medici Cycle in the Louvre, conceived in 1622. A black chalk copy of the mask of *Night*, in the Kupferstichkabinett, Dresden,[6] has been attributed to Rubens but is more emphatic and coarse than his authentic drawings.

1. Vasari 1568, III, p.741: 'il dolore, & la malinconia di chi perde cosa onorata, & grande'.
2. Goldscheider 1957, p.17.
3. See B. Cleaver in Oxford/London, 1988, pp.29–30, no.4, repr.
4. Formerly Robert von Hirsch. Sold London, Sotheby's, 20 June 1978, lot 34.
5. Inv.no.C 1967–46.

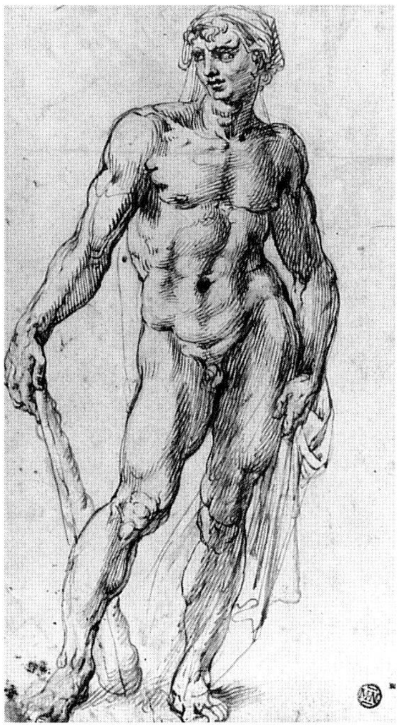

16

15 · Bartolomeo Passarotti (1529–1592) after Michelangelo, retouched by Rubens
The Punishment of Haman

Pen and brown ink, retouched with pen and ink, greyish wash and cream bodycolour; 42.1 × 21.5 cm. On a sheet with an arched top, laid down onto a slightly larger rectangular piece of paper.
Département des Arts graphiques, Musée du Louvre, Paris, inv.no.20267
Exhibited in Nottingham only

REFERENCES: Lugt 1949, II, p.22, no.1039; Held 1959, I, p.52; Jaffé 1966a, p.145, note 23; Jaffé 1977, pp.19–20; Logan 1978, pp.423, 433; Sérullaz 1978, p.86, no.82.

This drawing extracts the main figure from Michelangelo's fresco of the *Punishment of Haman* on one of the corner spandrels of the Sistine Ceiling, executed in the second stage of work between 1510 and 1512 when the figures became increasingly large and assertive. Haman, the Agagite, chief minister of King Ahasuerus, died on the gallows he had prepared for his enemy Mordecai (Esther 7: 9). However, in the fresco, Haman is shown crucified, which must be because he was intended as a prefiguration of Christ.

This drawing in the Louvre has sometimes been dated before 1600 and is said to be based on an anonymous engraving reissued by Antonio Lafreri in 1555.[1] Matters were complicated by the emergence of a second and similar drawing, currently on deposit at the Fitzwilliam Museum, Cambridge, which has been published as a duplicate by Rubens,[2] an opinion that has been convincingly refuted.[3] These drawings raise a number of questions about their relation to each other, to Michelangelo's fresco, to the engraving, and to Rubens.

Neither the Louvre drawing nor the second version were in fact based on the print, which reduces the figure to a few simple blocks of shading and lacks the detailed surface musculature found in the underdrawing on the Louvre sheet. This is a sixteenth-century work that Rubens retouched. In my opinion it is one of the Michelangelo copies made by Bartolomeo Passarotti, whose emphatic pen style combined areas of neat cross-hatching with others that are heavier and more vigorous. By contrast, the second version is the work of one hand and a weak copy of the Louvre drawing before retouching.

Rubens reworked the Louvre drawing with grey wash and cream bodycolour, making some limited changes with pen and ink. He used the tip of the brush to add curved lines on the branch at Haman's left shoulder, extra locks of hair, and shading on the trunk of the tree. Rubens used cream bodycolour to reduce the size of Haman's feet and to change the contours of his legs, as well as to give a greater sense of structure and animation to his torso and head.

This kind of intervention is close to the changes that he made to the drawing, in Berlin, of a *Nude Youth with a Cornucopia* after Mantegna.[4] This is particularly evident in the use of long, almost feathery strokes of the brush placed on either side of the figure. In neither of these drawings was Rubens concerned with imposing his own personality on the model, and this fits with a date of around 1615 during the most cautious phase of his interventions on earlier drawings.

1. Lugt 1949, II, p.22, no.1039; Held 1959, I, p.52.
2. Jaffé 1966a, pp.131, 145, note 23; Jaffé 1977, pp.19–20.
3. Logan 1978, p.433.
4. Inv.no.KdZ 1551. Mielke/Winner 1977, pp.37–9, no.6, repr.

16 · Bartolomeo Passarotti after Michelangelo, retouched by Rubens
Hercules

Pen and ink over faint traces of black chalk, retouched with wash and bodycolour; 30.5 × 17 cm
Département des Arts graphiques, Musée du Louvre, Paris, inv.no.20213
Exhibited in Edinburgh only

REFERENCES: Lugt 1949, II, p.27, no.1073; Tolnay 1964, pp.129–32, 134; Châtelet-Lange 1972, p.455; Jaffé 1977, pp.19, 105, note 6; Logan 1978, p.434; Logan/Haverkamp-Begemann 1978, pp.94–5; Sérullaz 1978, pp.90–1, no.91; Cox-Rearick 1995, pp.310–13.

This drawing has been identified as a copy of Michelangelo's lost marble statue of *Hercules*. Both Condivi and Vasari dated it to shortly after the death of Lorenzo de'Medici in 1492.[1] It was Michelangelo's first life-size marble in-the-round, but it is not known who commissioned it. The Strozzi were certainly the first owners, and Piero Strozzi called it 'our giant'.[2] Much to Michelangelo's displeasure the family gave the work to Giovanni Battista della Palla, who in turn presented it to François I around 1530. By the early seventeenth century the statue had been moved from the Cour de la Fontaine at Fontainebleau to the Jardin d'Etang. Rubens may have seen it during one of his visits to the chateau in the early 1620s.

The Louvre drawing is a sixteenth-century sheet that was retouched by Rubens,[3] and the supple underdrawing bears no relation to his use of the pen. The contours were reworked with the tip of the brush in dark brown wash, and areas that needed change were blocked out with cream bodycolour, also applied in small touches to add relief to the figure and animation to the face. The left shoulder was made bigger to prevent the right one from appearing disproportionately large. The figure must originally have looked as though it was about to fall over and the retouching made it stand more

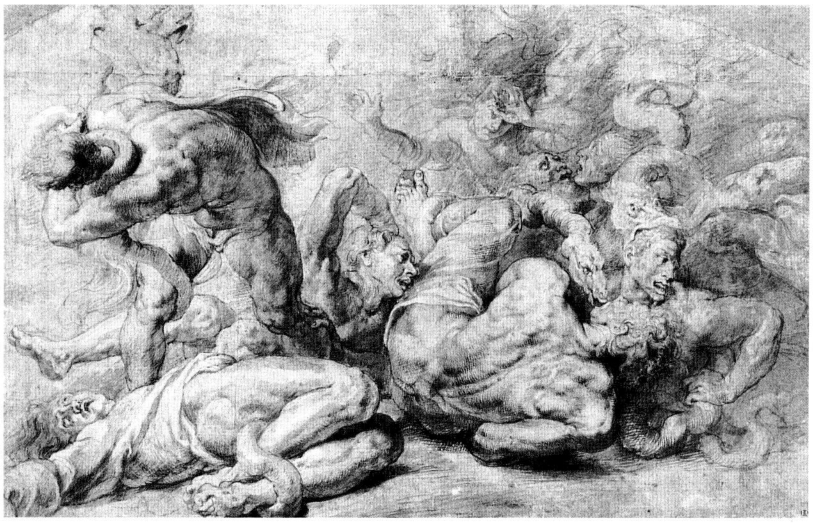
17

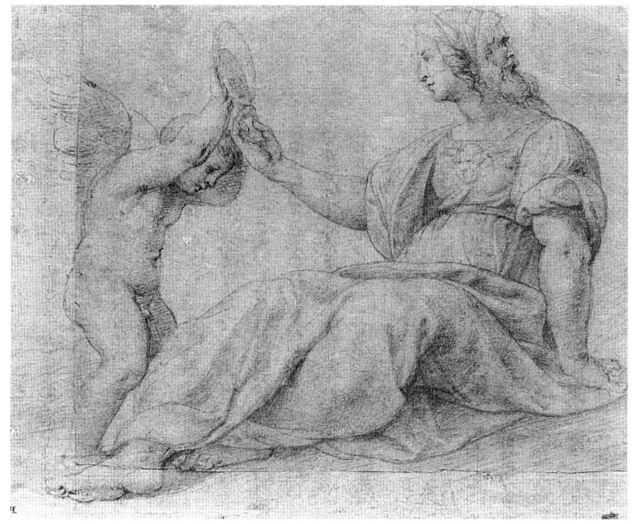
19

firmly on the ground. Most significantly, the straight stick originally held in the right hand was changed into a knotted club, so that the figure was transformed into a youthful and unbearded Hercules. This observation alone demolishes earlier arguments that the drawing was made directly from the Fontainebleau *Hercules*.[4]

Since the Louvre drawing exaggerates the musculature of this figure, making it fleshy and disturbingly pliable, it is hard to be certain of the exact prototype. A large model now in Casa Buonarroti, Florence, has been identified as the source.[5] But the proliferation of copies after Michelangelo's *Hercules* during the sixteenth century meant that it entered the repertoire of models available to artists.

It is here proposed that the drawing is by Bartolomeo Passarotti, whose interest in the work of Michelangelo is well-known. Heavy pressure on the pen produced dark, biting lines, and the pliability of the body is typical of his work. By comparison, a copy of Michelangelo's *Haman* [cat.no.15], here also attributed to Passarotti, is a diligent record of its model while the Louvre *Hercules* is a free variant.

The drawing has been dated to 1600,[6] or 1600–8.[7] But it is closer to the retouching on several other pen drawings which belong to the period 1615 to 1620. These interventions correct rather than transform the originals, and they fit well with Rubens's retouchings on *modelli* for engravings for which a precise chronology exists.

1. Condivi 1553, fol.7r.; Vasari 1568, III, p.720.
2. See Cox-Rearick 1995, p.462, note 145: 'del gigante di casa'.
3. As observed by Logan/Haverkamp-Begemann 1978, pp.94–5; and Logan 1978, p.434.
4. Tolnay 1964, pp.129–32.
5. Châtelet-Lange 1972, p.455.
6. Jaffé 1966a, pp.130–1.
7. Logan 1978, p.434.

17 · Anonymous Draughtsman after Michelangelo, retouched by Rubens

A Group of Eight Men and Women Plagued by Serpents

Pen and ink on paper cut up into sections and laid down on a new sheet, reworked with black chalk, brown wash and white bodycolour; 38.5 × 59.6 cm
The British Museum, London, inv.no.1895-9-15-1055

REFERENCES: Rooses 1886–92, V, p.225, no.1424; Hind 1923, p.7, no.4; Rowlands 1977, p.31, no.16; Jaffé 1977, p.21; Logan, 1987, p.69; C. Miele in Haverkamp-Begemann/Logan 1988, pp.87–9, no.21; D'Hulst/Vandenven 1989, pp.85–6, no.22; D. Jaffé in Canberra/Melbourne 1992, p.190.

Rubens's drawing is a free version of Michelangelo's *Worship of the Brazen Serpent*, one of the spandrels on the Sistine Chapel ceiling, and it shows the boldness with which he filled the difficult triangular shape of these frescoes with wildly foreshortened figures who seem almost to float. The subject concerns the disobedience of the Israelites towards Moses and Aaron and the plague of poisonous snakes sent to punish them by Jehovah (Numbers 21: 4–9).

Rubens cut up a neat pen and ink copy of the fresco and rearranged it with the addition of some new pieces of paper. The main sections that he retained contain the upper body of a man who bends forward, appearing to be strangled rather than bitten by a snake, and the man seen from the back, recoiling from a serpent who seems almost to kiss him on the lips. A distraught figure with outstretched arms in the background was based on a similar one in the fresco, but Rubens did not reuse the pen and ink copy here, preferring to work fast in chalk and wash across several sections of paper.

An intermediary, vertical stage in Rubens's organisation of his material can be reconstructed by looking at the way in which the pieces of paper were trimmed, since the lower edge of one fragment, on the left, is cut in exactly the same irregular shape as the top edge of another to the right. From this it appears that at one time Rubens placed the figure of the man bending forward directly above the man who is seen lying on the ground, recoiling in horror from the serpent.

Rubens's drawing is so radical in its reorganisation of Michelangelo's design that it is doubtful whether it remains a depiction of the Old Testament story, and the brazen serpent itself is nowhere to be found in the new composition. Nevertheless, the impact of some individual figures from this model can be seen in Rubens's own paintings of the *Brazen Serpent*, in particular a work now in the Courtauld Institute Galleries, London, of *c.*1609–10, and the much later interpretation of the same subject in the National Gallery, London, dateable to the late 1630s.

Although the drawing has been dated previously to the end of Rubens's visit to Italy,[1] or shortly after his return to Antwerp in 1608,[2] it is more like a final comment on Michelangelo's design than a study that might have led to Rubens's early version of the *Brazen Serpent*, already mentioned.[3] Adaptations of this kind had a life of their own in Rubens's work and the vigour and freedom of his treatment points to a dating in the 1630s.

1. Held 1980, I, p.463, under no.335; C. Miele in Haverkamp-Begemann/Logan 1988, p.87, under no.21.
2. Rowlands 1977, p.31, under no.16.
3. For the contrary view, see D'Hulst/Vandenven 1989, p.86, under no.22.

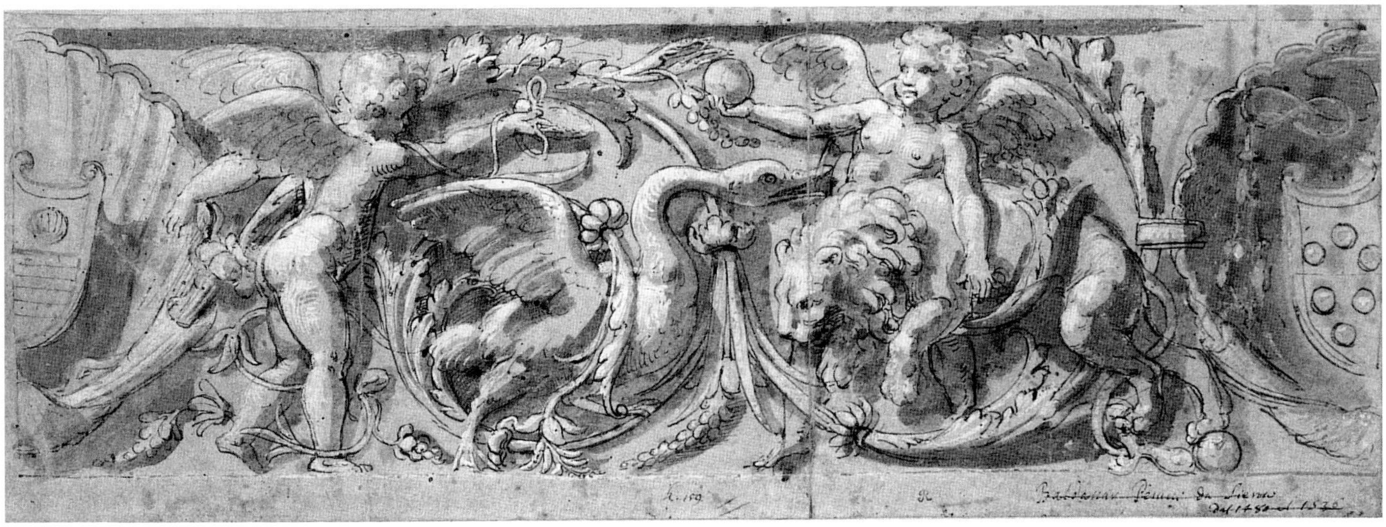

18

BALDASSARE PERUZZI

18 · Baldassare Peruzzi (1481–1536)
A Frieze with the Arms of Cardinal Ercole Rangone

Pen and ink with wash, heightened with white; 13.2 × 35.1 cm. Inscribed *Baldassar Perucci da Siena dal 1480 al 1536* by Rubens.
The British Museum, London, inv.no.Pp.2–96

REFERENCES: Pouncey/Gere 1962, cat. vol., pp.142–3, no.245; Jaffé 1964, p.396, note 32; Frommel 1967–8, pp.104–5, no.61; Wood 1994, pp.337, 349, note 26.

This drawing has been identified as containing the arms of Cardinal Ercole Rangone (d. *c*.1527) on the left, together with those of the Medici, on the right. When the design was repeated in a frieze the two would have been joined together. Putti playfully try to restrain the heraldic supporters of the Rangone and Medici families, the swan and lion. Rangone owed much to a Medici pope, Leo X, who made him a cardinal on 1 July 1517 in recognition of Rangone's mother's kindness after the battle of Ravenna in 1512.

The drawing is exhibited here because it was owned (but not retouched) by Rubens, who inscribed Peruzzi's name at the lower right. It belongs among a small group of drawings identified by him in this way [see also cat.nos.20, 27, 44, 45, 60, 66, 71, 73], and it is the only example where he included the artist's dates. This type of decorative design is rare in Rubens's collection, but he may not have retouched such sheets and it is his intervention which usually provides the only way of knowing whether or not he owned a particular drawing.

RAPHAEL

19 · Anonymous Sixteenth-Century Draughtsman after Raphael (1483–1520), retouched by Rubens
Prudence

Red chalk, retouched with red wash and yellowish bodycolour; 18 × 21.2 cm. The core section (16.2 × 18.7 cm) expanded by an L-shaped piece of paper at left and lower edges, 2.5 cm in width at the top left and 1.8 cm in height at the lower right.
National Gallery of Scotland, Edinburgh, inv.no.D 1787

REFERENCES: Jaffé 1967, p.101; Jaffé 1977, pp.24–5; Andrews 1985, I, p.71, no.D 1787; J. Lloyd Williams in Edinburgh 1999, p.68, no.28.

This drawing is a copy of one of the female personifications that Raphael painted above the window of the so-called Jurisprudence wall in the Stanza della Segnatura in the Vatican, dateable to the second half of 1511. Prudence was one of the four Cardinal Virtues. Raphael placed her at the centre of the fresco, flanked by Fortitude, on the left, and Temperance, on the right. Prudence's conventional attribute is the mirror, which allows her to see herself truthfully, and which Raphael included, held up in front of her by a winged child. Her Janus-like head, which makes her appear a beautiful young woman at front and a venerable old man at back, allows her to look in two directions at once with circumspection.

The core drawing which Rubens obtained and enlarged is so distinctive in quality and close to Raphael's draughtsmanship that it must have come from his studio.[1] The handling of red chalk recalls a slightly later study by Raphael, now in the Albertina, Vienna,[2] for one of the angels in the Chigi Chapel frescoes at Santa Maria della Pace, Rome. Despite the inherent softness of the medium, it was used here with the precision of metalpoint, as can be seen from the sharp and crisp outlines, and the way that internal modelling was created through blended cross-hatching.

Rubens expanded the drawing substantially on the left and at the bottom by joining it to an L-shaped piece of paper. He was content to make a few rapid notations on the new margins to suggest the infant's wings, buttocks, and foot, as well as Prudence's right foot which he drew naked rather than with a shoe.

Rubens made only a limited intervention on the rest of the drawing. He showed Prudence's chin jutting out less prominently, and he enlarged the mirror into which she gazes. A more substantial change was made to Prudence's right hand, which in the fresco is uncomfortably twisted round so as to rest on the palm and is largely covered over by draperies. Rubens drew a new hand, turning it around to make it rest on the knuckles. A few touches of red wash gave greater depth and relief to the draperies, but Rubens respected the core drawing and did not transform it into his own manner.

A dating of around 1615 is proposed here for Rubens's enlargement of the drawing, since it reflects the more cautious method of his earliest reworkings and lacks the increasingly assertive approach found from the 1620s onwards, a chronological development supported by examining the retouched *modelli* for engravings.

1. The suggestion of 'a mid- to late-sixteenth-century Italian artist' made by J. Lloyd Williams in Edinburgh 1999, p.68, under no.28, is, in my opinion, too late.
2. Inv.no.17573. See Oberhuber 1972, pp.593–4, no.398, repr.; Mitsch 1983, p.110, no.35, repr.

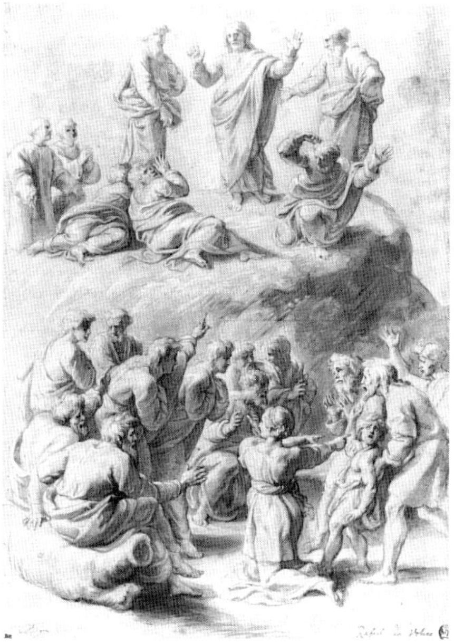

20

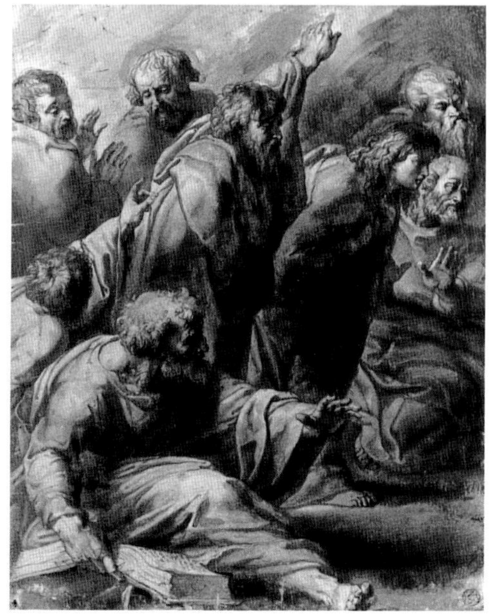

21

20 · Anonymous Draughtsman after Raphael, retouched by Rubens *The Transfiguration*

Pen and ink with grey and white wash, retouched in ink, greenish-brown wash, yellowish bodycolour, and white heightening; 41 × 28.6 cm. Inscribed *Rafael da Vrbino* by Rubens.
Département des Arts graphiques, Musée du Louvre, Paris, inv.no.20355
Exhibited in Edinburgh only

REFERENCES: Lugt 1949, II, pp.24–5, no.1060; Oberhuber 1962, pp.116, 122–6; Jaffé 1977, p.26; Logan 1978, p.436; Logan / Haverkamp-Begemann 1978, p.94; Sérullaz 1978, p.100, no.103; J. Foucart in Nancy 1990, pp.41, 43, 45; Cordellier / Py 1992, p.534, no.906.

This drawing records the second main preparatory stage in the development of Raphael's *Transfiguration* commissioned in 1517, first placed in S. Pietro in Montorio, Rome, but now in the Pinacoteca Vaticana. It is closely connected to a Raphael school *modello*, now also in the Louvre, which has sometimes been attributed to Gianfranceso Penni,[1] who, it is believed, was allowed to make detailed compositional drawings for Raphael. The copy was considered to be entirely by Rubens,[2] until persuasively identified as simply retouched by the artist.[3]

The *modello* is close to the finished altarpiece, but is far from identical. In both, the composition is divided into two sections with Christ revealing his divinity to James, Peter, and John, on Mount Tabor above. This episode is combined with the story that immediately follows it in the synoptic gospels, concerning the failure of the Apostles to heal a boy possessed by an evil spirit (Matthew 17: 14–21; Mark 9: 14–29; Luke 9: 37–44). The seated figure in the left foreground (Saint Matthew in the altarpiece) is shown perched on a large tree-trunk and nearly all the heads of the Apostles differ between *modello* and painting.

The underlying copy is easy to see in the upper section of the design which is the least retouched. This basic work on the sheet was carried out in pen with grey wash and may also have contained some delicate white heightening, as can be seen from the drapery folds of the Apostle lying at Christ's feet.

Rubens added a greenish-brown wash to strengthen areas of shadow throughout the drawing. This is evident to the right of Mount Tabor, on the powerful shadows cast across the foreground by the fallen tree-trunk, and from small accents added to the figures. A major change is to be found on the skirt of the kneeling woman in the foreground, which was once conical in shape but was curved inwards by Rubens. He also used pen and ink to strengthen and animate many of the faces on the lower level of the composition. The face of the possessed youth was made more violently distorted by Rubens who may have had the final altarpiece at the back of his mind when making this change.

The retouching on this particular drawing is the most discreet of the three related to the *Transfiguration* which Rubens owned and reworked.[4] His intervention was fastidious and delicate, seeming to be the result of careful deliberation. Since it is even more cautious than the interventions found on retouched drawings in the period 1618 to 1623, a date in the Italian period or shortly after Rubens's return to Antwerp is proposed here.

1. Inv.no.3954. See Oberhuber 1962, pp.122–3 (as Penni); Cordellier / Py 1992, p.534, no.905 (as 'atelier de Raphaël?').
2. Jaffé 1967, p.103; Jaffé 1977, p.26.
3. Logan 1978, p.436; Logan / Haverkamp-Begemann 1978, p.94.
4. See also cat.no.21. The third drawing is Louvre, inv.no.20189; Cordellier / Py 1992, p.534, no.904, repr.

21 · Anonymous Draughtsman after Raphael, retouched by Rubens *Eight Apostles*

Black chalk with brown wash, retouched in brown wash, and heightened in cream and white bodycolour; 35.2 × 27.2 cm
Département des Arts graphiques, Musée du Louvre, Paris, inv.no.20276
Exhibited in Edinburgh only

REFERENCES: Lugt 1949, II, p.25, no.1061; Jaffé 1967, p.103; Jaffé 1977, p.26; Logan 1978, pp.425, 436; Sérullaz 1978, pp.98–9, no.101; J. Foucart in Nancy 1990, pp.43, 45; Cordellier / Py 1992, p.537, no.910; A. Balis in Brussels / Rome 1995, p.303, no.169.

This drawing is a detailed copy of eight of the nine Apostles from the lower left-hand corner of Raphael's *Transfiguration*, now in the Pinacoteca Vaticana, Rome. It provides a careful record of the original, even including the threads placed as markers between the pages of the book in the foreground. The frowning head at the top right-hand corner was moved slightly lower so as to remove the Apostle who, in the final altarpiece, points towards the possessed boy. This change was part of the initial copy and not introduced by Rubens when he retouched the sheet.

Not all the disciples can be securely identified.[1] There has been agreement that the man seated in the left-hand foreground is Saint Matthew, who provided a detailed account of the Transfiguration and the healing of the possessed youth in his Gospel, which is displayed prominently. The scowling head at the top right-hand corner is said to be Judas Iscariot. The youthful Apostle, below, and the man to his right with short grizzled hair and beard, have been called John and Peter,[2] but they are included in the upper part of the altarpiece as witnesses to the Transfiguration on Mount Tabor.

Rubens set to work on top of an elaborate copy in black chalk and brown wash which paid close attention to effects of light and dark. It does not resemble a sixteenth-century Italian drawing and was probably recent in date. The outlines were first established in some detail, as can be seen from the hands of the Apostle at upper left, where even the fingernails are delineated.

Rubens added a brown wash to clarify the placing of the figures and to redraw faces. He also used the tip of the brush to describe curling locks of hair with dark brown ink. Finally, Rubens applied heightening in both cream and white bodycolour. This is evident on the head of one of the Apostles which was made smaller. Thick heightening was added to the balding top of Saint Matthew's head, and small accents in yellowish or cream bodycolour can be seen on the draperies, intensifying their metallic shimmer.

The drawing has been identified as a copy made in front of the original during Rubens's first visit to Rome of 1601,[3] and associated with the preparation of his own *Transfiguration* for the church of the Santissima Trinità, Mantua, now in Nancy.[4] But Rubens's retouching is closer to his corrections on *modelli* in the period 1618 to 1622, redefining key details such as faces, hair, feet and hands with crisp lines in pen and ink or the tip of the brush.

1. See, for example, Cordellier / Py 1992, p.532.
2. This identification is maintained in Joannides 1983, pp.128, 242, no.437.
3. The most insistent statement along these lines is Huemer 1977, p.118.
4. For example, see Jaffé 1967, p.103; Jaffé 1977, p.26.

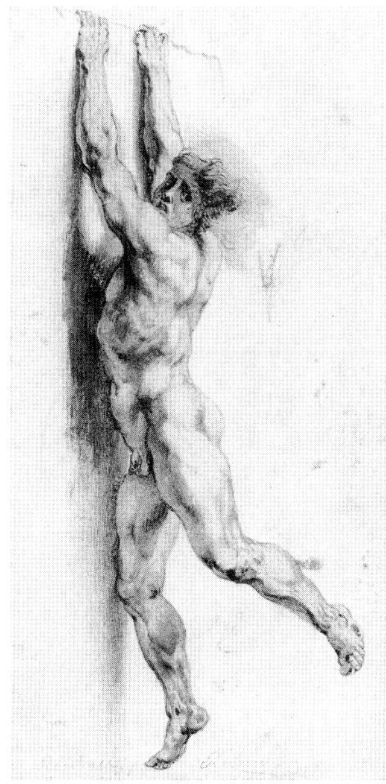

22

22 · Anonymous Sixteenth-Century Draughtsman after Raphael, retouched by Rubens

A Naked Man Clinging to a Wall

COLOUR ILLUSTRATION ON PAGE 16

Brush and wash with traces of white heightening, retouched with brown wash and yellowish and white bodycolour; 22.4 × 11.1 cm
The British Museum, London, inv.no.Oo.9–23

REFERENCES: Hind 1923, p.21, no.49; Jaffé 1967, pp.101–2; Jaffé 1977, p.25; Logan 1977, p.412; Rowlands 1977, p.40, no.33; Held 1980, I, p.75, under no.42; Logan 1983, p.416; Mitsch 1983, p.116, under no.38; D. Jaffé in Canberra / Melbourne 1992, p.189, no.72.

This drawing shows a man making a precarious descent to safety from a high wall. The figure was taken from Raphael's *Fire in the Borgo* in the Stanza dell'Incendio in the Vatican – a fresco begun in 1514 but not completed until 1517. The story is found in the *Liber Pontificalis*, and tells of a conflagration that was miraculously extinguished when Pope Leo IV (847–855) made the sign of the cross. The subject allowed Raphael to paint half-clothed men and women rushing from the flames in agitation, some gathering their children out of harm's way, others bringing water to quench the fire, and a few climbing over a wall to safety.

This drawing does not show the figure as in the fresco but, instead, undraped, as if drawn from the model, and must derive from a preparatory study. The most closely related work is a damaged red chalk drawing in the Albertina, Vienna,[1] sometimes said to be Raphael's original. It follows that the sheet in the British Museum may be an early sixteenth-century drawing from Raphael's workshop which Rubens retouched.[2] The underdrawing was made with a fine brush in wash, and the use of delicate parallel lines to create blended tone does not look like Rubens's way of working. It was retouched with broader areas of brown wash, some contours were scooped out in cream bodycolour, and touches of this were placed on the body to create a more brilliant sense of relief. There is a halo of yellow bodycolour around the man's head which allowed his hair to fly out sideways rather than hang down (as in the Albertina drawing). The face was transformed from a relatively placid mask into a more agonized expression of pathos, with deeply furrowed brow. The left arm was made more undulating and muscular with white bodycolour applied to block out the underdrawing. A similar change was made to the chest so that it is more prominent, and the exertion of the figure becomes palpable. In short, Rubens did not change the pose, but his retouching gave the figure a heightened sense of muscular tension and physical action.

Rubens used the figure clinging to a wall in two of his own works. It appeared in the *Battle of the Milvian Bridge with the Defeat of Maxentius*,[3] one of the designs for the set of tapestries on the life of the Emperor Constantine, designed in 1622, and in the unfinished *Miracles of Saint Benedict* in Brussels,[4] perhaps dateable to the early 1630s. It follows logically that Rubens's intervention on the drawing can be placed around 1622, when he first turned his attention to using this figure in a context of his own devising.

1. Inv.no.4882. See Oberhuber 1972, p.109, no.423, repr. pl.26; Mitsch 1983, p.116, no.38, repr.
2. The retouching was noted in Logan 1977, p.412; Logan 1983, p.416.
3. As observed by Pope Hennessy [1970], p.242; Jaffé 1977, p.25.
4. Inv.no.809. See Vlieghe 1972–3, I, pp.110–15, no.73, repr. fig.125.

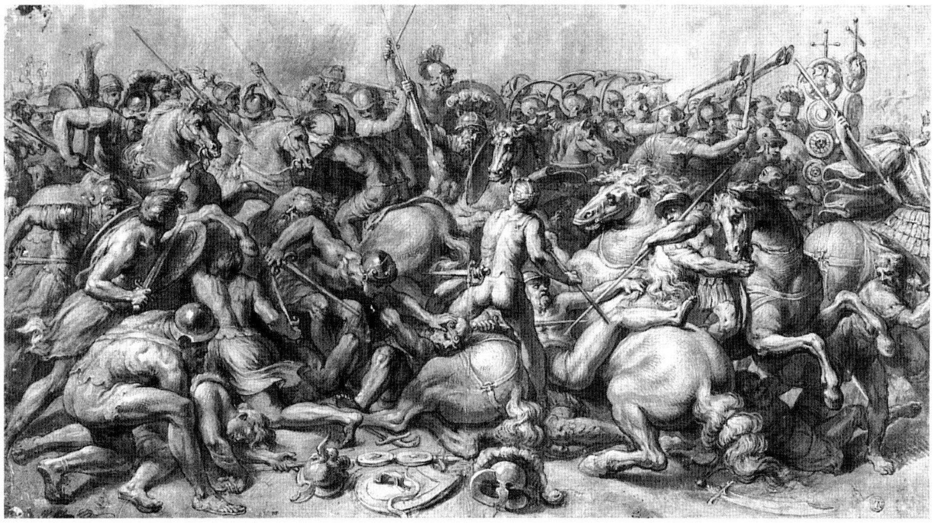

23

23 · Anonymous Sixteenth-Century Draughtsman after Raphael, retouched by Rubens

Battle of Horsemen and Foot Soldiers

Pen and ink with wash over black chalk on beige prepared paper, retouched with brown and yellowish wash, with heightening in cream and white bodycolour; 33.2 × 58.3 cm
Département des Arts graphiques, Musée du Louvre, Paris, inv.no.20375
Exhibited in Nottingham only

REFERENCES: Lugt 1949, II, p.29, no.1083; Jaffé 1977, p.30; Freedberg 1978, p.90, note 19; Logan 1978, p.436; Sérullaz 1978, p.98, no.100; Cordellier/Py 1992, p.552, no.949.

This drawing copies the left-hand side of Raphael's fresco of the *Victory of Constantine at the Milvian Bridge* in the Sala di Costantino in the Vatican. It was long considered Raphael's last great work, which, as Vasari established, had been executed posthumously by Giulio Romano and Gianfrancesco Penni,[1] and can be dated 1520–21. The panoramic composition, conceived as a fictive tapestry, dominates the long wall of the room which contains four episodes showing Constantine as defender of the Christian faith.

This story occupied a key place in the early history of Christianity. On the eve of battle in 312, the Emperor Constantine (288–337) was told in a dream to place the cross rather than the Roman eagle on the standards of his legions, and, on the day, the forces of the Emperor Maxentius fled before the Christian symbol.

The underlying drawing was made in pen and ink with wash over black chalk, and can be seen on the heads of the soldiers blowing trumpets and horns at the upper right, as well as on the nearby standards. This copy is so close to the fresco it must have been made from the finished work. The feet of flying angels above Constantine remain visible in black chalk, at the upper right, and the design is interrupted along the right edge, which suggests it once recorded all of the composition but was subsequently cut in half and trimmed at the top. The original size must have been approximately 44.2 × 116.6 cm.

Rubens strengthened the copy, but he also introduced some changes, particularly to the group at the bottom right-hand corner. His heightenings are largely yellowish, cream or white but some have a pink tint, as on the back, shoulders and right arm of the warrior seen from behind at the centre of the drawing. The most brilliant highlights are on the warriors' helmets and the eyes and nostrils of the horses, giving life to the intense drama of the battle. An extraordinary sheen and vibrancy is given to both men and animals, like a low relief in bronze.

The *Victory of Constantine* influenced Rubens's own battle subjects, notably his *Constantine Defeating Licinius*, designed in 1622 for a cycle of tapestries which allowed Rubens to measure himself against the Sala di Costantino. This suggests when Rubens made his retouching. It belongs among a group of compositions, here dated to the 1620s, that were reworked to give greater volume and animation to the figures. The dark tonality and densely pigmented surface marks it out as close to his intervention on a copy of a *Fall of the Giants* [cat.no.35] associated with Giulio Romano, and both drawings must have been reworked at around the same time.

1. Vasari 1568, II, p.336.

24 · Anonymous Draughtsman after Raphael or Perino del Vaga (1501–1547), retouched by Rubens

Two Women Walking and Two Women Running

Pen and ink with wash, retouched in black chalk, brown wash and cream bodycolour; 15.6 × 18.2 cm. An irregularly shaped section cut out and replaced at the lower edge.
Christ Church, Oxford, inv.no.0678

REFERENCES: Jaffé 1966a, pp.138, 147, note 47; Byam Shaw 1976, I, p.123, no.380; Jaffé 1977, p.46; Ravelli 1978, p.476–8, no.985b; B. Cleaver in Oxford/London 1988, p.54, no.14.

This drawing combines two separate groups from the fictive reliefs painted on the dados (*basamenti*) of the west wall in the Logge, located on the second floor of the Cortile San Damaso in the Vatican, a project commissioned by Pope Leo X. Work is documented between the spring of 1518 and the summer of 1519. These illusionistic reliefs are now almost entirely destroyed and have to be reconstructed from early copies.

The figures on the left were taken from *Joshua Renewing the Covenant at Shechem*, painted on the west wall of the tenth bay. This scene depicts a gathering of the Israelites when Joshua, nearing the end of his life, reminded them they should make a solemn covenant to serve Jehovah (Joshua 24: 1–28).

The figures on the right were taken from the ninth *basamento*, devoted to the history of Moses. The subject is uncertain because the central portion of the fresco was destroyed at an early date by the insertion of a doorway, but it is likely to have been the *Destruction of the Sons of Aaron* (Leviticus 10: 1–2).[1]

Work on the Logge was undertaken by a team of artists under Raphael's direction.[2] Vasari singled out Perino del Vaga as one of the

24

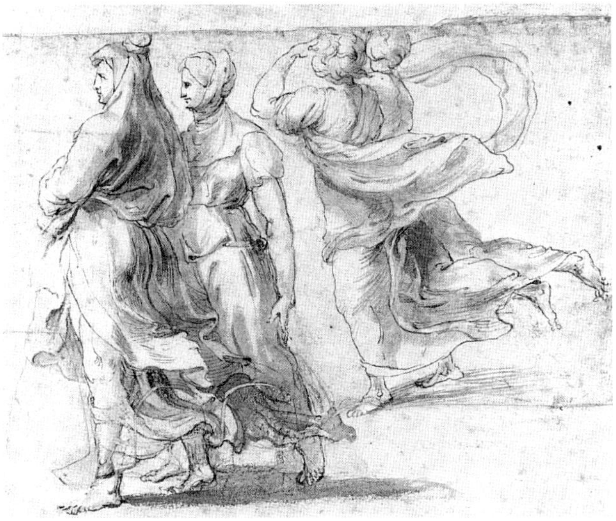

25

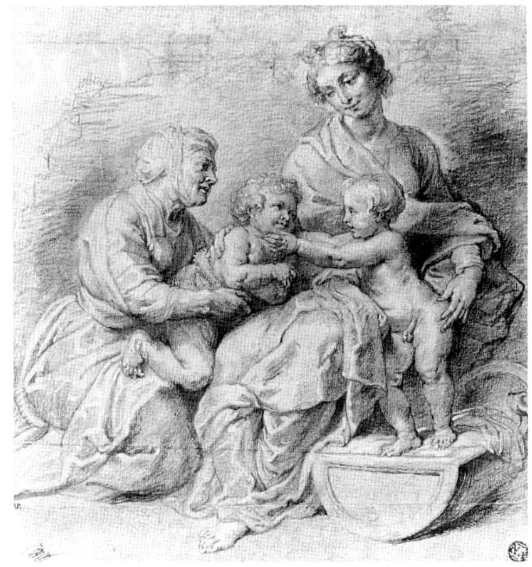

most able, and said that he had painted the vault and dado of bay ten.[3] Raphael must have provided drawings for the narratives on the vaults, but may have given his assistants a free rein in the design of the less prominent dados.

The underdrawing in pen and ink with pale brown wash is by a sixteenth-century hand. The main intervention was made by trimming round the feet of the woman at the far left so as to insert a new piece of paper in order to lengthen her robes and legs.[4] These revisions were made roughly in black chalk and then worked over in grey and brown wash and bodycolour. The robes of the main figures were strengthened by adding touches of brown wash in the shadows and cream bodycolour as highlights, unifying the sheet, and a heavy fold of drapery was added onto the skirts of the woman at far left. The reworking animates the figures and gives a remarkable lightness to their fluttering robes.

This intervention is characteristic of Rubens and reveals an impatience that points to a relatively late point in his career. It can be compared to another retouched sheet which combined female figures from different parts of a composition, in that case by Polidoro [cat.no.28], and an even more richly reworked sheet of *God the Father* [cat.no.68] which was reused in one of Rubens's compositions of the late 1620s. All three drawings are likely to have been retouched during that decade.

1. See Davidson 1985, pp.78–9.
2. See Cordellier/Py 1992, pp.396–7.
3. Vasari 1568, II, p.352.
4. B. Cleaver in Oxford/London 1988, p.54, under no.14, is needlessly cautious as to whether Rubens made this alteration.

25 · Anonymous Sixteenth-Century Draughtsman after Raphael, retouched by Rubens

The Virgin and Child with Saint Elizabeth and the Infant Saint John the Baptist

Red chalk, retouched in red ink and wash, heightened with cream bodycolour; 27.1 × 24.6 cm
Département des Arts graphiques, Musée du Louvre, Paris, inv.no.20186
Exhibited in Nottingham only

REFERENCES: Lugt 1949, II, p.24, no.1057; Jaffé 1967, p.103; Jaffé 1977, p.23; Haverkamp-Begemann 1978, pp.47–8; Logan 1978, pp.429, 435–6; Sérullaz 1978, pp.97–8, no.99; Cordellier/Py 1992, p.508, no.880.

This composition by Raphael has been dated around 1518–19, a period when he designed several depictions of the Virgin and Child but delegated their execution to his studio. There has been no agreement as to the exact model for the Louvre drawing. A highly-finished drawing in red chalk survives at Windsor Castle,[1] sometimes attributed to Giulio Romano,[2] which may have been used for a related engraving by Jacopo Caraglio.[3] There are also several painted versions with smaller figures in a landscape setting. The most famous is the *Petite Sainte Famille* in the Louvre, sometimes said to have been made by Gianfrancesco Penni from Raphael's design,[4] but also attributed to Giulio.[5]

Recently the opinion has taken root that the Louvre drawing was based on Caraglio's engraving.[6] In fact it is a retouched sheet,[7] that was originally closer to the Windsor drawing than this print, since the drapery folds are softer and less angular, the locks of hair on Christ's head are less spiky, and Saint Elizabeth bends forward solicitously rather than sitting erect.

Strips were added to the sheet at both top and bottom, presumably by Rubens and perhaps to repair damage. He would not bother to do this unless it was an earlier Italian drawing of some value, perhaps even from Raphael's studio, and the fact that it is drawn in red chalk supports the idea that it was an early facsimile of the Windsor sheet.

Rubens transformed the Virgin's face, turning it so that she looks down at the infant Christ rather than sideways towards Saint Elizabeth. He gave the cradle an arched headboard which does not appear in any other version. Thick cream bodycolour was applied to the strap under Saint Elizabeth's chin, round the top of the Virgin's head, and along her left shoulder to make its outline more pronounced. The overall effect was to make the draperies look silken, a pictorial effect that Rubens relished, here and elsewhere.

He did not make use of this composition until late in his career. The adaptation is to be found on the outer shutters of the Saint Ildefonso altarpiece painted for the church of St James on the Coudenberg, Brussels, in 1630–1, and now in Vienna. Rubens turned the figure of Christ into the infant Saint John by reversing him,[8] and his outstretched arms no longer give a blessing but entreat one. The creamy richness of the impasto, as well as Rubens's interest in the composition at this time, points to a date around 1630.

1. Inv.12740. Popham/Wilde 1949, p.320, no.833.
2. S. Ferino [Pagden] in Mantua 1989, p.251.
3. Bartsch XV, p.69, no.5.
4. Inv.1499. Dussler 1971, pp.49–50.
5. S. Béguin in Paris 1983–4, pp.104–7, no.14.
6. See Jaffé 1967, p.103.
7. Haverkamp-Begemann 1978, pp.47–8; and Logan 1978, pp.429, 435–6.
8. Pope Hennessy [1970], p.243; repeated by Vlieghe 1972–3, II, p.93, under no.118.

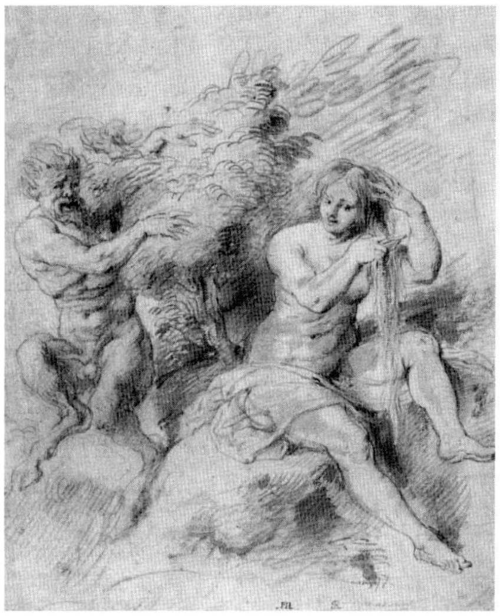

26

26 · Rubens after Raphael or Giulio Romano (*c.*1499–1546) *Pan and Syrinx*

Red chalk with red wash and cream bodycolour; 21.7 × 17.4 cm
The British Museum, London, inv.no.1910–2–12–192

REFERENCES: Hind 1923, p.15, no.28; Jaffé 1967, pp.99–100; Oberhuber 1972, p.147, under no.454a; Jaffé 1977, p.23; Logan 1977, p.412; Rowlands 1977, p.48, no.44.

This drawing reproduces a composition painted by Raphael and his workshop during 1516 in the bathroom or *Stufetta* of Bernardo Dovizi, Cardinal Bibbiena (1470–1520) in the Vatican. The walls and vault contain grotesque ornament and panels with mythological subjects taken from Ovid and Bion, some mildly erotic. The *Pan and Syrinx* has been defaced by the pious in the course of time.

Although Raphael was in charge, much of the work was delegated to his assistants. A preparatory drawing in red chalk for the *Pan and Syrinx*, generally given to Giulio Romano, survives in the Louvre.[1] Recent attempts to attribute this and other drawings for the commission to Raphael[2] have met with a frosty reception,[3] and he probably did no more than provide quick sketches.

Despite Raphael's dependence on his workshop, he took pride in these compositions and they were engraved immediately. The printmakers did not work from the frescoes themselves, but from the red chalk drawings which could only have been made available with Raphael's cooperation. The reversed engraving of *Pan and Syrinx* is unsigned but has been attributed to Marcantonio Raimondi,[4] and, more recently, to Marco Dente.[5] Some scholars have claimed that Rubens's drawing was based on this engraving,[6] but, if so, they have not explained why he should have drawn it unreversed. More likely it was made from the drawing now in the Louvre, since Rubens probably never visited the *Stufetta* which was kept secret for centuries. Alternatively, he could have seen a repetition of this design in the frescoed loggia of the villa decorated for Cristoforo Stati around 1519–20, now detached and in the Hermitage, St Petersburg.

In my opinion, the drawing is entirely by Rubens and the faint traces of the red chalk underdrawing are from his hand.[7] He drew over this fluently in red wash, adding a few touches of a darker red chalk on top, and applying broad patches of yellowish bodycolour on Syrinx's stomach, legs, and right arm, intended to give a silken sheen to female flesh.

When Rubens came to depict the story of Pan and Syrinx himself, he preferred the most dramatic and climactic moment in the story, when the god lunges forward to seize Syrinx and she flings herself away to evade his grasp. This can be seen from several cabinet paintings of the late 1610s in which Rubens painted the figures and Jan Brueghel the Elder provided the landscape backgrounds. More than twenty years later Rubens depicted the subject again for the Torre de la Parada in Madrid, a lost canvas executed to his designs by Erasmus Quellinus (1607–1678). But the drawing was not made with any of Rubens's surviving versions of the subject in mind. Nevertheless, a dating can be proposed to the mid-1630s, when he used the brush to draw with an attack and fluency that recalls his oil sketches on panel.

1. Inv.4035. See Oberhuber 1972, p.147, no.454a, repr. fig.148; Cordellier/Py 1992, pp.325–7, no.478, repr.
2. See Gnann 1999, p.108, no.47, repr.
3. See Monbeig-Goguel 1999, pp.496, 498.
4. Bartsch XIV, p.245, no.325.
5. See Shoemaker/Broun 1981, p.188, no.64, repr.
6. Jaffé 1967, pp.99–100; Jaffé 1977, p.23; Rowlands 1977, p.48, no.44.
7. For the contrary view, see Logan 1977 p.412.

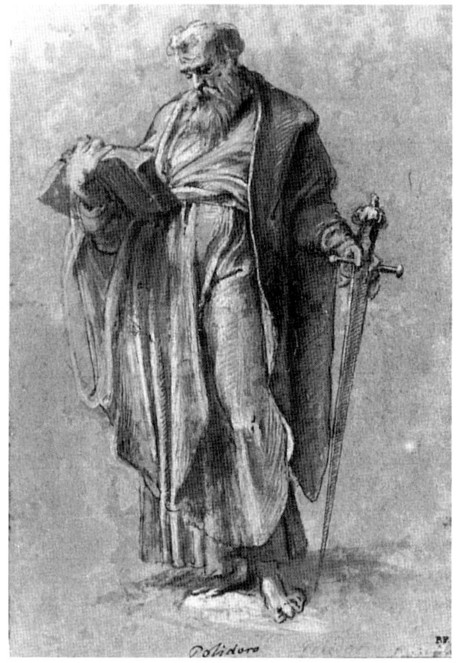

27

POLIDORO DA CARAVAGGIO

27 · Polidoro da Caravaggio (1490/1500–?1543), retouched by Rubens *Saint Paul the Apostle*

Pen and ink with some white heightening and squared for transfer in black chalk, retouched with brown wash and cream and white bodycolour; 20.9 × 13.9 cm
Inscribed *Polidoro* in Rubens's hand.
Département des Arts graphiques, Musée du Louvre, Paris, inv.no.20244
Exhibited in Nottingham only

REFERENCES: Jaffé 1964, p.391; Jaffé 1966a, p.135; Marabottini 1969, I, pp.291, note 258, 349, no.212; Jaffé 1977, p.48; Logan 1978, p.434; Ravelli 1978, pp.275–6, no.433; Sérullaz 1978, p.92, no.93; Wood 1994, p.337.

This drawing shows Saint Paul the Apostle holding his attributes: the sword of his martyrdom, and the Epistles of which he was author. There has been no agreement as to whether this drawing is an original by Polidoro, or a copy, nor whether it is entirely by Rubens or simply retouched by him. It contains faint traces of squaring in black chalk which prove it was a working study intended for enlargement.[1] No related painting by Polidoro is known.

A second version survives, present whereabouts unknown, which is the same size but has been trimmed to leave more space at the top and less on either side of the figure. It has been said that this was the work which Rubens copied,[2] but, since it corresponds precisely with the underdrawing on the Louvre sheet, it is surely a copy made before later reworking. The crucial question is therefore whether Rubens was responsible for the retouching on the Louvre drawing.

The *Saint Paul* was reworked with brown wash and creamy-yellow bodycolour. The figure was enlarged on the left and originally had a straighter, less swollen silhouette. Small tablets were turned into a supple and weighty book, and the right hand was changed to support the volume by its spine. The fluted folds of drapery on the saint's robes were made more massive by adding dark brown wash in the shadows and brilliant cream bodycolour on the highlights. Paul's left foot was made larger and his craggy profile was turned into a three-quarter view, which made the figure less uncomfortably twisted in pose. This intervention is typical of Rubens. In addition, the attribution to Polidoro written on the recto is in Rubens's own hand and confirms that he both owned the drawing and knew who had made it.

It has been suggested that the *Saint Paul* was used by Rubens for the figure of Saint Amandus on the exterior shutter of the *Raising of the Cross* altarpiece,[3] completed in 1611 for the church of Saint Walburga, and now in Antwerp Cathedral, but the similarity is not very great. The date of Rubens's intervention on the Louvre *Saint Paul* has to be based on comparison with other retouched drawings. Precise parallels can be made with the way Rubens added dark accents on faces, hands, and feet, and his use of cream bodycolour on drapery folds, when retouching both Italian copies and *modelli* for engravings in the late 1610s and early 1620s.

1. As noted by Wood 1994, p.337.
2. Jaffé 1966a, p.135.
3. Jaffé 1977, p.48.

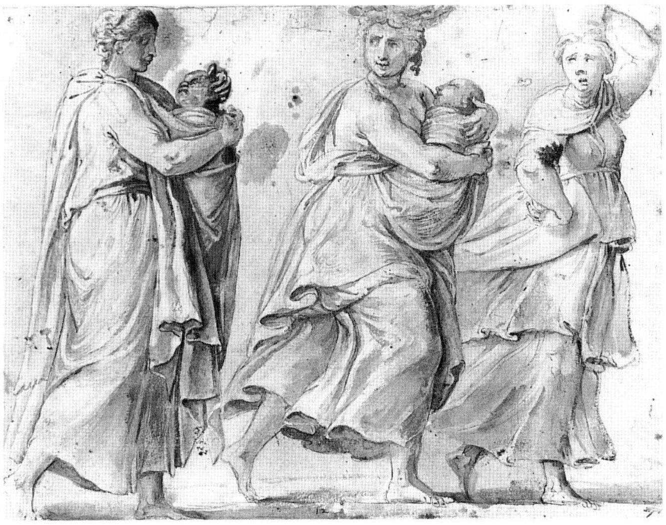

28

28 · Anonymous Sixteenth-Century Draughtsman after Polidoro da Caravaggio, retouched by Rubens

Two Women Carrying Infants, and One with a Basket, Walking to the Right

Pen and ink with wash over faint traces of black chalk, retouched with brown wash and cream bodycolour, perhaps with some oils; 21.3 × 27.1 cm
Visitors of the Ashmolean Museum, Oxford, WA PII 485

REFERENCES: Parker 1956, I, p.242, no.485; Marabottini 1969, I, p.291, note 258; Ravelli 1978, p.364, no.659; B. Cleaver in Oxford/London 1988, p.56, no.15.

This drawing contains three figures extracted from the monochrome frieze painted by Polidoro and Maturino above the windows of the first floor of the façade at Palazzo Gaddi, Rome; a work dateable around 1526, but now destroyed. This portion of the frieze depicted a crowd of men, women, and children, preparing to make a long sea journey that will eventually take them to Latium.

The women on the left and in the middle of the drawing were placed in the fresco on either side of two men carrying a heavy load of barrels, but their positions were swapped in the copy. The woman on the right of the drawing was to be found among the figures at the far left of the frieze, part of a group of similar women carrying vases and bundles on their heads. The remains of the underdrawing reveal a neat and dry use of the pen, and comparison with other early copies after Polidoro suggests that it was a faithful record of the figures by a Roman draughtsman of the mid-sixteenth century.[1]

Rubens added brown wash throughout the drawing with some vigour, strengthening the draperies, and also enhancing contours with the tip of the brush, so that the sheet gained a rich sense of surface and almost silken texture. A change can be seen in the dress of the woman on the right, which was originally pulled in further making her look delicate and unstable. However, her outline was thickened by Rubens with a few lines dragged across the paper in dark brown wash. Heavier and more oily touches are evident on the faces of the other two women, and particularly on the head of the child at the left, as well as on the fingers of his mother's hand which were thickened with dense pigment. The slightly vacant expressions of the faces as conceived by Polidoro, and still evident on the head of the woman on the right, became more alert and animated when reworked by Rubens.

The drawing is unusual in having been always accepted as a sixteenth-century sheet retouched by Rubens. His concern with the weight and corporality of these figures, as well as the vigour and extent of his intervention, points to a date in the 1620s. Comparison can be made with the *God the Father* said to be by Federico Zuccaro [cat.no.68] which shares Rubens's bold use of cream and yellowish bodycolour as a means of strengthening and changing the design. Because that figure was adapted in an oil sketch of the late 1620s, its dating is reasonably secure.

1. Ravelli 1978, p.364, no.659.

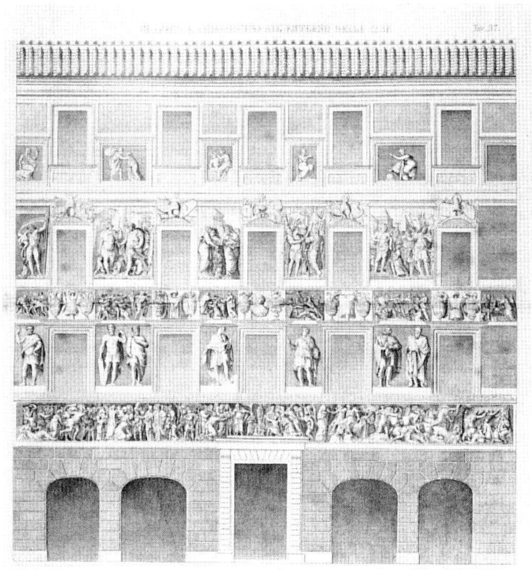

29

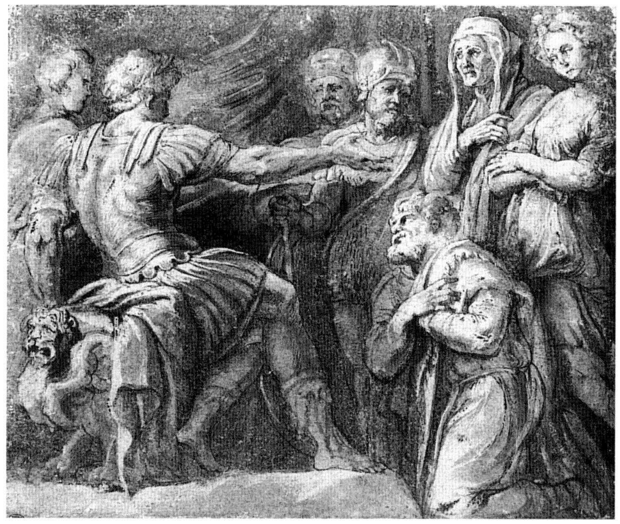

30

POLIDORO'S FAÇADE AT PALAZZO MILESI

29 · Enrico Maccari after Polidoro da Caravaggio *Façade of Palazzo Milesi, Rome*

Steel engraving from E. Maccari, *Secolo XV. XVI. Saggi di architettura e decorazione italiana illustrata da M. Giovanni Iannoni. Graffiti e chiaroscuri esistenti nell'esterno delle case riprodutti in rame*, Berlin-Rome, n.d.
The British Museum, London, inv.(168 c.15) 1954–2–11–4 (37)

REFERENCES: Pericoli Ridolfini 1960, p.40, no.56; Ravelli 1978, p.367, under nos.667–8.

Enrico Maccari's nineteenth-century engraving records the painted façade of Giovanni Antonio Milesi's house in Rome, commissioned from Polidoro and Maturino in the mid- to late 1520s, shortly before the Sack in 1527 when both artists fled the city. Rubens owned and retouched drawings of no fewer than nine scenes painted on this façade, five of them in the present exhibition [cat.nos.30–4]. Maccari's engraving is included here in order to help reconstruct the commission.

Although known as Palazzo Milesi, the building was a substantial house rather than a palace and it owed its fame more to its painted decoration than its architecture. Polidoro worked in monochrome and with the cheapest of materials – a mixture of painted and incised fresco – but his illusionistic decorations looked magnificent, and Vasari referred to the vases 'of gold' and figures that seem 'truly made of metal'.[1] Polidoro drew on a rich repertoire of Roman motifs, both decorative and historical. He visualised narrative in terms of classical relief sculpture, but he treated his sources freely, exaggerating the elegance of his figures, the sinuous shapes of precious vases and the splendour of ancient weapons.

The most celebrated part of the decoration was a frieze devoted to the story of Niobe [cat.nos.31, 33, 34] which ran the full width of the building on the first floor, above the entrance and the arcaded openings of the shops at street level. Above this, and between the windows of the main floor, were large figures of famous men from antiquity, depicted as fictive statues on pedestals. The frieze between the first and second floors was divided into smaller units with anthropomorphic panoplies constructed from suits of armour on poles. These were flanked by large vases which became well-known in the late sixteenth century through a series of ten engravings by Cherubino Alberti (1553–1615).[2]

Polidoro's choice of subjects appears random and even obscure at first sight. But there may be thematic connections between some of the narratives. For example, the scene where Cronus (Saturn) castrates his father [cat.no.32] is linked to the episode directly above where Saturn is seen again, now himself a parent and devouring his own children in case they usurp him in turn. Similarly, *The Continence of Scipio* [cat.no.30] has a link to the scene above where Gaius Fabritius Luscinus refuses the gifts of King Pyrrhus, since both narratives show strong-minded protagonists resisting temptation. If the famous men of antiquity between the windows of the main floor could be identified, it seems probable that they too would emerge as part of these themes intended to be read along six vertical axes.

1. Vasari 1568, II, p.201: 'un'infinità di figure di bronzo, che non di pittura, ma paiono di mettallo'.
2. Bartsch XVII, p.110, nos.161–70.

30 · Anonymous Sixteenth-Century Draughtsman after Polidoro da Caravaggio, retouched by Rubens *The Continence of Scipio*

Pen and wash over black chalk on green paper, heightened with white, retouched with brown and greenish wash and some white bodycolour;
17.3 × 20.1 cm
Département des Arts graphiques, Musée du Louvre, Paris, inv.no.20249
Exhibited in Nottingham only

REFERENCES: Benesch 1954, p.201; Logan 1978, p.438.

This composition formed one section of the frieze between the first and second floors of the Palazzo Milesi façade [see cat.no.29]. Polidoro's subject has sometimes been identified as the family of Darius before Alexander,[1] but, if so, it should be Darius's mother, Sisygambis, who kneels, not a bearded man, and she should be accompanied by Darius's wife and children. Polidoro's composition shows a young woman and an older couple who are petitioning the enthroned commander. This makes it closer to the Continence of Scipio. Scipio had captured a beautiful woman, but, on learning that she was to be married, he reunited her with her betrothed, Allucius (sometimes called Indibilis). The woman at the far right must be the bride, the kneeling man, her father, and the old woman at her side, her mother. This is confirmed by the very literal use that Giulio Romano made of Polidoro's composition around 1531–2 in his *Continence of Scipio* on the ceiling of the Sala del Imperatore, also called the Sala di Cesare, at Palazzo Te in Mantua.

The underdrawing was done in pen and wash on green paper which established a mid-tone and helped create a sense of volume. Rubens's retouching was limited to changing the contours of some figures with the tip of the brush and adding greenish wash to strengthen relief. He also added a few touches of pale

31

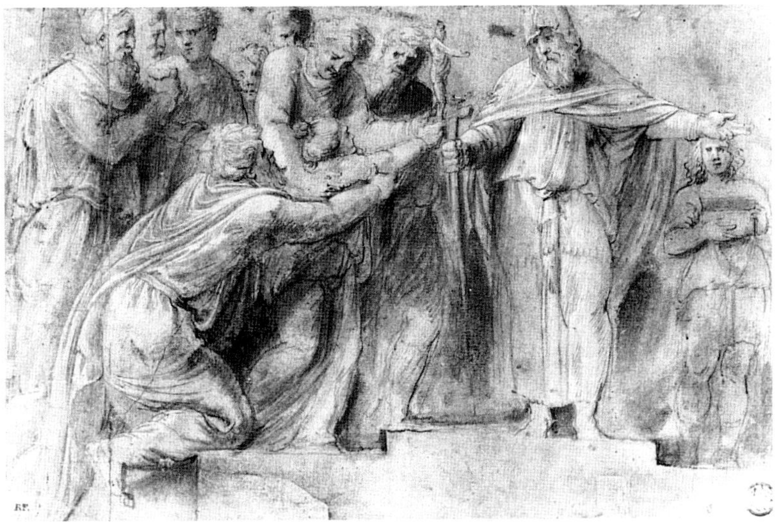

bodycolour, particularly on Scipio's throne. The only face to be noticeably altered was that of the man in armour holding a baton whose hand also seems to have been added at this stage.

Rubens worked on his own version of *The Continence of Scipio* around 1617–20, now lost,[2] but known from an oil sketch in a private collection, and an engraving.[3] His early drawings for this work in Berlin,[4] and Bayonne,[5] show him adopting a compressed composition like Polidoro's, rather than his final spacious and frieze-like design. These sketches adopt a low viewpoint placing Scipio's throne on a dias near the front of the picture space, packing the figures together and pushing them towards the surface so that any sense of recession is minimised. The connection is closest in the Bayonne drawing, where a bulbous vessel with floridly curved handle recalls the famous vases on the Palazzo Milesi façade. Rubens's restrained retouching points to a date not long before he started work on his own version of the subject.

1. See Ravelli 1978, pp.286 (nos.457–9), 420–2 (nos.820–8).
2. See McGrath 1997, II, pp.257–63, no.49.
3. Voorhelm Schneevoogt 1873, p.140, no.35.
4. Inv.no.KdZ 5,685. See Held 1959, I, p.110, no.38, repr. pl.40; McGrath 1997, II, pp.263–4, no.49a, repr. fig.183.
5. Inv.no.1414 (formerly 1436). See Held 1959, I, p.110, no.39, repr. pl.41; McGrath 1997, II, pp.264–5, no.49b, repr. fig.184.

31 · Anonymous Sixteenth-Century Draughtsman after Polidoro da Caravaggio, retouched by Rubens

A Crowd of Nine Worshippers with a Votive Offering Before a Priest

Pen and brown ink on prepared paper, heightened with white, retouched with brown wash; 16.5 × 24.2 cm
Département des Arts graphiques, Musée du Louvre, Paris, inv.no.20245
Exhibited in Edinburgh only

REFERENCES: Pericoli Ridolfini 1960, p.40, no.89; Jaffé 1964, pp.391, 396, note 30; Marabottini 1969, I, p.368; Jaffé 1977, p.48; Ravelli 1978, p.388, no.721; Logan 1978, p.438.

The Louvre drawing records a section of the main frieze at first floor level from the façade of Palazzo Milesi [see cat.no.29]. Niobe, the wife of Amphion, King of Thebes, and daughter of Tantalus, tried to stop the Theban women from worshipping Latona (Leto), saying she should take their place because she was a grand-daughter of Jupiter. Her presumption and impiety were punished by Latona's children, Apollo and Diana.

The character of the underdrawing is evident from the white heightening which was applied in very long, fine lines. This can be seen in the cloak of the man kneeling in the left foreground, the man standing behind him at the far left, and the robes of the priest. The underdrawing has been called 'undistinguished',[1] but it is not as heavy-handed as many early copies after Polidoro's work, and the draughtsman was able to convey the gracefulness of his invention, as seen from the supple pose of the man kneeling in the foreground.

Rubens's intervention is evident in broadly handled areas of shadow and incisive touches on the faces. He completely redrew the youth with the incense box at the far right and he created a step, not in the original, to balance the one to the left in order to give this acolyte longer legs. Rubens worked far more loosely than the draughtsman responsible for the underlying copy and also more confidently, applying brown wash with the tip of the brush. The strength of this retouching lies in his ability to match the sinuous and elegant quality of Polidoro's figures with the fluency of his intervention, which is refined and slightly impatient.

Rubens's retouching is less emphatic than many of the changes that he made on drawings during the 1610s, although the long and feathery lines drawn with the brush offer some parallels. This sheet is also less densely re-worked and richly highlighted than many retouched drawings of the following decade, but the speed of execution and abbreviation of forms points to a date around 1620.

1. Jaffé 1964, p.391; Jaffé 1977, p.48.

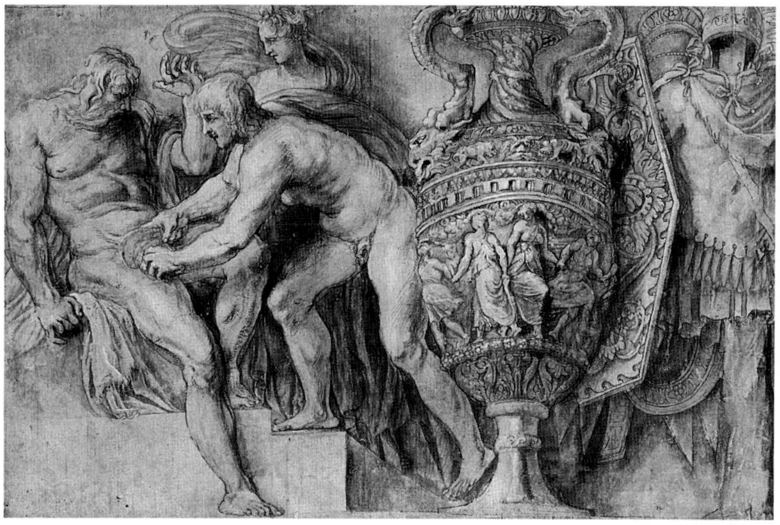

32

32 · Anonymous Sixteenth-Century Draughtsman after Polidoro da Caravaggio, retouched by Rubens

The Castration of Uranus by Cronus

COLOUR ILLUSTRATION ON PAGE 17

Pen and ink with brown wash, retouched with brown and yellowish wash and cream bodycolour;
27.6 × 41.1 cm
Private Collection

REFERENCES: Jaffé 1977, p.48.

This drawing records one of the scenes from the frieze between the first and second floors on the façade of Palazzo Milesi [see cat.no.29]. The union of Gaea (or Terra, the earth) and her son Uranus (or Coelus, the heavens) produced the race of giants who were thrown down to the underworld by their father. In revenge, Gaea gave her youngest son, Cronus, a sickle which he used to castrate his father (Hesoid, *Theogony*, 133–87). The drawing not only contains this episode, but also the large vase and part of a trophy of arms included to the right of this scene on the frieze.

This drawing is the work of a sixteenth-century copyist and has been extensively retouched by Rubens. The underlying tight and dry pen work remains legible, particularly on the right-hand side. This is by the same hand who drew a copy, also reworked by Rubens, now in the Art Gallery of Ontario, depicting the adjacent section from this frieze with the *Rape of the Sabines*,[1] and the two sheets may once have been joined together. The same copyist was responsible for two other drawings after this façade that Rubens retouched now in the Louvre,[2] and the Hermitage, St Petersburg,[3] depicting vases, trophies and panoplies of arms.

The figures on the left were far more densely reworked by Rubens than the vase and weapons on the right. He redrew the main outlines of Uranus and Cronus in dark brown and then worked up their bodies and draperies with paler brown and yellowish wash to give them more definition. Uranus had his right wrist thinned, both hands redrawn so that his fingers became smaller, and the upper part of his right leg made more shapely. The same process can be seen on the figure of Cronus, both of whose arms were subtly redrawn, the size of his head was increased, and his right leg made more curvaceous. Internal modelling on these figures was applied with an ochre wash and then hatched with the tip of the brush in a darker brown. The vase received more summary attention, but Rubens did add some dark brown accents and small patches of cream bodycolour to the decoration of the dancing Muses or Hours, based by Polidoro on the famous relief of the *Borghese Dancers* now in the Louvre. This economic use of heightening brought a sense of the play of light to this surface.

The close relation between this drawing and the *Rape of the Sabines* already mentioned, raises the question of when both works were retouched. Rubens intervention went beyond merely strengthening the design, as was characteristic of his retouchings during the 1610s, and this bold and assertive reworking points to a date in the 1620s or even early 1630s.

1. Ravelli 1978, p.476, no.985, repr.; D. McTavish in Toronto 1981–2, p.52, no.44, repr.
2. Inv.no.20247. Lugt 1949, II, p.36, no.1125, repr. pl.XLVII; Ravelli 1978, p.432, no.862, repr.
3. Inv.no.28532. Jaffé 1964, pp.391–2, repr. pl.23; Jaffé 1977, p.48; Ravelli 1978, pp.284–5, no.456, repr.; Wood 1994, p.337, repr. fig.4.

33 · Anonymous Sixteenth-Century Italian Artist after Polidoro da Caravaggio, retouched by Rubens

A Man Leading a Horse

COLOUR ILLUSTRATION ON FRONT COVER

Pen and ink with brown wash, heightened with white, retouched with brown wash and white bodycolour;
42.7 × 23.5 cm
The British Museum, London, inv.no.1895–9–15–653

REFERENCES: Hind 1923, p.20, no.47; Pouncey / Gere 1962, cat. vol., pp.129–30, no.225; Jaffé 1977, p.48; Logan 1977, p.412; J. Müller Hofstede in Cologne 1977, I, p.298, no.78A; Rowlands 1977, p.40, no.32; Ravelli 1978, pp.386–7, no.712.

This is a copy after one of the figures from the frieze devoted to the story of Niobe at first floor level on the façade of Palazzo Milesi [see cat.no.29]. The man with a horse linked two different parts of the narrative: a group of Thebans offering gifts to Niobe on the left, and, to the right, a crowd worshipping the statue of Latona, a group copied on another sheet which Rubens owned and retouched [cat.no.31].

Although sometimes said to be entirely by Rubens,[1] this drawing has been persuasively identified as a sixteenth-century copy that he retouched.[2] The underdrawing in pen and wash remains easily legible throughout, with a wiry use of line and heavily shaded contours that cannot be paralleled in Rubens's own work.

Rubens reworked the sheet boldly and to great effect, although with remarkable economy. He used dark wash to change contours and applied brilliant white bodycolour to increase the sense of volume and relief of both man and horse, greatly extending the tonal range and impact of the drawing. Decisive lines were added on the horse's head and mane, and broader washes of white bodycolour were placed on its chest to make it swell more assertively. Further touches were used to thicken the horse's leg, and tiny spots of

33

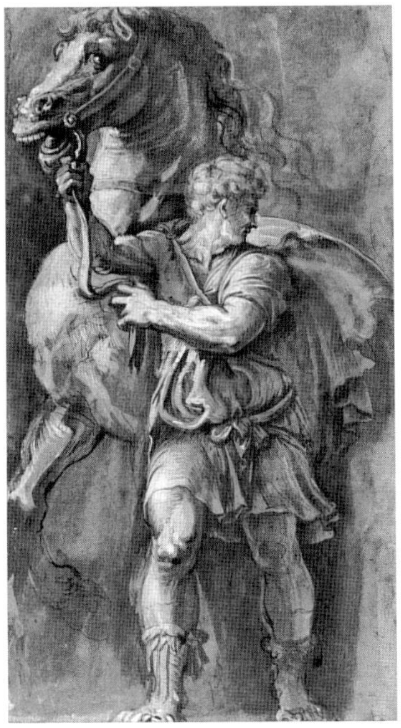

34

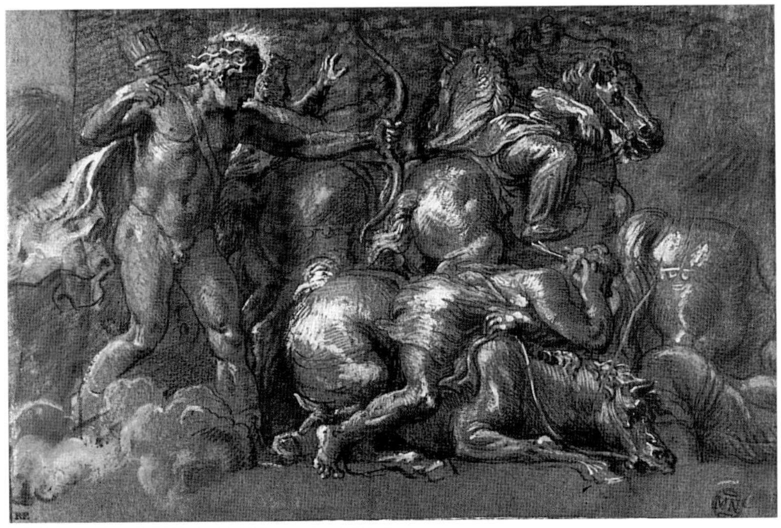

brilliant white were applied to animate its eyes, teeth, and nostrils. Brown wash was used to redefine the man's legs, altering their outline, and the volume of his body was strengthened by adding heavy strokes of white bodycolour to his left forearm and as highlights on the knuckles of his right hand. The retouching on this sheet reveals the confidence of a hand – and the habits of a mind – skilled in adding a few touches of paint to workshop pictures in order to bring them to life.

Previous attempts to date the British Museum drawing have placed it in the period 1600–8,[3] assuming that it was made by Rubens in Rome from the original. But it is perverse to think that Rubens would go to all the trouble of making a tight and dry copy before covering it over with impatient and vigorous changes. The bold character of this retouching does not look like Rubens's drawing style in Italy, or even after his return to Antwerp, and can only be explained if placed much later, around 1630.

1. Hind 1923, p.20, no.47; Jaffé 1977, p.48; J. Müller Hofstede in Cologne 1977, I, p.298, no.78A.
2. Logan 1977, p.412; Ravelli 1978, pp.386–7, no.712.
3. Hind 1923, p.20, no.47; Jaffé 1977, p.48, caption to pl.130; J. Müller Hofstede in Cologne 1977, I, p.298, no.78A.

34 · Anonymous Sixteenth-Century Draughtsman after Polidoro da Caravaggio, retouched by Rubens *Apollo Killing Two of the Sons of Niobe*

Black chalk on blue paper, retouched with green-brown wash and heightened with cream and white bodycolour; 16.3 × 24 cm
Département des Arts graphiques, Musée du Louvre, Paris, inv.no.20246
Exhibited in Edinburgh only

REFERENCES: Lugt 1949, II, p.27, no.1071; Jaffé 1977, p.48; Logan 1978, pp.434, 437; Ravelli 1978, p.400, no.751.

This drawing records a section from the frieze devoted to the story of Niobe from the façade at Palazzo Milesi [see cat.no.29]. It shows Apollo aiming his bow at the sons of Niobe, who have made a futile attempt to escape on horseback. The remainder of the composition, not visible here, contains the vengeful Diana shooting dead Niobe's daughters, and the mother herself seated with one of her terrified children trying to hide in her lap.

The drawing has been attributed entirely to Rubens,[1] but was more likely retouched by him.[2] The underdrawing is in black chalk on blue paper. A strip was added along the left-hand edge, and was used to make Apollo's cloak billow out differently from the fresco. Rubens applied greenish bodycolour in areas of shadow, and then redrew a number of outlines in wash with the tip of the brush. The original copyist had followed the way that the lower edge of the composition was cut off very sharply by Polidoro (because it was designed to be seen from below), but Rubens enlarged the legs and hooves of two of the fallen horses, redrew the most prominent animal's head and added touches of white on its eye and nostril to accentuate the poignancy of its dying moments. Other areas where white bodycolour was added by Rubens are the nimbus around Apollo's head and the highlights on his cloak which unify the join between the two pieces of paper. The blue paper actively contributes to the interplay between black chalk and the retouching in dark wash, greenish bodycolour, and white heightening, so that Rubens was able to create a rich and shimmering effect.

Another copy of Polidoro's *Death of the Children of Niobe*, also in the Louvre, extends the composition at the right with the figures of Diana, Niobe and her daughters, and has been attributed to Rubens as well.[3] However, despite being better known than the present drawing, its retouching slavishly follows Polidoro's design, and the heightening was applied in a neat and pedestrian way. This restoration may have been the work of Prosper Henry Lankrink (*c*.1628–1692) who owned the sheet in the late seventeenth century.

The retouching of the drawing exhibited here conveys an almost silken treatment of texture, a softness and malleability of form, and a colouristic richness despite the use of a limited range of pigments, all of which points to a date for Rubens's intervention around 1630.

1. Jaffé 1977, p.48.
2. Lugt 1949, II, p.27, no.1071; Logan 1978, pp.434, 437.
3. Inv.no.20299. Entirely by Rubens according to Lugt 1949, II, p.27, no.1072, repr. pl.XLIII; Jaffé 1977, p.48; Sérullaz 1978, pp.91–2, no.92, repr. Retouched by Rubens according to Logan 1978, pp.429, 434; Ravelli 1978, pp.401–2, no.758, repr. pl.LXIX.

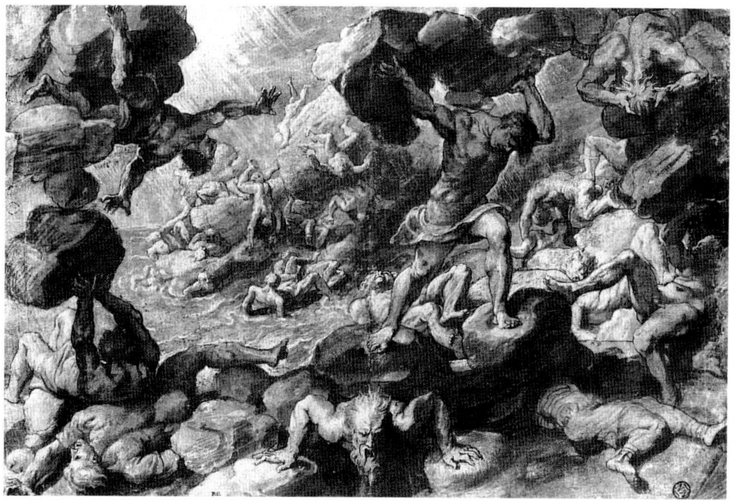
35

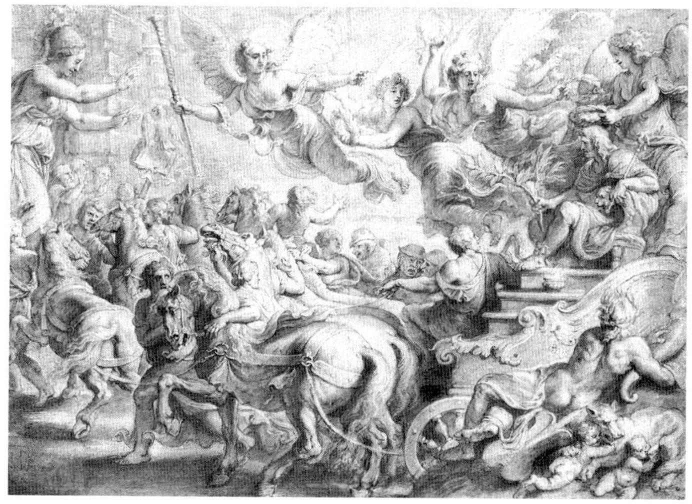
36

GIULIO ROMANO

35 · Anonymous Sixteenth-Century Draughtsman perhaps after Giulio Romano (*c*.1499–1546), retouched by Rubens

The Fall of the Giants

Pen and ink with wash, retouched with wash and bodycolour, heightened with white; 27.5 × 40 cm
Département des Arts graphiques, Musée du Louvre, Paris, inv.no.20177
Exhibited in Edinburgh only

REFERENCES: Lugt 1949, II, pp.26–7, no.1070; Burchard/d'Hulst 1956, p.41, no.23; Jaffé 1956, p.318; Jaffé 1958, p.326; Jaffé 1977, p.43; Logan 1978, pp.429, 433; Sérullaz 1978, pp.81–2, no.78; Held 1980, I, pp.276–7, under no.190.

This composition has been attributed to Giulio Romano, and identified as a hypothetical project for the decoration of a room at Palazzo Te at Mantua painted in 1532–4.[1] But Giulio made his giants seem monstrous through their heavy, fleshy bodies, thick lips, flaring nostrils and furrowed brows; by contrast, this design lacks any sense of the grotesque. The story tells of a race of giants who decided to launch an assault on heaven. They heaped the rocks from two mountains together, piling Mount Pelion upon Mount Ossa, to construct a staircase to Olympus. Jupiter retorted by crushing them under an avalanche of the rocks that they had erected (*Metamorphoses* I: 152–8).

The composition is recorded in an anonymous sixteenth-century engraving attributed to Cornelis Bos,[2] for which a pen and ink *modello* survives in the Rijksprentenkabinet, Amsterdam.[3] The Louvre sheet is almost exactly the same size and must have once been a replica of this *modello*. Rubens extensively retouched the drawing under discussion, and, since it derived from a model by a Netherlandish artist for an engraving by a northern printmaker, it is likely that he obtained it after his return to Antwerp in 1608.

Rubens reworked the Louvre drawing using brown wash and cream bodycolour, giving it a rich tonal range, clarifying the space of the composition and the volume of the figures. He threw the head of the giant, at the centre of the lower edge, into deep shadow and brought his satyr-like expression alive through crisp touches of heightening. He also intensified the way that the silhouetted arms of the falling giant at the upper right are seen against a vivid burst of light, making the scene far more dramatic.

Rubens made very literal use of three of the giants in his treatment of the same subject for the Torre de la Parada of 1636.[4] But there is something expedient and hasty about the adaptation, in keeping with Rubens's general approach to this commission. It may be that Rubens retouched the Louvre drawing at this time, but the elaborate tonal character of the retouching is closer to comparable reworked sheets from the 1620s. In this case, unusually, there may have been an interval between the retouching of a drawing and its re-use.

1. See Gombrich 1935, p.135, repr. fig.103; K. Oberhuber in Mantua 1989, pp.172–5.
2. See Schéle 1965, pp.205–6, no.237, repr. pl.62; Massari 1993, pp.54–5, no.45, repr.
3. Boon 1978, text vol., p.203, no.538, repr.
4. As noted by Lugt 1949, II, p.26, under no.1070.

36 · Rubens after Giulio Romano

The Life of Scipio Africanus: Scipio Welcomed Outside the Gates of Rome

COLOUR ILLUSTRATION ON PAGE 17

Pen and ink with wash and white heightening, retouched with brown wash, and grey, cream and white bodycolour with some heightening in oil; 41.9 × 57.3 cm
Private Collection

REFERENCES: Rooses 1910, p.198; Lugt 1949, II, p.29, under no.1081; Jaffé 1958, p.326; Van Gelder 1965, pp.5–20; Jaffé 1977, p.43; Jestaz/Bacou 1978, p.137, under no.XXII.2.

This drawing records a design from one of *The Life of Scipio* tapestries woven for François I of France. The original was melted down for its gold and silver thread in 1797 and is now best studied from a drawn *modello* in the Louvre, known as the *petit patron*.[1] Giulio followed Appian's description of Scipio's triumph (*Punic Wars* IX 66), but added the figure of Roma, at the far left, welcoming the procession into the city, and the River Tiber, at lower right, reclining with a cornucopia and a paddle, accompanied by Romulus and Remus with the she-wolf.

Rubens worked on top of a sixteenth-century sheet which reproduced the *petit patron* very precisely (and was almost exactly the same size), as revealed by some exposed outlines in fine pen and wash, similar to Giulio's workshop drawings. The underdrawing agrees precisely with the *petit patron*, as can be seen on the horse in the foreground whose legs were originally thinner and shorter, its mane and tail less long and sinuous, and the edge of the saddle cloth scalloped.

Rubens made a number of embellishments. A second stem was added to the olive branch held by Scipio which was given thick leaves, and an eagle was added to his sceptre. The chariot's rim was made thicker and given richer decoration with scrolls and foliage. The Tiber's

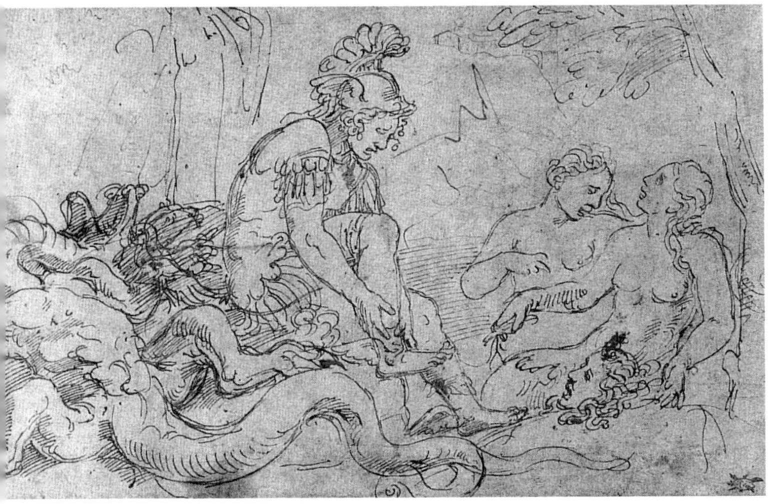

37

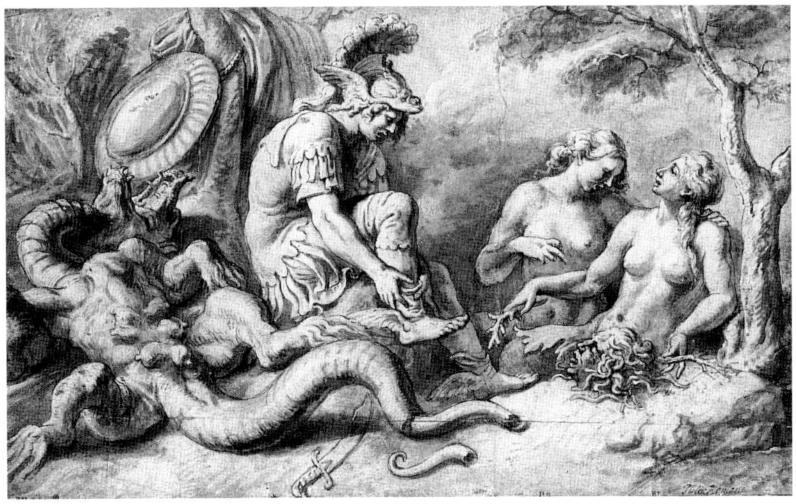

38

headband was replaced with a laurel wreath. The wolf beside him was made to look more ferocious and her mouth opened to reveal her fangs. Lastly, the simple walls of Rome were given heavy rustication and the glimpse of a column with a doric capital.

Rubens's intervention shows that he respected Giulio's invention while transforming it into his own pictorial language. He did not alter the sometimes rubbery poses, but made them look less physically uncomfortable. The greatest change, however, was the suggestion of a shimmering play of light on surfaces. His very delicate use of pigmentation gives the drawing a silvery sheen. The thickness of some of the most densely-worked highlights and the slight cracking on their surface suggests that he used oil to achieve the richest pictorial effect possible.

It has been said that Rubens used this composition as a model for his *Triumph of Henri IV* in the Uffizi, Florence,[2] dateable to 1628, but the influence is more significant in his earlier *Triumph of the Church* of *c.*1626 from the Eucharist tapestry cycle, which similarly contains a great chariot drawn by eight horses led by women. By adapting Giulio's triumph, Rubens turned what could have been a static allegory into an event with a sense of imperial magnificence and the momentum of a procession. These connections suggests the drawing was retouched in the 1620s, as is supported by its technique, almost in grisaille, which has much in common with his oil sketches from this decade.

1. Inv.no.3536. See D'Astier 1907, pp.107–8; Hartt 1958, I, p.303, no.265, repr. fig.479; Bacou 1983, p.55, no.59, repr.
2. Van Gelder 1965, p.18; Jaffé 1977, p.43.

37 · Giulio Romano

Perseus Disarming and the Origin of Coral

Pen and ink, some outlines indented, over traces of black chalk, on blue paper; 19.2 × 31.6 cm
The British Museum, London, inv.no.1895-9-15-645

REFERENCES: Hartt 1958, I, p.306, no.308; Jaffé 1958, pp.327–8; Pouncey / Gere 1962, cat. vol., pp.65–7, no.87; Jaffé 1977, p.44; Rowlands 1977, p.57, no.51.

The purpose for which Giulio made this drawing is not known, but a list of pictures in the Gonzaga collection at Mantua mentions a 'Perseo che taglia la testa a Gorgone', among works from his hand.[1] The drawing has been compared to his designs for the Camerino dei Cesari in Palazzo Ducale, Mantua,[2] of the 1530s. It is exhibited here for comparison with cat.no.38.

Perseus is shown seated, pulling off his winged sandals after a hard day's work beheading the Medusa (whose face turned anyone who looked at it to stone) and rescuing Andromeda from the sea monster. The defeated corpse of that bizarre creature is seen lying on its back. Perseus has set down Medusa's head, with its hideous and still-living snaky locks, on the shore. Her blood turned the seaweed to coral, and this so amazed the sea nymphs that they dipped twigs into it in order to make more of this astonishing red stone (*Metamorphoses* IV: 740–9).

1. Luzio 1913, p.153.
2. See Hartt's opinion cited in Pouncey / Gere 1962, cat. vol., p.66, under no.87, and reiterated by Rowlands 1977, p.57, under no.51.

38 · Anonymous Draughtsman after Giulio Romano, retouched by Rubens or Erasmus Quellinus II (1607–1678)

Perseus Disarming and the Origin of Coral

Pen and ink with brown wash, retouched in brown, yellow and grey-green wash, heightened with white bodycolour, on discoloured blue paper; 24.9 × 39.2 cm
The British Museum, London, inv.no.1851-2-8-322

REFERENCES: Jaffé 1958, pp.327–8; Pouncey / Gere 1962, cat. vol., p.66, under no.87; Jaffé 1977, p.44; Rowlands 1977, pp.56–7, no.50; Freedberg 1978, p.84; D. Jaffé in Canberra / Melbourne 1992, pp.191–4, no.76.

This composition is known from a lively pen and ink preparatory sketch by Giulio [cat.no.37], which shows how the design evolved and how the larger and more detailed version, under discussion, was retouched. In the earlier sketch, the monster's head was placed too close for comfort behind Perseus's back and was moved to insert his shield, which, in the later version is positioned hanging on the tree. The monster's tail was first shown extended and then redrawn with its tip curved around, but, in the later version, it was depicted as if sliced off in the fight with Perseus.

The larger sheet was originally a tight and highly finished drawing strengthened with brown wash and white heightening. It was retouched in dark wash to deepen the shadows, with some greenish wash used to add foliage in the background, while yellow wash was applied on the bodies as a mid-tone. Finally, thick touches of white bodycolour were used to add brilliance.

The artist who retouched the larger drawing made few changes to the design, with the following exceptions. (1) The sea monster's neck was enlarged along its left edge. (2) The lower contour of the right arm of one of the nymphs was thickened. (3) Her middle finger was made to point directly at the head of

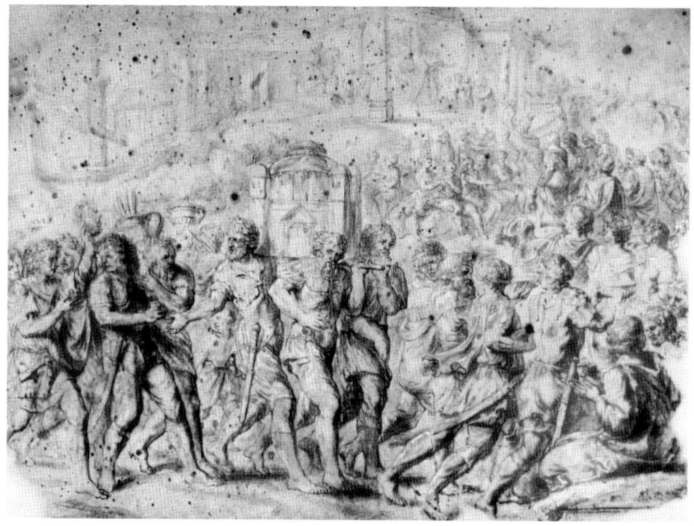

39

Medusa. (4) A large flat leaf on the tree to the right was given small dabs of greenish wash to look more like foliage. (5) The folds of Perseus's cloak on a tree were extended with touches of brown wash. (6) The shrubs at the upper left were added using a similar technique.

The retouching has been attributed to Rubens and given a wide range of dates from early in his Italian period, ranging from 1600 and 1605,[1] to the 1630s.[2] But it lacks his ability to enliven detail, animate faces and hands, and suggest a variety of textures. The faces are mask-like, fingers look wooden, and, paradoxically, only the dead monster has any life. The changes listed above are very limited by comparison with those found on the mass of Rubens's retouched sheets. In particular, the way in which the foliage at the upper left and right is drawn with shapeless touches of wash is identical to similar passages in the *Saint Andrew led to Martyrdom* after Guido Reni at Chatsworth, which to my mind, is not by Rubens, but from the hand of Erasmus Quellinus II or perhaps his son, Jan Erasmus Quellinus (1634–1715). If the *Perseus* was retouched by Quellinus, it suggests he could make a good job of imitating the general effect, but not the detail, of Rubens's interventions.

1. Jaffé 1977, p.44, caption to pl.112.
2. D. Jaffé, 'Drawings' in Canberra/Melbourne 1992, p.194, caption to no.76.
3. Inv.no.489. See Jaffé 1965a, p.28 (as Rubens 1608); Jaffé 1977, p.99; J. Wood in Oxford/London 1988, pp.10–11 ('modified by someone in Rubens's studio').

39 · Anonymous Draughtsman after Giulio Romano, retouched by an Artist in Rubens's Workshop

The Life of Scipio Africanus: The Triumph with Models of Captured Cities and Precious Objects Carried in Procession, also known as the *Ascent to the Capitol*

Red chalk counterproof, retouched with red wash and cream bodycolour; 43.8 × 57.5 cm
The British Museum, London, inv.no.1972 U.675

REFERENCES: Hind 1923, p.21, no.50; Jaffé 1958, p.329; Van Gelder 1965, pp.16, 20; Jaffé 1977, p.42; Logan 1977, p.412; Rowlands 1977, p.43, no.36; Jestaz/Bacou 1978, p.113, under no.XIV, 1.

This drawing records a design by Giulio for one of the tapestries depicting *The Triumph of Scipio* woven for François I between 1532 and 1535. The destruction of the tapestry in the eighteenth century means that the most reliable guide to the design is Giulio's drawn *modello*, known as the *petit patron*, now in the Louvre.[1]

This episode was based on a passage in Appian's *Punic Wars* (VIII, ix 66). The procession is shown winding up towards the Temple of Jupiter Optimus Maximus, whose statue is visible behind the portico. The temple was the most venerated in Rome because Jupiter was viewed as the special protector of the city and the empire. A random selection of monuments can be seen nearby, including the obelisk of Rameses II and the equestrian statue of Marcus Aurelius (then popularly identified as depicting Constantine),[2] which was located at the Lateran during the period when Giulio was in Rome. Giulio's evocation of the Capitol also contained Trajan's Column from the Forum with the bronze statue of the emperor clearly visible. It seems that Giulio was not much concerned with topographical and historical accuracy.

The drawing is a counterproof that reverses Giulio's design and may have been made from a red chalk copy of the *petit patron*, which is similar in size. The soft and fuzzy character of the counterproof is easiest to see at the upper part of the sheet, rather than on the foreground figures which were extensively retouched. The drawing has been washed and also abraded in the course of time, and, although the reworking proved more resilient than the underdrawing in chalk, it now reads disjointedly.

The use of brush and wash resembles Rubens's manner in the late 1620s when his figures took on a soft, simplified and malleable character, but this sheet is fussy by comparison, being over-concerned with the description of drapery and facial expression. Unusually for Rubens, the retouching fails to revise the design and seems more concerned with clarifying the underdrawing. The figures retain the puppet-like appearance found in Giulio's *petit patron*, with disjointed limbs, heads that do not fit onto bodies or are too small, and angular poses. A case can be made that the drawing relates to Rubens's draughtsmanship of the late 1620s, but, to my mind, it is more likely to be by someone in his workshop.

1. Inv.no.3544. See Jestaz/Bacou 1978, pp.111–12, repr.
2. See Bober/Rubinstein 1986, pp.206–8, no.176, repr.

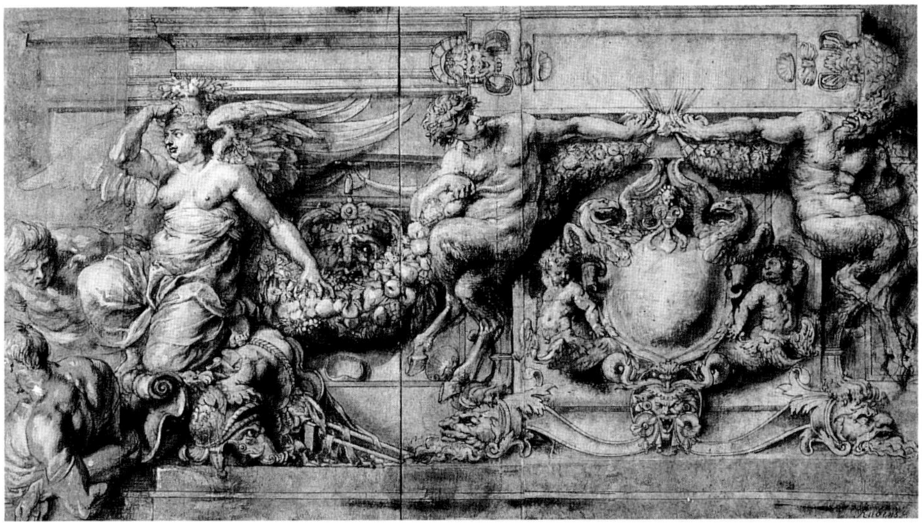

40

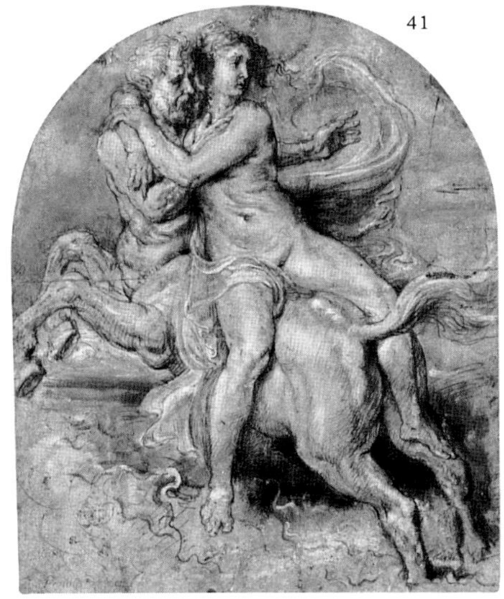

41

PERINO DEL VAGA

40 · Anonymous Sixteenth-Century Draughtsman after Perino del Vaga (1501–1547), retouched by Rubens

Part of a Frieze with a Winged Woman and a Blank Cartouche Supported by Satyrs

Pen and ink with wash, retouched with black chalk, brown wash and yellow and white bodycolour; 36.5 × 64.1 cm. The main section extended by a strip (8.5 cm wide) at left.
The British Museum, London, inv.no.1994–5–14–43. Formerly N.G. 853 K, left-hand section, and 853 M, right-hand section; renumbered as 1972 U.792.

REFERENCES: Pouncey / Gere 1962, cat. vol., pp.114–15, no.194; Van Gelder 1965, pp.5, 7–9; Jaffé 1977, p.47; Rowlands 1977, p.58, no.53; E. Parma in Mantua 2001, p.283, under no.153.

The drawing in the British Museum records part of Perino del Vaga's design for a panel to decorate the lower section of the altar wall (*basamento*) in the Sistine Chapel, which had been left bare when Michelangelo finished work on the *Last Judgement* in 1541. Vasari says the design was to be woven in tapestry.[1] Perino was given the commission and received two payments in November 1542,[2] but, although he produced a cartoon on canvas, it seems the project was never realised because of his death in October 1547. Not one but two full-size canvases survive, now attached to the walls of the second Sala of the Galleria Spada, Rome. One, the original, contains a papal tiara and keys in the central cartouche, while the other, a replica from the 1630s, has a basket of fruit.[3]

This drawing has been identified as retouched by Rubens ever since the eighteenth century.[4] The sheet is made up of several pieces of paper, with the main section drawn on a double sheet which must always have constricted the winged female figure. Rubens solved the problem by adding a strip of paper on the left which also allowed the inclusion of two bound captives.

Rubens made substantial changes to the two male terminal figures flanking the cartouche. These were originally joined at the waist to bulging consoles with lion feet. He did not like these strange hybrids and turned them into satyrs who perch cross-legged. While the figure on the left remains youthful, the one on the right was aged, and Rubens gave him horns, a pointed goatee, and showed him sticking out his tongue. He also changed the cartouche, adding shadow to suggest a curved surface, and white heightening to strengthen the two infants with the bodies of winged sea horses. The eagles above were given wings. The festoons were made more substantial by the addition of highlights, which were also placed on the eyes of the mask, thereby making it look alive.

The substantial strip that Rubens added on the left provides the best guide to the date of his enlargement and retouching. The outlines of the bound captives were first drawn quickly in black chalk and are like his figure drawings from the late 1610s. Assured touches of brown wash and white heightening make the captives look as solid as the precise penmanship of the core section which Rubens did not bother to imitate. The retouching has parallels with his assured and abbreviated use of chalk, wash, and bodycolour of around 1620 and should be dated accordingly.

1. Vasari 1568, II, p.366.
2. See Davidson 1966, p.51, under no.49.
3. See E. Parma in Mantua 2001, pp.282–3, under no.153.
4. Mariette 1741, p.93, no.814.

41 · Anonymous Draughtsman after Perino del Vaga, retouched by Rubens

Nessus and Deianeira

COLOUR FRONTISPIECE

Pen and ink, retouched with brown wash and blue-grey, green-grey and cream bodycolour, heightened with white; 25.2 × 20.3 cm
The British Museum, London, inv.no.1893–7–31–19

REFERENCES: Hind 1923, p.20, no.46; Pouncey / Gere 1962, cat. vol., p.116, no.196; Jaffé 1977, p.47; Logan 1977, p.412, Rowlands 1977, p.40, no.31; D. Jaffé in Canberra / Melbourne 1992, pp.190, 193.

This drawing is remarkable for the palpitating sense of life given to the figures and the touchingly intimate way in which they cling together. When Hercules and Deianeira, the daughter of the river god Oeneus, journeyed to the river Evenus, it was so swollen they could only cross with the help of Nessus, a centaur, who acted as ferryman. But Nessus decided to abduct Deianeira and Hercules slew him with an arrow (*Metamorphoses* 9: 101–133).

The design has been given to Perino del Vaga on the basis of an early inscription. In addition, the words *bruzza sorzi* in a sixteenth-century hand on the verso confirm this is an earlier sheet that Rubens reworked. The pen and ink underdrawing is legible on the front legs of the centaur, which are described with a sinuous outline and wiry, slightly scratchy hatching, unlike Rubens's fluent use of the pen. This sheet was badly damaged at an early stage in its history and the way it was repaired and retouched fits Mariette's description of how Rubens liked to restore drawings.[1]

The drawing was reworked by applying blue-grey bodycolour to the sky and the expanse of water, using the pigmentation of the paper to suggest flesh tone. A greenish-grey wash was added to the shadows, and yellowish-cream bodycolour applied to Deianeira's body;

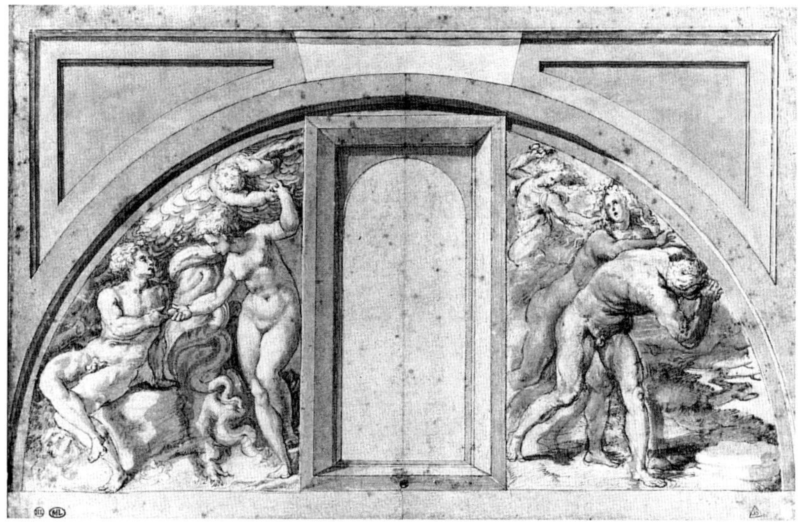

42

remarkable skill was used to suggest the pull on her body as she twists around, her hips being redrawn to make the torsion of her pose more anatomically convincing. Outlines were redrawn with the tip of the brush and dark brown wash, locks of Deianeira's hair were made to float out sideways and the two faces were transformed into Rubens's manner, with expressions that are animated and apprehensive. Finally, delicate touches of white were used to give a pearly brilliance to the forms, and to convey the transparency and lightness of Deianeira's drapery.

The authorship of the underdrawing is a problem since little remains legible to establish whether it is by or after Perino. Some similarities can be found with a drawing by him in the Ashmolean Museum, Oxford,[2] depicting another figure who twists round on the back of a rearing horse, a preparatory study for the fresco of *Marcus Curtius* on the ceiling of the Loggia degli Eroi at Palazzo Doria del Principe, Fassolo, near Genoa, dateable to the 1530s.

The drawing – whether said to be entirely by Rubens or retouched by him – has been placed as early as his Italian period,[3] and as late as 1621 to 1630.[4] The combination of delicacy and vigour in the application of wash and bodycolour cannot be paralleled in Rubens's early drawing style, and has far more in common with that of the 1630s.

1. Mariette 1741, pp.92–3.
2. See Parker 1956, cat. vol., p.391, no.730, repr. pl.CLXII; E. Parma in Mantua 2001, p.220, no.109, repr.
3. Jaffé 1977, p.47; Logan 1977, p.412.
4. Dated *c.*1621–30 by D. Jaffé in Canberra / Melbourne 1992, caption to no.74.

FRANCESCO SALVIATI

42 · Francesco Salviati (1510–1563), retouched by Rubens

The Fall of Man and the Expulsion from the Garden of Eden

Pen and ink with yellowish-brown and grey wash over some black chalk, heightened with white; retouched in wash with cream and greenish bodycolour; 19 × 29 cm
Département des Arts graphiques, Musée du Louvre, Paris, inv.no.RF 593
Exhibited in Edinburgh only

REFERENCES: Cheney 1963, II, p.547; Jaffé 1965a, p.21; Monbeig-Goguel 1972, pp.117–20, no.140; Jaffé 1977, p.50; Sérullaz 1978, pp.116–17, no.121; Mortari 1992, p.250, no.440.

This drawing depicts a lunette pierced by a tall round-headed window within a deep embrasure. It is clearly a *modello* for a specific location. The two episodes on either side of the window are linked by the theme of original sin. On the left is the Fall of Man (Genesis 3: 1–6), and, on the right, the expulsion from the Garden of Eden (Genesis 3: 23–4).

Salviati painted these subjects several times in the 1550s, notably at San Salvatore in Lauro, Rome, and in the Chigi Chapel in Santa Maria del Popolo, Rome, but the Louvre drawing is unrelated to any of these. However, there is a parallel in theme and shape with Rosso Fiorentino's lunettes of the *Creation of Eve* and *Fall of Man* in the Cappella Cesi, Santa Maria della Pace, Rome. The contract was drawn up on 26 April 1524 when Salviati was only fourteen years old, but Rosso was sacked after finishing the work, which Vasari called the worst he ever painted.[1] The chapel was not completed until the 1540s and the drawing may be a proposal to replace Rosso's unsatisfactory frescoes. If so, it can be dated with some precision to 1541–3 when Salviati returned to Rome for his second stay in the city.[2]

The underlying drawing was made in pen and ink with brown wash, as well as some delicate white heightening. Rubens concentrated his retouching on the two main episodes. His principal intervention was on the Expulsion, where he used cream and slightly greenish bodycolour to block out Eve's right arm in order to move it across her chest in a gesture of self-protection. Her left leg was moved to the right and entirely redrawn so as to anchor her more firmly to the ground, and Adam's left leg was shifted in the opposite direction so as to give his pose more complexity and torsion. As a result, three or perhaps four pairs of legs can be made out rather than the two which might be expected. Adam's foreshortened torso was heavily reworked in bodycolour and brown wash, and an area of ochre oil paint covers his left arm which was entirely redrawn so as to clench his hands in front of his face. The window embrasure and spandrels above were a later addition, the latter being drawn on a shaped piece of paper that was stuck down onto the sheet, probably by Pierre-Jean Mariette who owned the drawing in the eighteenth century.

Rubens's intervention on this sheet was bold and energetic, although on an almost miniature scale. It shows him imposing his own graphic style on top of that of Salviati, as though impatient with the delicacy and precision of the original. Such an assertive intervention points to a date, late in Rubens's career, of after 1630.

1. Vasari 1568, II, p.207.
2. This is marginally earlier than the dating to the late 1540s or early 1550s found in Cheney 1963, II, p.547.

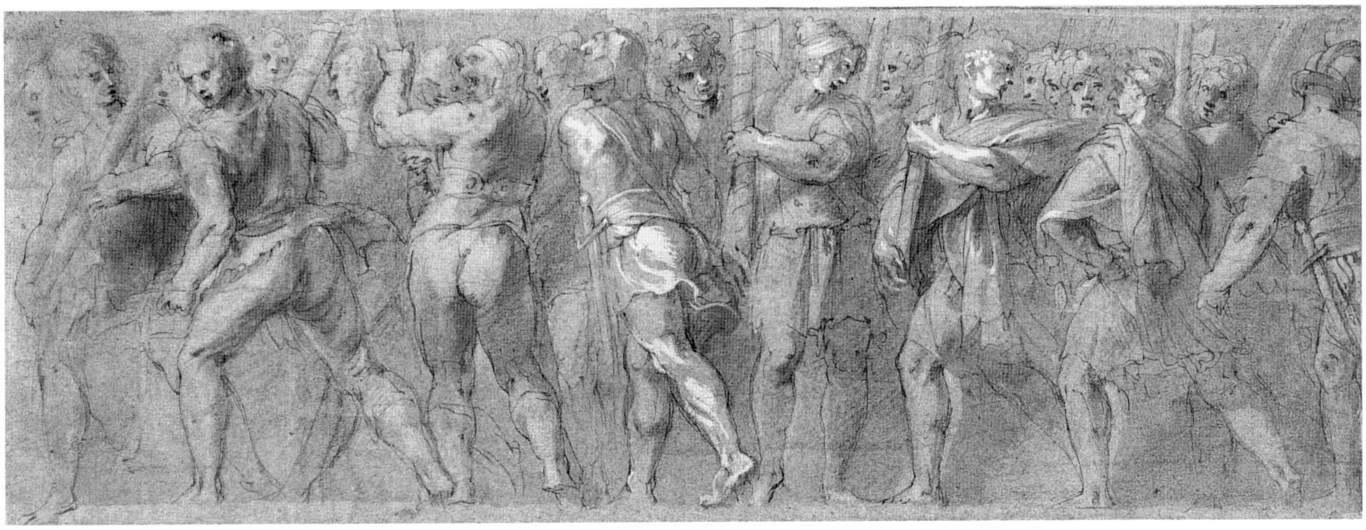

43

TADDEO ZUCCARO

43 · Taddeo Zuccaro (1529–1566), retouched by Rubens

A Procession of Lictors

Pen and ink and wash, retouched with black chalk and green and white bodycolour, 16.4 × 42.2 cm
The British Museum, London, inv.no.1895–9–15–1043

REFERENCES: Rooses 1886–92, v, p.208, no.1396; Hind 1923, p.20, no.48; Pouncey / Gere 1962, cat. vol., pp.172–3, no.288; Jaffé 1965a, p.25; Gere 1969, p.164, no.103; Ravelli 1978, p.475, no.980; Gere / Pouncey 1983, cat. vol., p.204, no.325.

This drawing shows a procession of twenty men carrying fasces (bundles of rods containing an axe); one is in armour, one has a sword, and another wears a lion-skin headdress. A related drawing in pen and wash, also in the British Museum,[1] shows three captives being led to execution by a procession of soldiers. Since these drawings are alike in format and figure scale, they were probably intended for the same unidentified commission. The low viewpoint suggests that both designs were conceived for a painted façade and were meant to be viewed from below.

In the early nineteenth century this drawing was attributed to Perino del Vaga, 'touched by Rubens',[2] and then given entirely to Rubens,[3] but in the mid-twentieth century it was attributed to a follower of Polidoro da Caravaggio,[4] and then to the young Taddeo Zuccaro, working around 1550.[5] The survival of the related drawing of a procession of soldiers with prisoners, mentioned above, which is convincingly attributed to Taddeo on grounds of style, makes the authorship of the drawing under discussion secure.

A Procession of Lictors was quite lightly drawn before being retouched. It was strengthened with wash on the main figures and black chalk was added to the shadows. Brilliant white highlights were given to the figure near the centre who has a sword at his waist; in addition, a few touches were placed on the noses and foreheads of adjacent heads. This reworking strengthened the relief of the design, but did not change it in detail. The only significant alteration is on the figure with a sword whose foot was enlarged with white bodycolour.

The reworking is quite limited but has been plausibly attributed to Rubens. Its fluency and reticence point to a time towards the end of the 1610s, when he also intervened on *modelli* for engravings with a similar restraint, and before the more encrusted and impatient interventions of the 1620s and 1630s.

1. Inv.no.1946–7–13–579. See Pouncey / Gere 1962, cat. vol., p.172, no.287, repr. pl.271 (as 'follower of Polidoro da Caravaggio'); Gere 1969, pp.165–6, no.105, repr. pl.5 (as Taddeo Zuccaro); Gere / Pouncey 1983, cat. vol., p.204, no.326, repr. pl.311 (as Taddeo Zuccaro).
2. See William Young Ottley's sale (anon), London (T. Philipe), 11–14 April 1804, lot 307.
3. See Lawrence, Inventory, fol.84, case 6, drawer 2, as Rubens ('67. A Roman procession with Lictors, on blue paper').
4. Pouncey / Gere 1962, cat. vol., pp.172–3, no.288.
5. Gere 1969, p.164, no.103; Gere / Pouncey 1983, cat. vol., p.204, no.325.

44 · Taddeo Zuccaro, retouched by Rubens

The Marriage of the Virgin

Pen and ink with wash, retouched with brown wash and cream bodycolour; 28.5 × 41.6 cm. Inscribed *f. Zuccaro* in ink by Rubens.
Département des Arts graphiques, Musée du Louvre, Paris, inv.no.4521
Exhibited in Nottingham only

REFERENCES: Jaffé 1965a, pp.21, 30, note 4; Gere 1969, pp.98, 99, 202, under no.213; Jaffé 1977, p.51; Sérullaz 1978, pp.117–18, no.122; Wood 1994, pp.340, 342; Acidini Luchinat 1998, I, p.132, note 8.

This drawing in the Louvre corresponds with the central portion of a wider horizontal composition known from a drawing in the Rosenbach Foundation, Philadelphia.[1] The Protoevangelium records that when it was time for the Virgin to marry, all the available suitors were given a rod to hold, and when Joseph touched his it flowered, a miracle witnessed by Mary and the seven virgins who were her companions. The Rosenbach drawing includes ten disappointed suitors and ten virgins on either side of the central group.

The purpose for which Taddeo conceived the horizontal version is not known, but the figures of the Virgin, Joseph, and the High Priest reappear in his fresco of *c.*1558–9 in Santa Maria dell'Orto, Rome, where they are also placed in front of a shallow niche, although the narrower format of the fresco meant that the group had to be compressed. The commission was awarded to Taddeo, but, according to Vasari, he only painted one fresco, an *Adoration of the Shepherds*, delegating the remainder to his younger brother, Federico.[2] Vasari suggested that the latter was proficient enough to design and execute these works independently, but it is likely, given that drawings by Taddeo survive for one of the other scenes, that he provided Federico with sketches from which to work.

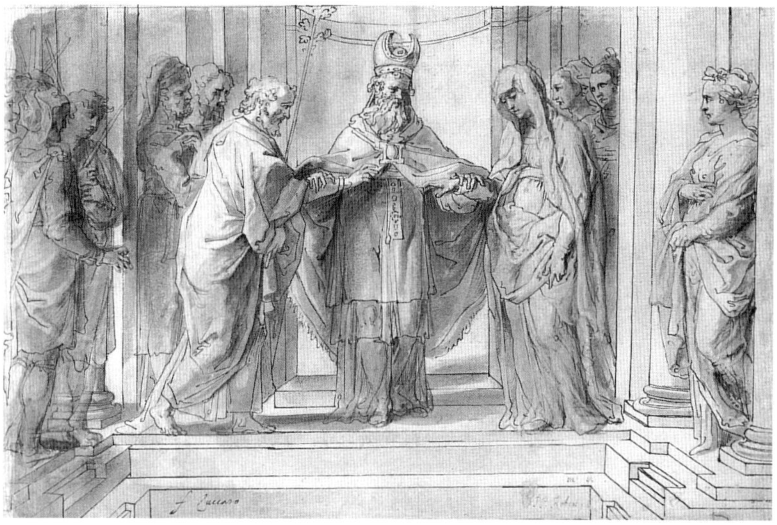

44

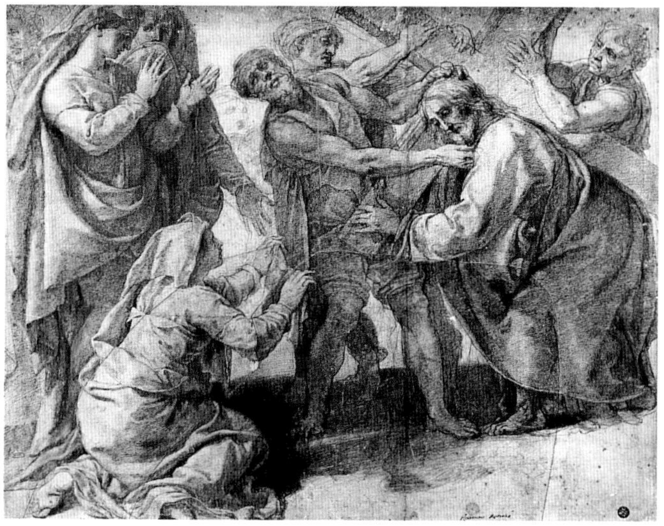

45

Rubens's reading of Vasari could explain the attribution to Federico that he wrote at the lower left.

The underdrawing in pen and ink is regular and mechanical, and the steps and columned portico are drawn with a ruler. Rubens's retouching gave the drawing a greater sense of depth, enhancing the texture and softness of the draperies, and enlivening the most important faces. The Virgin was extensively redrawn, and similar retouching can be found on the left arm and robe of the woman at the far right, seen stepping through the colonnade. The crowd of disappointed suitors on the left was more impatiently shadowed with some broad touches of wash, and the leg of the third man from the left was entirely redrawn by Rubens to make him stand more firmly.

Rubens's intervention on the Louvre drawing is deft, fluent and a little impatient. It belongs among a group of drawings that were retouched entirely with the brush, where the aim of the reworking was to give an almost silken richness to draperies and to increase the three-dimensionality of the figures. This type of reworking is very different from the more linear changes made to some sheets, here dated to the 1610s, which were predominantly concerned with design and composition, and, as a result, this retouching should be placed in the late 1620s.

1. Inv.472/22, nos.24, 25. See Gere 1969, p.202, no.213; Gere 1970, pp.133–4, no.28, repr. pl.17a-b.
2. Vasari 1568, III, p.691.

GIROLAMO MUZIANO

45 · Girolamo Muziano (1532–1592), retouched by Rubens

Christ Carrying the Cross with Saint Veronica Presenting the Sudarium

Red chalk, retouched with red wash, heightened with some white bodycolour; 47 × 58.7 cm. Inscribed *Hieronimo Muciano* by Rubens at lower right. Département des Arts graphiques, Musée du Louvre, Paris, inv.no.5101
Exhibited in Edinburgh only

REFERENCES: Da Como 1930, p.53; Bierens de Haan 1948, p.96, under no.83; C. Monbeig-Goguel in Paris, 1977, p.108, no.77; Logan 1978, pp.426, 428–9; Logan/ Haverkamp-Begemann 1978, p.94; Sérullaz 1978, p.115, no.118; Wood 1994, p.340.

This drawing is among the largest and most impressive by Girolamo Muziano to have survived. It depicts Christ carrying his cross to Golgotha (John 19: 17) and stumbling, but not falling, under his burden. Saint Veronica is shown kneeling in the left foreground with the cloth she used to wipe his face, the *sudarium*, which took the imprint of his likeness.

Muziano's drawing is related to the altarpiece that he painted for the Cathedral at Orvieto, delivered on 30 April 1557, and now in the Museo dell' Opera del Duomo in the city. The main difference is that the drawing only records the lower half of the altarpiece, which has a tall vertical format and arched top. In the painting Muziano turned the Virgin round so as to face the spectator, showing her swooning, supported by the two Maries, and gave Christ the crown of thorns whilst the men lifting the cross wear Roman helmets. The altarpiece was engraved by Cornelis Cort (*c*.1533–1578) in 1567,[1] as Rubens almost certainly knew.

Muziano's drawing is made up of three pieces of paper cut and joined in a complicated way. He removed a large section running from Saint Veronica's right foot to the bottom edge of the cross and down through Christ's robe. The second major change was the removal of a large part of the left-hand side of the drawing, and its replacement with the section containing the three holy women, and the heads of Saint Veronica and the executioner. The large size, extreme refinement of handling, and elaborate physical construction of this work suggest that it was intended as a *modello* for the altarpiece.

Rubens knew that this was a drawing by Muziano because he wrote the artist's name in ink at the lower right-hand edge. He reworked it with brush and red wash, and his most noticeable intervention was on Christ's face where a few lines drawn with the tip of the brush gave it a more pathetic character. He also redrew the left foot of Christ, who at one time had an under garment which trailed on the ground. The fact that the two executioners at the centre of the composition have five legs rather than the more usual four suggests either that Muziano changed his mind or that Rubens intervened. Pinkish wash was applied in areas of shadow, and some white bodycolour was mixed into the red chalk of the Virgin's robe to help separate her from Saint Veronica.

Rubens clearly admired this drawing and did little to change its basic visual character. His retouching is not unlike his intervention on several other red chalk drawings, including one by Annibale Carracci [cat.no.72] which he reused in two dateable commissions of the early 1620s and 1630s. This points to the probable date of Rubens's work on the entire group.

1. Bierens de Haan 1948, pp.96–7, no.83, with discussion of some early copies and adaptations.

Artists Working in North Italy

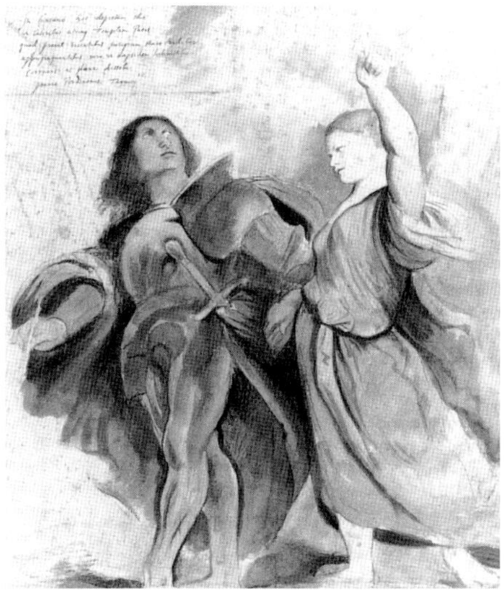
46

PORDENONE

46 · Rubens after Giovanni Antonio da Pordenone (1483/4–1539)
The Emperor Augustus and the Tibertine Sibyl

COLOUR ILLUSTRATION ON PAGE 26

Black and red chalk, with grey-blue, brown, green and yellow watercolour; 40 × 33 cm. Inscribed in Rubens's hand at upper left: *In concavo hoc depictum est / a lateribus utrinq[ue] Templum Pacis / quod procol visentibus integrum stare videtur / approprinquantibus vero et hapsidem* [= *apsidem*] *subeuntibus / corruere ac plane dissolvi*[.] */ pinxit Pordenonus Tarvisji.*
Département des Art graphiques, Musée du Louvre, Paris, inv.no.RF 702
Exhibited in Edinburgh only

REFERENCES: Rooses 1886–92, V, pp.201–2, no.1383; Glück/Haberditzl 1928, pp.10, 28, no.1; Lugt 1949, II, p.25, no.1065; Jaffé 1977, p.39; Sérullaz 1978, p.93, no.94; Warnke 1986, pp.191–7; Pilo 1988, pp.116–23; Cohen 1996, I, p.144; II, p.573, under no.32.

The Louvre drawing is a copy of two main figures from Pordenone's fresco of the *Emperor Augustus and the Tibertine Sibyl* painted in 1520 in the Malchiostro or Annunciation Chapel in the Duomo, Treviso. The story showed that Christ's birth was not only announced to the Jews, but to the Gentiles. When Augustus was declared a mortal god, he consulted the Tibertine Sibyl who prophesied the coming of a child who would be greater than all the gods of Rome, and he witnessed a vision of the Virgin with the infant Christ (*Ara coeli*).

Pordenone painted a broken column and a fragment of an entablature in the foreground alluding to the ruins of the Templum Pacis which the sibyl also prophesied would fall at the moment when the Virgin gave birth. Although Rubens copied only the two protagonists, his Latin inscription reveals that he recognised Pordenone's allusion: 'In this concavity is painted on both sides the Temple of Peace, which seems to those who observe it from a distance to be whole, but to those who go closer and enter the apse has clearly collapsed and is obviously ruined.' The inscription is similar to other texts found on drawings from Rubens's Italian period, and shows he was thinking about the meaning of works that he studied, about their setting and location, about visual problems of representation, and also about literary associations drawn from his reading.

Pordenone took some trouble in depicting ancient Rome in the background, but showed Augustus wearing modern armour. Rubens copied this in a summary way, as if not of interest, and only lightly indicated the imperial sceptre in Augustus's hand. He may have recalled Rogier van der Weyden's depiction of Augustus as a Burgundian knight on the Bladelin Altarpiece, now in Berlin. More recent Italian depictions had showed the emperor in, at least, vaguely classical dress.

Rubens drew the outlines of this drawing in chalk and added broad areas in coloured wash, a greyish tint being used on Augustus's armour and green on the sibyl's dress. Despite the energy of this copy it has some raw and awkward qualities, which point to a very early date almost immediately after Rubens's arrival in north Italy. The copies that he made in 1601 from the prophets and sibyls on the Sistine Ceiling [cat.nos.9, 10] are equally large and also use black chalk for the main outlines with red reserved for flesh.

TITIAN

47 · Rubens or Anthony van Dyck (1599–1641) after Titian (1488/90–1576)
The Emperor Charles V

Oil on canvas; 75 × 55.5 cm
The Courtauld Institute Gallery, London
inv.no.P.1978.A5.351

REFERENCES: Seilern 1955, pp.23–4, no.13; Müller Hofstede 1967, pp.71–4, 76, 79–80, 93, note 158; Seilern 1971, pp.21–2, no.13; Jaffé 1977, p.69; Jaffé 1989, p.152, no.31; J. Wood in Canberra/Melbourne 1992, pp.140–2, no.40.

Titian's *Emperor Charles V on Horseback*, now in Madrid, commemorated the imperial victory at Mühlberg in 1547, and it interested Rubens as both the likeness of a great Habsburg ruler and a prototype equestrian portrait. In September 1548 Titian wrote to Antoine de Granvelle (1517–1586) to tell him that in six days he would hand the portrait over to his patron. When Rubens first visited Spain in 1603 it was displayed at the Madrid Alcázar, and he must have seen it there for the second time in 1628–9.

The technique of this copy suggests a date of 1603. The paint surface is dense, contours are drawn in a dark lake and the shadows on flesh areas are painted thickly. The armour is a darker bluish-black than Titian's original, and the sheen of the metal is exaggerated through the thick use of white lead in the highlights. These explosive contrasts of light and dark are a hallmark of Rubens's early work.

Titian's *Charles V* influenced Rubens's own equestrian portraits, and he made his copy around the time he was commissioned to paint the Duke of Lerma (1552–1625) on horseback, a work now in Madrid. Rubens returned to the Titian when he was back at the Spanish court in

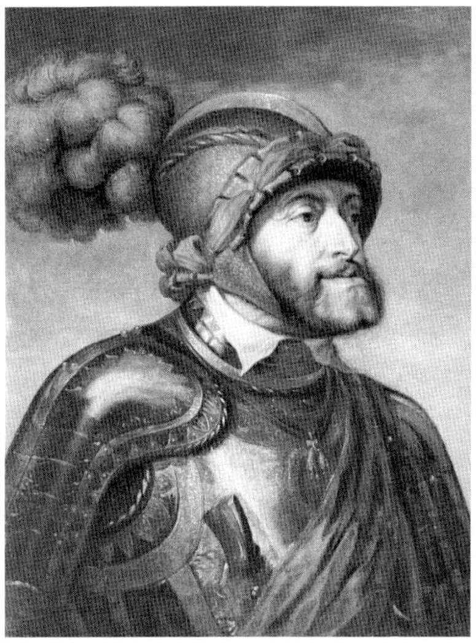

47

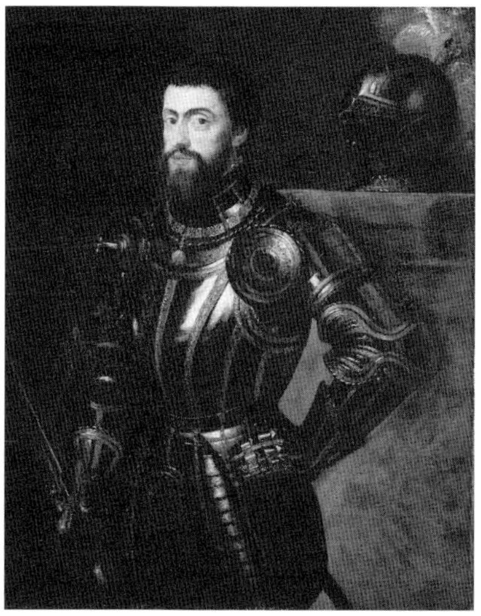

48

1628–9 and was required to paint an equestrian portrait of Philip IV, now destroyed but known from a copy in Florence. This work was intended to hang facing Titian's *Charles V* in the New Room at the Alcázar.[1] However, the most exact use that Rubens made of this prototype was in his *Battle of Tunis*, now in Berlin, dateable to 1635, where a small version of the emperor on horseback provides a calm focus of imperial authority amidst a seething mass of warriors.[2]

In the 1640 inventory of Rubens's collection, a head of Charles V in a helmet after Titian was described as by Van Dyck.[3] Since the younger artist never travelled to Spain he cannot have copied the original. Another version, now in a private collection, New York, includes slightly more of the figure than the Courtauld version. It follows that this may have been the work painted by Rubens in 1603, that the Courtauld version was copied from it by Van Dyck, and that his version was kept by Rubens in his own collection.

The current condition of these two copies may be misleading particularly since the Courtauld version has been transferred to a new canvas. The sky can be seen on both sides of the head, but there should be trees on the left, and the background appears to have been once a pale ochre, closer to the mellow skies in Titian's original than the pale blue now on the surface. The collar has sharper and more twisted points, but, as this appears in both versions, all it suggests is that one was made from the other. On balance, it seems safer to retain the attribution of the Courtauld version to Rubens, given that the other picture, although once of good quality, has been even more badly damaged.

1. Volk 1980, p.172; Orso 1986, pp.58, 70–1.
2. See Held 1982, p.334.
3. See Glück 1937, p.174, note 27; Muller 1989, pp.110–11, under no.79.

48 · Rubens after Titian

Charles V in Armour with a Drawn Sword

COLOUR ILLUSTRATION ON PAGE 21

Oil on canvas; 118.8 × 92.6 cm
Private Collection

REFERENCES: Burchard 1950, pp.28–30, no.26; Müller Hofstede 1967, pp.38–47; Wethey 1969–75, II, p.192, under no.L-3; Wethey 1987, p.14; Jaffé 1989, p.152, no.35; Muller 1989, pp.60, 106, no.52; Vergara 1999, pp.100, 201, note 26.

Titian's portrait of Charles V (1500–1558) with an unsheathed sword shows him bareheaded, wearing full armour with a breastplate and two circular, spiked armpit defenses (besagews). It was probably the first of the many portraits that he painted of this sitter but the chronology is far from resolved. The original has traditionally been dated to shortly before Charles's coronation in Bologna on 24 February 1530,[1] but Titian wrote several letters from Venice in these months, and some scholars have argued that Titian did not paint the emperor until their second meeting in 1533.[2] Titian must have been instructed to depict Charles in armour, and, as Rubens would have realised, this follows a northern tradition in imperial portraiture.

In 1561 Titian's portrait was recorded at Simancas,[3] where it appears to have remained, and which was located conveniently near Valladolid where Rubens spent much of his time during his first visit to Spain in 1603. It was later moved to the Madrid Alcázar, and appears to have been destroyed in one of the all-too-frequent fires in the Spanish royal palaces.

Rubens's copy has a thick and opaque paint surface. The handling is simplified and bold with powerful contrasts of light and dark and the elimination of half tones. A range of touch is evident in the picture, since the face is handled softly in comparison to the bolder treatment of the armour. There is a vivid contrast between the red velvet and the black armour with its brilliant sheen and gold damascened bands. These areas are powerfully differentiated from the pale and soft flesh of the face. An early dating for Rubens's copy has been accepted by most writers, with one recent exception.[4]

Rubens's main interest in the portraiture of Charles V was stimulated by the accession of Philip IV in 1621 and his increased dealings with the Spanish Habsburgs. Echoes of this particular work can be found in some of his half-length portraits, such as one in a private collection of the Cardinal-Infante Ferdinand (1609–1641), dateable to the mid-1630s. Rubens was required to paint several imaginary portraits of Charles V, and in each case he showed the emperor in armour and holding a naked sword in his right hand. The most important of these formed part of the decorations for the Ceremonial Entry of the Cardinal-Infante into Antwerp in 1635. The Triumphal Arch of Philip included a seated portrait of Charles V painted by Cornelis de Vos (*c*.1584–1651) to Rubens's designs, now in the Akademie, Vienna. Even more prominent was a large statue of Charles V holding a drawn sword in one hand and a globe (*Reichsapfel*) in the other, which was carved as one of twelve images of great Habsburg rulers for the Portico of the Emperors.

1. For example, see Wethey 1987, pp.79–80, note 67.
2. See Hood/Hope 1977, pp.551–2; Hope 1980, p.76; Hope 1988, p.49.
3. Beer 1891, p.clxxiii, no.196.
4. Vergara 1999, p.201, note 26.

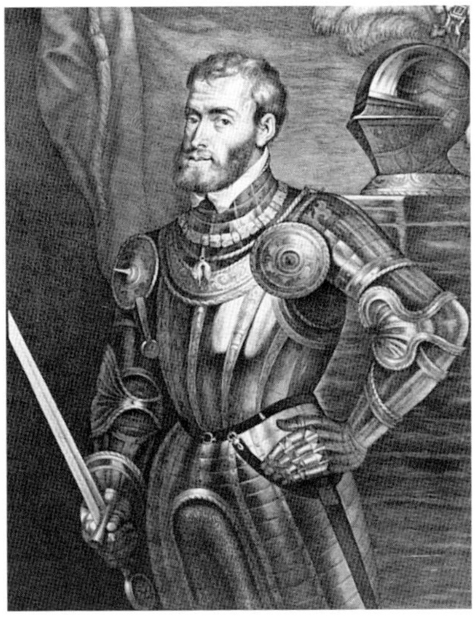

49

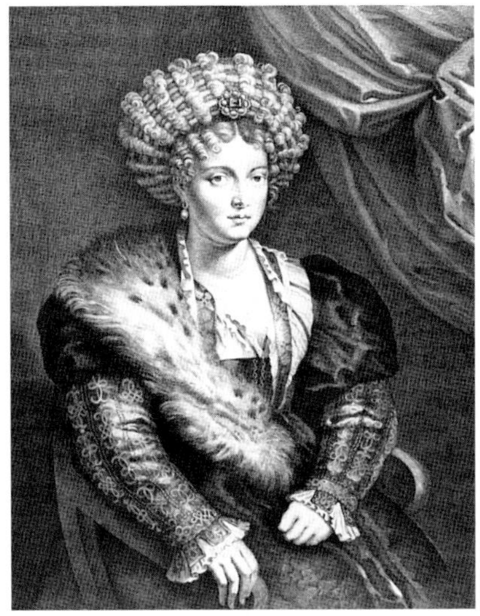

50

49 · Lucas Vorsterman (*c*.1595–1675) after Rubens, after Titian

Charles V in Armour with a Drawn Sword

Engraving; 43.5 × 32.3 cm. First state before letters.
The British Museum, London, inv.no.1862–7–12–50

REFERENCES: Voorhelm Schneevoogt 1873, p.170, no.144; Hymans 1893, pp.24, 157, no.150; Van den Wijngaert 1940, p.103, no.731; Burchard 1950, pp.31–2, no.27; Bodart 1977, p.76, no.138; Schuckman 1993, p.141, no.144.

Rubens waited some time before issuing this print after his copy of *Charles V with a Drawn Sword* [cat.no.48] painted in 1603. Lucas Vorsterman's engraving can be dated between 1618, when he started work for Rubens, and 1620, because it does not bear the print privilege which Rubens obtained in that year.[1] It has been argued that the formula *cum privilegiis* was used frequently and could point to a later date,[2] but this ignores the fraught and chronologically precise history of Vorsterman's and Rubens's partnership.

The engraving is a vivid and faithful record of Rubens's copy with the exception that Charles's head was replaced with one derived from Titian's later portraits of 1548. It has been suggested that the exact model was Titian's lost *Charles V in Armour with a Baton*, known from several copies (one of which, in the collection of Wilfried Goepel, Detmold, has been wrongly attributed to Rubens).[3] But Vorsterman could have used a number of different models, including Enea Vico's 1550 engraving of the head of the emperor after Titian.[4] A similar head, although wearing a laurel wreath, appears in a woodcut by Christoffel Jegher of the mid-1630s,[5] which was almost certainly taken from a model provided by Rubens, and is in fact very close to the near-contemporary portraits of the emperor that he designed for the ceremonial entry of the Cardinal-Infante into Antwerp in 1635, which may all share a common source.

The changed head in Vorsterman's engraving has led scholars to invent several imaginary pictures. It has been suggested that either Titian or Rubens could have painted a second, lost version in which the likeness of the emperor was brought up to date,[6] but this overlooks the degree of freedom found in seventeenth-century reproductive printmaking, and treats Vorsterman's print as if it ought to be a photograph of Rubens's copy. There are substantial differences of detail between the two, including the curtain found in the engraving, the different shape of the helmet, and the narrower and taller proportion of the print. These could all be used to argue that Vorsterman worked from a different model, but, to my mind, they suggest that absolute fidelity was not at issue. The inscription gives credit where credit is due to both Titian and Rubens, but the engraving was saleable as an image of Charles V as much as it is the record of a particular work of art. The head was surely changed in the process of designing the print so as to make use of the most familiar, easily recognisable and distinctive likeness of the emperor in his maturity.

1. See Hymans 1893, p.24, and Burchard 1950, p.31, under no.27.
2. Vergara 1999, p.100.
3. First published by Müller Hofstede 1967, pp.47–58, repr. fig.8.
4. Bartsch xv, p.339, no.255.
5. Voorhelm Schneevoogt 1873, p.170, no.145.
6. Wethey 1969–75, II, p.191–2, under no.L–3; Burchard 1950, p.31–2, under no.27.

50 · Lucas Vorsterman after Rubens, after Titian

Isabella d'Este in Black

Engraving; 42 × 31.8 cm. State II. Inscribed 'ISABELLA ESTENSIS. FRANCISCI GONZAGAE MARCH. MANTOVAE VXOR'; at left *F. Titiani Prototypo. P.P. Rubens exc*, at right *Cum Privilegijs*.
The British Museum, London, inv.no.1875–7–10–1983

REFERENCES: Voorhelm Schneevoogt 1873, pp.180–1, no.230; Hymans 1893, pp.24, 171, no.172; Van den Wijngaert 1940, pp.103–4, no.738; Müller Hofstede 1967, p.91, note 127; Schuckman 1993, p.168, no.165, repr.

Titian painted two portraits of Isabella d'Este (1474–1539), wife of Francesco Gonzaga, 4th Marquis of Mantua, who, as Rubens knew, had made her court famous for its learning, poetry, music, and, not least, its art collections. The second of the portraits showed her in a black dress with blue sleeves and is now in Vienna, but the painted copy which Rubens made from it is lost. Rubens kept his version throughout his life because it was recorded in the inventory of his collection compiled in 1640,[1] but it is now only known from this engraving by Lucas Vorsterman.

Isabella commissioned her portrait from Titian in 1534 when she was sixty years old. She found sitting for artists tiresome, and she was not too concerned with exactitude in a likeness. Instead of having herself painted as she then looked, Isabella instructed Titian to use a portrait by Francesco Francia (*c*.1450–1517/18), now lost, which had been painted in 1511 when she was thirty-seven. In the circumstances, it is not too surprising that Titian's portrait of Isabella appears vapid and doll-like in expression, which is disappointing given her forceful personality.

Titian's portrait is also a picture of her costume. He showed Isabella wearing a magnificent black dress trimmed with ermine, worn over a white chemise and with a fur stole.

Her blue sleeves are embroidered in white and gold in a pattern of interlaced knots which had been designed as her personal device. She wears a headdress, known as a *zazara*, made of hair and fabrics, of a type which she herself is said to have invented, but which became fashionable in north Italy during this period. Titian delivered the portrait in 1536 and it appears to have satisfied the sitter.

Titian's portrait entered the Gonzaga collection in Mantua, where it was presumably known to Rubens during his period as court artist there. The work was not sold to Charles I in the late 1620s with the rest of the Mantuan pictures, but passed to the Southern Netherlands and entered the collection of the Archduke Leopold Wilhelm (1614–1662),[2] where it was wrongly identified as Caterina Cornaro, Queen of Cyprus,[3] no doubt because of the turban-like headdress. Rubens probably painted his copy while in Mantua, around 1605, although it could be argued that it was made in Antwerp during the 1630s if Titian's original was taken there immediately after the dispersal of the Mantuan pictures. On the other hand, an early date would fit with Vorsterman's most intensive period of work for Rubens between 1618 and 1620. His engraving [cat.no.49] after Rubens's copy of Titian's *Charles V with a Drawn Sword* is similar in technique and was surely made at the same time.

1. Muller 1989, p.107, no.57.
2. Recorded in Teniers 1660, no.75.
3. Berger 1883, p.cvii, no.367.

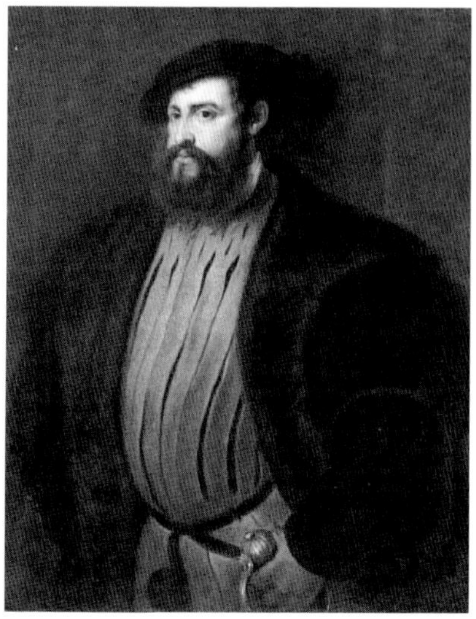

51

51 · Rubens after an Anonymous Italian Artist (perhaps Titian) *Portrait of an Unknown Man*

Oil on canvas; 97.5 × 76.5 cm
The Courtauld Institute Gallery, London
inv.no.P.1978.AS.354

REFERENCES: Seilern 1969, pp.11–14, no.299; Wethey 1969–75, II, p.159, under no.X-25; Jaffé 1989, p.171, no.123.

Little more can be said about this work than that it is probably by Rubens and a copy after an Italian sixteenth-century artist. A bust-length version of the portrait was recorded in a reversed engraving by George Vertue dated 1724 with an inscription identifying the sitter as Hernán Cortéz (1485–1547) and the artist as Titian. It was then owned by Sir Paul Methuen (1672–1757), and remained in his family's possession until the mid-nineteenth century when it was seen by Gustav Waagen who recorded it as a Titian, although he did not accept the attribution.[1] Not long after it was sold to the dealer William Buchanan.[2] Another version survives in Weimar, but has no early history before it appeared for sale in Vienna in 1820.

Vertue's identifications have recently been taken seriously,[3] but perhaps in ignorance of the vagaries of eighteenth-century British antiquarians, not to mention the imaginative identifications found on portraits in British country houses. It is true that Titian was sometimes asked to paint people of the very highest rank from portraits made by other artists, but which of his rich and important patrons would have gone to such lengths to obtain a likeness of Cortéz, and why are there no contemporary records of such a remarkable commission? Nor is there any real similarity to authentic likenesses of Cortéz. An alternative suggestion that the artist responsible might be Antonis Mor (1516/20–1576) is even less persuasive.[4]

A recent technical investigation of the painting has thrown new light on its making. The canvas does not follow the standard preparation of Antwerp suppliers. The ground is unusually thick and contains a large amount of coarse lead white. X-radiographs reveal that it was applied with a broad knife in fan-shaped movements. These distinctive arcs are also found in the preparation of some of Velázquez's canvases, such as the *Forge of Vulcan* painted in Italy in 1630 and the equestrian portrait of Philip IV, painted in Spain in 1634–5, both now in Madrid. Artists bought their canvases ready primed and there were variations between different locations, which may help establish where the Courtauld work was painted.

The painting has been dated between 1608 and 1612,[5] If so, Rubens painted it from a model available in Antwerp after his return from Italy, since he usually made full-size copies from originals. The smoothness of handling found on the face is comparable to Rubens's signed and dated *Cupid Sharpening his Bow* after Parmigianino of 1612 in Munich [fig.9] and some of his own portraits of this decade. An assessment of the Courtauld picture is not made easy because of serious abrasion to the surface, and areas such as the fur-trimmed robe and right arm can now be read only with difficulty.

1. Waagen 1838, III, p.104.
2. Information from James Methuen-Campbell on file at the Courtauld Institute Galleries.
3. Seilern 1969, pp.11–14, no.299.
4. Wethey 1969–75, II, p.159, under no.X-25.
5. Seilern 1969, pp.12, 14; Jaffé 1989, p.171, no.123.

52

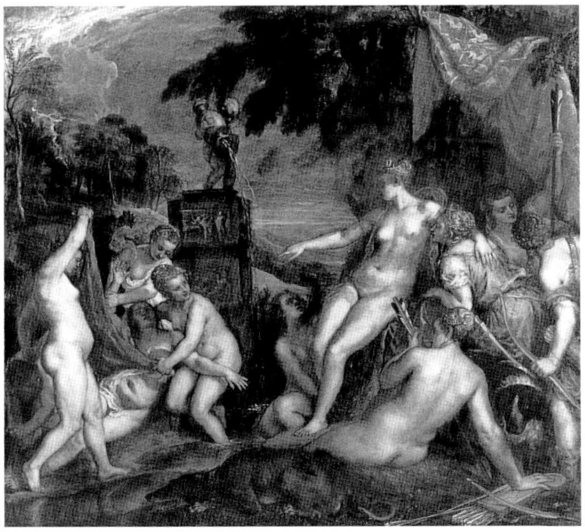

53

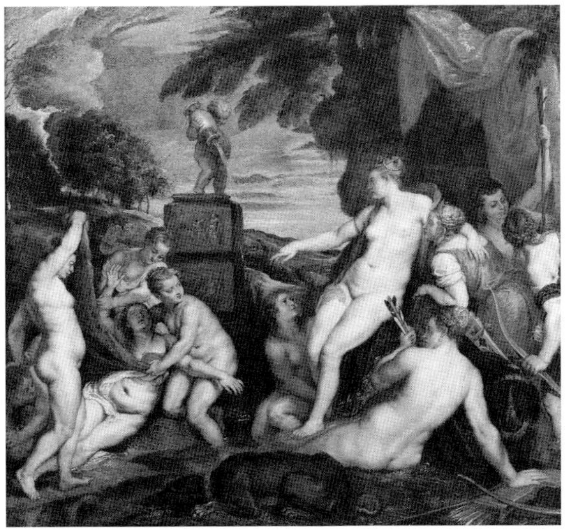

52 · Titian
Diana and Callisto

Oil on canvas; 187 × 204.5 cm
Duke of Sutherland loan, 1946,
National Gallery of Scotland, Edinburgh
Exhibited in Edinburgh only

REFERENCES: Crowe / Cavalcaselle 1877, II, pp.275–84; Panofsky 1969, pp.154–5, 158–60; Wethey 1969–75, III, pp.141–2, no.10; Brigstocke 1993, pp.183–6; Hope 1980, pp.128–34.

Titian's *Diana and Callisto* belongs to a group of his works known as the *poesie* (subjects drawn from legend or myth) which show the entanglements of mortals with the gods and provided an opportunity for the artist to paint the human figure, particularly the female nude, on a large scale. This canvas marks a shift in his use of colour from a relatively subdued if rich palette to a more dazzling range of hues that suggests he was responding to the work of younger artists in Venice, particularly Paolo Veronese. Despite Titian's appetite for the visual pleasures of the material world, this work shows that he did not flinch from depicting the pain that Diana inflicted on Callisto who had offended her. Together with its pendant of *Diana and Actaeon*, also in the Sutherland Collection, *Diana and Callisto* was painted for the man who emerged as Titian's foremost patron in the mid-sixteenth century, Philip II of Spain (1527–1598). These canvases are now among the most famous mythological paintings of the late Renaissance, but, in the context of this exhibition, it should be borne in mind that during the sixteenth and early seventeenth centuries they were little known outside the Madrid court.

This work depicts a story from Ovid's *Metamorphoses* (II: 401–531) and *Fasti* (II: 153–192) concerning Callisto, the daughter of Lycaon, King of Arcady. Diana's attendants were expected to be as chaste as their mistress, but Callisto was deceitfully seduced by Jupiter in the guise of Diana. Callisto's pregnancy was discovered some months later when forcibly undressed by her companions, and, as a result, she was banished by the goddess. Titian depicted the cruel moment when Callisto's companions pulled back her robes to reveal her swollen belly, and made her sprawl vulnerably on the ground before the unforgiving and imperious Diana, who is seated to the right.

This work dates from between 1556 and 22 September 1559 when Titian wrote to Philip II that it was about to be delivered, together with its pendant and an Entombment now in Madrid. The paintings were consigned to García Hernández, secretary to the king, at Genoa in October and despatched to Spain.[1] Cassiano dal Pozzo, an Italian visitor, saw them at the the Alcázar of Madrid in 1626 in the first of the king's private apartments (*quarto bajo*), known as the *bóvedas* because of their vaulted ceilings, on the ground floor of the north-east corner of the building.[2] It was here that Rubens saw the *Diana and Callisto* in 1628 and where he painted a full-size copy which is included in the present exhibition [cat.no.53].

1. See the documents in Crowe / Cavalcaselle 1877, II, pp.515–17.
2. Volk 1981, pp.519, 526.

53 · Rubens after Titian
Diana and Callisto

COLOUR ILLUSTRATION ON PAGE 23

Oil on canvas; 186 × 198 cm
The Right Hon. the Earl of Derby

REFERENCES: Knowsley 1801, p.17; Scharf 1875, pp.62–3, no.113; Wethey 1969–75, III, p.142, under no.10; Jaffé 1971, pp.43–6; Jaffé 1977, p.34; Held 1982, pp.306, 324, 339, note 27; Jaffé 1989, p.315, no.978; Muller 1989, p.103, no.43.

Rubens had not gained access to the paintings in the king's private apartments when he first visited Madrid in 1603,[1] but on his return as a diplomat in 1628–9 he was able to paint this full-size copy of Titian's *Diana and Callisto* [see cat.no.52]. A drawing by him now in the J. Paul Getty Museum, Los Angeles [fig.14],[2] contains six studies from Titian's *poesie*, two of them from the *Diana and Callisto*, which must also have been made during the later visit. The dating is confirmed by Francesco Pacheco who, in 1649, listed 'los dos banos' amongst Rubens's copies from 1628–9, and clearly referred to these pendants, both of which show women bathing.[3]

The copy is very faithful to Titian's original but could never be confused with it because Rubens used a cooler colour range and a bluish tone in flesh painting, not to mention a softer treatment of tonality. On the other hand, he carefully reproduced the most vivid areas of local colour in Titian's original: the red collar on the dog, the lilac boots of the woman at far right, and the almost orange quiver that spills arrows in the right foreground. In addition, the reliefs on the fountain – where Rubens might have introduced some changes – follow Titian very closely. In 1875 Sir George Scharf wrote that Rubens had added three small figures in the sky in addition to the lightning at upper left,[4] but they are no longer visible.

Rubens made some changes to Titian's design. At the lower left-hand corner, he pulled back the left foot of the standing woman so that she no longer seems to be about to kick the helpless Callisto. Rubens made a bending woman at the far left wipe Callisto's right foot with a red cloth, and he omitted her red boots. Not least, Rubens made Callisto's face more pathetic, her eyes swollen and red with tears trickling down her cheeks.

Rubens's own later treatment of this story, now in the Prado, Madrid, shows him depicting Callisto's plight with more sympathy than Titian, a change already introduced in the painted copy. Rubens did not depict Callisto humbled on the ground and naked, as had

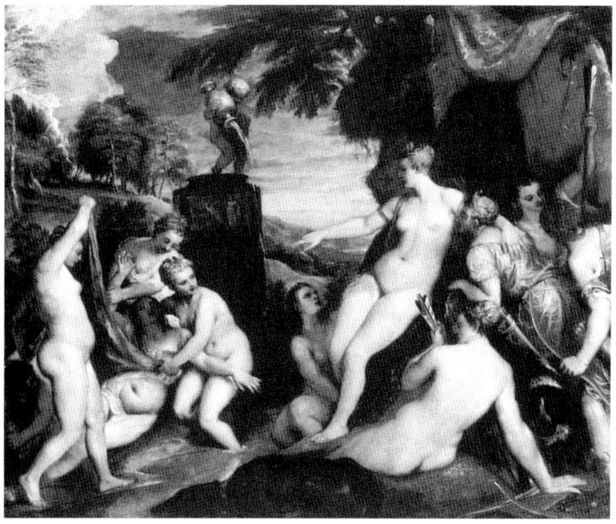

54

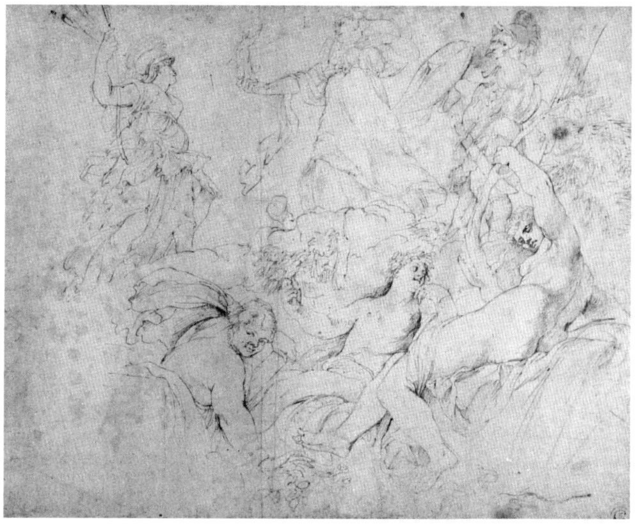

55

Titian, but standing fully dressed and supported by her companions, only her down-turned head suggesting her shame. Diana stands on the left and stretches out her arms in a gracious and affectionate manner, unlike Titian's haughty goddess. Rubens may have wanted to surpass Titian as a painter, but by this point in his career he had turned his back on the Venetian master's cruel interpretation of the myth.

1. Volk 1983, p.142
2. Inv.no.82.GB.140. See Held 1986, pp.137–8, no.175, repr. col. pl.5.
3. Pacheco 1649, bk.I, chap.VIII, p.100.
4. Scharf 1875, pp.62–3, no.113.

54 · Anonymous Spanish Artist after Titian

Diana and Callisto

Oil on canvas; 171.5 × 194.3 cm
Knole, the Sackville Collection (The National Trust), inv.no.166
Exhibited in Nottingham only

REFERENCES: Bridgman 1817, p.40; Brady 1839, p.125; Sackville West 1906, pp.41–2; Phillips [1930], II, p.415.

Recent restoration of this copy at Knole has revealed it as one of the most accurate and sensitive ever made after Titian's *Diana and Callisto* [cat.no.52], only surpassed by Rubens's version [cat.no.53]. It could have been painted in Titian's studio before the original was sent to Spain, but a Venetian contemporary would surely have imitated his technique more closely. The original was in Spain from 1559 to 1704 when Philip V presented it to the French ambassador, the duc de Gramont. The copy under discussion, together with its pendant of *Diana and Actaeon*, was at Knole soon after 1700 and so must have been painted in Spain. For most people, access to the king's private apartments in the Alcázar would not have been easy, so the copyist must have had friends at court.

The pigments used could be either sixteenth or seventeenth century in date.[1] The canvas is of medium weight, with fine threads, but not tightly woven, and the artist took care to find a width that would not need piecing. It was painted on a red ground and did not imitate the fine white gesso or chalk layer used by Titian, although there may be a double ground on some areas of flesh which appear to have a whitish *imprimatura* (priming). Both ultramarine and azurite are detectable, the former on the distant hills and the latter in the sky. Both pigments were available in Spain although azurite was the more widely employed and ultramarine the more expensive.

The Knole copy could have been painted by Eugenio Cajés (1575–1634), whose father, Patricio (*c.*1540–1612), had been born in Arezzo and may have taught his son to paint in an Italian manner. Juan Bautista Martinez del Mazo (*c.*1613–1667) is another possibility, an artist well-known for his copies. A third artist, Juan de Alfaro y Gámez (1643–1680), was known to have been particularly skilled in reproducing works by Titian and Rubens to which he gained access as a pupil of Velázquez.

It is curious that copies said to be by Rubens after Titian's *Diana and Callisto* and *Diana and Actaeon* were recorded in the dispersal of Charles I's collection in 1650.[2] These are unlikely to have been the versions that Philip IV bought from Rubens's collection after his death [cat.no.53], but they might be the ones now at Knole, wrongly attributed. Marie de Rohan, duchesse de Chevreuse, brought paintings with her from Spain in 1638, and casts of antique busts from Aranjuez as well as several court portraits from Velázquez's workshop were sent to England in 1640. The Titian copies could have been an undocumented part of one of these consignments. At any rate, the pictures almost certainly arrived at Knole by inheritance from Lionel Cranfield, 3rd Earl of Middlesex (who had access to the royal collections) as part of six waggon loads of goods sent from his family seat, Copt Hall, in 1701.[3]

1. I am very grateful to Zahira Veliz for discussing this work with me.
2. Millar 1970–2, pp.187, 201.
3. See Phillips [1930], I, pp.480; II, p.402.

55 · Rubens or Anthony van Dyck after Titian

The Allegory of the City of Brescia

Pen and ink, heightened with white chalk by a later hand; 31.6 × 38.4 cm
The British Museum, London, inv.no.1897–4–10–12

REFERENCES: Hind 1923, p.14, no.25; Tietze-Conrat 1954, pp.209–10; Vey 1962, I, pp.224–5, no.155; Logan 1977, p.412; J. Müller Hofstede in Cologne 1977, I, p.282, no.71; Rowlands 1977, p.31, no.17; Held 1982, p.302; Held 1986, p.78, no.30; Logan 1987, pp.66, 68.

This drawing records one of the three octagonal canvases painted by Titian and his workshop in 1565–8 for the ceiling of the Great Hall of the Palazzo Comunale in Brescia, but it cannot have been made from the original which was destroyed as early as 1575.

Titian followed detailed instructions provided by his patrons, now known from a summary.[1] The upper section was to include a personification of Brescia with her right breast uncovered, holding a golden statue of Faith. She turned away from Mars and towards Minerva, described as a peace-maker, holding an olive branch. The lion's skin of Hercules was to be held by Brescia, and, although recently said to have been omitted,[2] is visible in the drawing draped over the edge of the cloud on which she stands. Mars's woodpecker is at his feet.[3]

The written programme required the presence of three daughters of the river with garlands of reeds and watery plants. In 1648 Ridolfi observed that Titian's Brescia was surrounded by the lakes and rivers of her region.[4] The programme specified they were to have an urns of iron, lead, and crystal respectively. These identified the nymphs with local rivers and the mineral deposits of the region.

The majority of scholars have attributed the drawing to Rubens and dated it between 1600 and 1608, but others have given it to Van Dyck as a work from his Italian period between 1622 and 1627.[5] The choice of pen and ink is unusual for Rubens who generally preferred red or black chalk when copying paintings. Van Dyck had no reservations about transcribing the soft and painterly effects of Venetian art into the harder medium of pen and ink. The elongation of bodies and exaggeration of faces is more like his work, but the drawing lacks his use of strong accents in wash, as seen throughout his Italian sketchbook, now in the British Museum, London, although a good comparison can be made with folio 116 verso, a copy after a lost Titian, the so-called *Lavinia with a Dish of Melons*, which has the same wiry character.

The opposition of the peacemaking Minerva and the warmongering Mars is a familiar one, but Rubens gave it new life, particularly in his political allegories of the 1630s. He may earlier have recalled Titian's allegory when designing the *Disembarkation at Marseilles* for the Medici Cycle, now in the Louvre, in 1622. Both works are arranged on two levels with nymphs in the foreground and an abrupt shift of focus to the figures above, where a young woman, in one case, receives the salutation of Minerva, and, in the other, that of another helmeted woman, who is a personification of France. Venetian art provided many models for this kind of composition, but, to my mind, the pivotal position of Brescia and Marie de'Medici in each work suggests a close visual link.

1. See Zamboni 1778, pp.139–41.
2. Wethey 1969–75, III, p.88.
3. Also wrongly said to have been omitted by Titian according to Wethey 1969–75, III, p.88, note 424.
4. Ridolfi 1914–24, I, p.177.
5. See Vey 1962, I, pp.224–5, no.155; Logan 1977, p.412; Logan 1987, pp.66, 68.

DOMENICO CAMPAGNOLA

56 · Domenico Campagnola (*c*.1500–1564), retouched by Rubens *The Assumption of the Virgin*

COLOUR ILLUSTRATION ON PAGE 15

Pen and brown ink, retouched with greyish wash and greyish-yellow bodycolour, and some dark brown ink; 30.9 × 19.6 cm
The British Museum, London, inv.no.1895-9-15-828

REFERENCES: Tietze/Tietze-Conrat 1944, p.128, no.486; Rowlands 1977, p.58, no.54a; Logan 1977, p.411.

In the mid-nineteenth century this drawing was given to Titian, but it is said to have had an early attribution to Domenico written on the verso.[1] Few drawings can be securely identified as his work, and recent accounts remain controversial since they are based on very different conceptions of the graphic output of his contemporaries in Venice.[2] Rubens was certainly interested in Domenico's drawings, and made very literal use of several prints after his landscapes during the 1630s [see cat.no.74]. His retouching on this sheet was first identified in 1869,[3] and is more substantial than may appear at a glance.

Domenico drew the *Assumption of the Virgin* in a reddish-brown ink. Rubens added confident lines in greyish wash, blocked out some areas, notably on the infants at upper left, using dense patches of greyish-yellow bodycolour, and, lastly, applied some very fine lines in dark brown wash to sharpen detail.

Rubens must have found it iconographically strange that Domenico placed clouds of child angels flying above the Virgin's head, rather than carrying her aloft, but this did not stop him creating seven more child angels. One pair were added immediately to the left of the Virgin, three more directly above, a further two were made to fly in with outstretched arms on the right. One of the infants seated on the

56

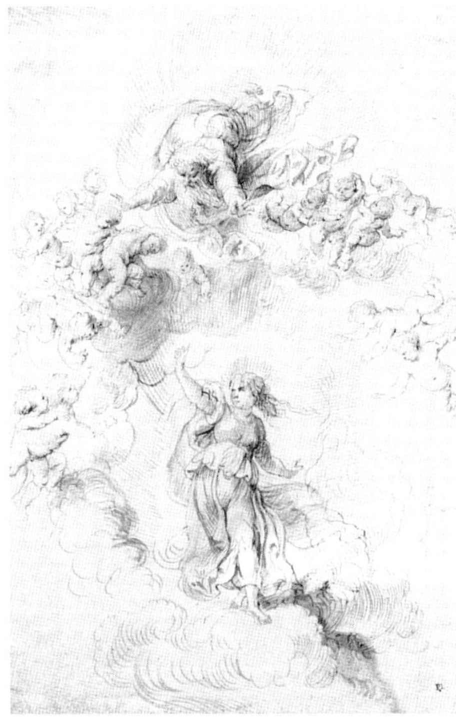

clouds was blocked out in bodycolour and may also be entirely Rubens's insertion.

Rubens also virtually created the billowing robes that made the Virgin and God the Father look much more grand. A swathe of draperies was added around the Virgin's right arm and to her left, but Rubens seems to have liked the twist in her pose and the way her right arm is flung upwards, which he did not change. God's cloak was made to float out on the left, and the end of his robe extended to fly out behind him as he hurtles downwards towards the Virgin.

Titian had placed God the Father directly above the Virgin in his *Assunta* in Santa Maria Gloriosa dei Frari, Venice, but Rubens may not have thought this suitable. When, in 1624, he decided to issue an engraving of his own altarpiece of this subject in the Kapellekerk, Brussels, now in Düsseldorf, of 1616–18, he added Christ (not God) at the top, who is seen opening his arms as if to embrace the Virgin,[4] with a pose not unlike that of Domenico's figure of God.

Rubens's intervention has some of the clarity and discretion of his retouchings from the late 1610s, but also the assurance of those dateable to the 1620s. Although no firm link can be made with any of Rubens's altarpieces depicting the same subject from this period, he was clearly interested in how it had been interpreted by Venetian artists. It follows that retouching may well date from the early to mid-1620s.

1. Robinson 1869, p.144, under no.383.
2. Compare W.R. Rearick in Florence 1976, pp.89–122, nos.50–82 and K. Oberhuber in Paris 1993, pp.431–50.
3. Robinson 1869, p.144.
4. See Logan 1999, p.233.

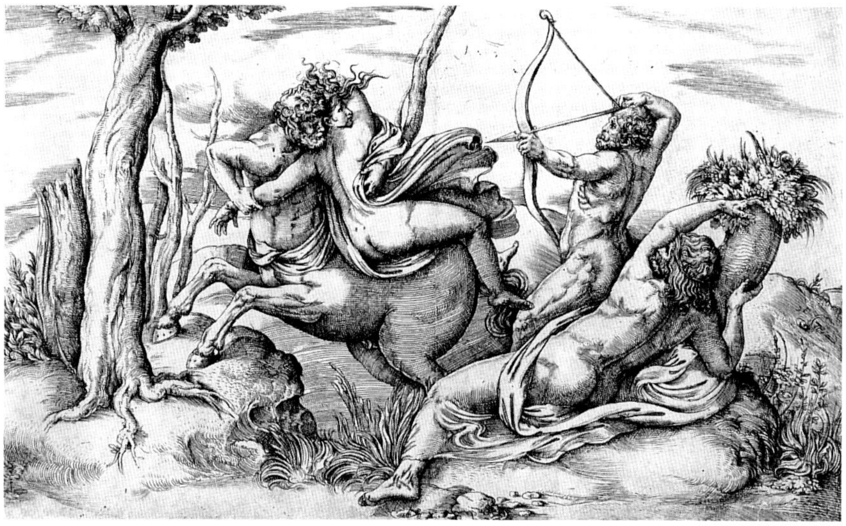

57

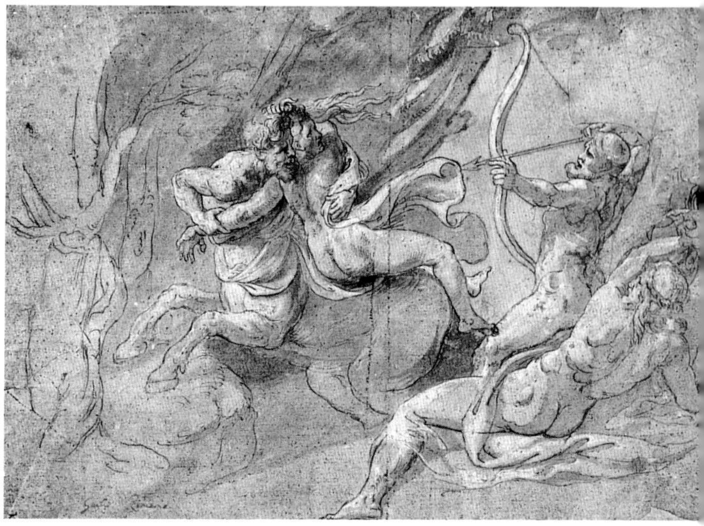

58

BATTISTA FRANCO

57 · Giovanni Battista Franco (*c*.1510–1561)

Hercules Slaying Nessus when he Attempts to Abduct Deianeira

Etching; 24.7 × 38.8 cm. Inscribed *Batista franco fece del antico*[.] *Franco forma*.
The British Museum, London, inv.no.1925-7-28-7

REFERENCES: Bartsch XVI, p.132, no.40; G.V. Dillon in Venice 1981, p.316, no.148.

This etching is inscribed as a work by Franco based on the antique, but no visual source has been identified. The story deals with the attempted abduction of Deianeira (daughter of the river god Oeneus) by the centaur Nessus while crossing the river Evenus, and Hercules's swift destruction of his rival (Ovid, *Metamorphoses* 9: 101–33; Philostratus, *Imagines* 16). Franco's composition contains all the main ingredients of the story, and Hercules is shown measuring the distance to his target, exactly as described by Philostratus, although Franco departed from tradition by not showing Nessus at the moment when the arrow struck. The etching is exhibited here for comparison with cat.no.58.

Franco made a number of prints after Giulio Romano's work during the 1540s, but, although the latter depicted this subject several times, none of his versions was the model for this etching, although Franco may well have been emulating his example as a designer of mythologies. One version by Giulio (which Franco certainly knew) was painted around 1527–8 as a fictive relief in the Sala dei Cavalli at Palazzo Te, Mantua, and is also known from a preparatory drawing in Stockholm.[1] In this case Giulio made his design look as static and as much like an antique relief as possible, which may explain the thinking behind Franco's inscription.

Franco's Deianeira can be compared, in reverse, to Giulio's stucco relief of Europa in the Sala del Aquile, also at Palazzo Te (also known from a preparatory drawing now in a private collection).[2] Both Deianeira and Europa ride side-saddle with their backs to the spectator, a pose ultimately derived from the famous Roman relief known as the *Letto di Policleto*,[3] but Franco's use of it is not specific enough to explain why his etching was inscribed 'fece del antico'.

1. Inv.no.348. See Hartt 1958, I, p.296, no.147, repr. fig.221; and K. Oberhuber in Mantua 1989, p.342, repr.
2. See Hartt 1958, I, p.297, no.164, repr. fig.224, as in the Ellesmere collection; C. Begley in New York 1999, pp.84–5, no.20, repr.
3. See Bober/Rubinstein 1986, p.127, no.94, repr.

58 · Giovanni Battista Franco, retouched by Rubens

Hercules Slaying Nessus when he Attempts to Abduct Deianeira

Pen and ink with wash over traces of red chalk, retouched with brown wash and white bodycolour; 24.8 × 35.4 cm
Devonshire Collection, Chatsworth, inv.no.87.

REFERENCES: Dimier 1900, p.480, under no.18; Jaffé 1964, pp.390, 395, note 26; Jaffé 1994b, p.86, no.795.

This drawing is closely related to an etching [cat.no.57] with an inscription that identifies Battista Franco's authorship. The drawing is similar to the etching but has enough small differences of detail to suggest that it was made in preparation for it, even though not in reverse. For example, Deianeira's flowing hair is different in each work, and there are variations in the shape of the tree on the left. The fine use of pen in the underdrawing is characteristic of Franco's delicate draughtsmanship.

Franco strengthened his pen and ink drawing with some pale brown wash and delicate white heightening but all the darker touches of brown which throw the main figures into relief were added at a later stage and are by a different hand. The tree trunks in the background, between the main figures, were largely drawn with the brush at this stage. Some touches of yellowish bodycolour were applied on the bodies of Deianeira and the river god, but these are difficult to read because the colour of the paper is now a similar tint. The retouching is most obvious on the entwined figures of Nessus and Deianeira; a few strokes of brown wash intensified the looks of alarm on their faces, which became far more expressive than in Franco's etching.

The retouching was limited, but effective, and the attribution to Rubens is at least plausible. As regards dating, it has been claimed that the sheet 'excited the attention of Rubens' in Italy,[1] but, although the restraint of this intervention points to a relatively early date the use of wash and bodycolour is closer to drawings he reworked around 1615, as well as being comparable to the earliest of his retouched *modelli* for engravings.

1. Jaffé 1994b, p.86, under no.795.

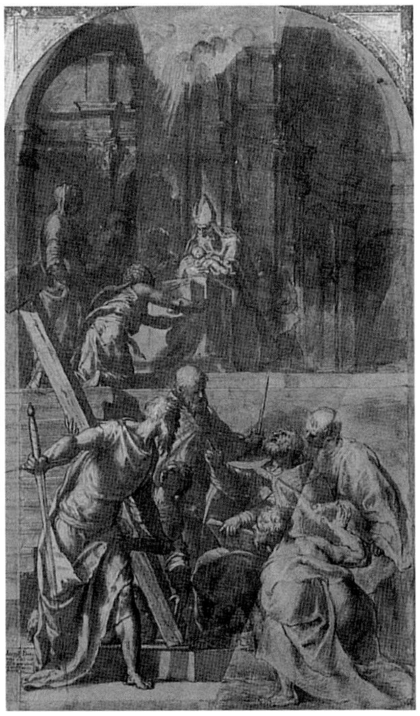

59

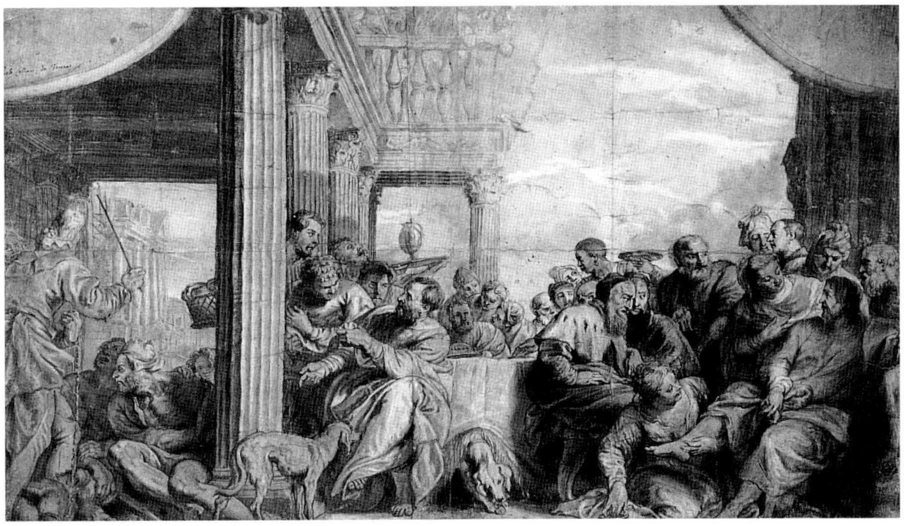

60

GIUSEPPE PORTA

59 · Giuseppe Porta, Il Salviati (*c.*1520–after 1573), retouched by Rubens

The Presentation of Christ in the Temple with Saints Paul, Helena, Nicholas of Bari, Gregory the Great, and Two Others

Pen and ink with wash over black chalk, traces of squaring in red chalk and heightening in white, retouched in black chalk, with brown, greenish-grey and cream bodycolour; 54.7 × 31.3 cm. The lower right-hand portion cut off and replaced.
Collection Frits Lugt, Institut Néerlandais, Paris inv.no.7617
Exhibited in Edinburgh only

REFERENCES: Jaffé 1955, pp.331–40; C. van Hasselt in London/Paris/Bern/Brussels 1972, pp.95–7, no.74; Jaffé 1977, pp.38–9; Logan 1978, p.430; Logan/Haverkamp-Begemann 1978, p.95; McTavish 1981, pp.149–54, 341–4, no.20; Byam Shaw 1983, I, pp.248–51, no.244.

This drawing is a preliminary study by Giuseppe Porta for his *Purification of the Virgin*, known as the *Pala Valier*, in Santa Maria Gloriosa dei Frari, Venice, painted around 1548. Fra Germano da Casale, the prior, ceded the altar previously dedicated to Saint Bernardino of Siena to a patrician, Niccolò Valier, in 1517. Casale specified that it be rededicated to the purification of the Virgin, but allowed Valier to include his family's name saints in the new altarpiece,[1] although Saint Bernardino had to be among them. Those who appear in the foreground of the drawing are Paul holding his sword of execution, Helena gazing at the True Cross, Saint Nicholas of Bari, and Gregory the Great with papal tiara (although he lacks this in the altarpiece).[2] The remaining two saints are problematic because the corner of the drawing was removed. In the altarpiece they are Saint Mark and Saint Bernardino, but the figures added by Rubens do not have attributes, although one is dressed as a deacon.

Ridolfi described Porta's altarpiece as depicting the purification of the Virgin,[3] reflecting the dedication of the altar. The event took place at the same time as the presentation of Christ in the temple. The way the high priest lifts him up and the reverence of his parents reveals they are witnessing the prophecy of Simeon.

The condition of this sheet before repair by Rubens is known from a copy now in the Graphische Sammlung, Munich.[4] He added a new section of paper at the lower right and drew on it in black chalk, brown wash, and greenish grey and white bodycolour to give the figures the same solidity as the remainder of the sheet. Rubens respected Porta's original and kept his intervention to a minimum on the rest of the drawing. Some wash was added to the burst of heavenly light, and an empty space to the right was completed so as not to leave a gap in the composition.

Rubens's intervention has been dated to his second visit to Rome around 1605–8,[5] but the added piece of paper has nothing in common with securely attributed drawings from this period. The figures are malleable, limbs and draperies appear soft, and forms are built up with brushstrokes in wash and bodycolour, all of which points to a date in the 1630s.

1. See Goffen 1986, p.241, note 17.
2. Ridolfi, I, 1914–24, p.242, identified this saint in the altarpiece as Augustine.
3. Idem. See also McTavish 1981, pp.144, 342.
4. Inv.no.21048.
5. Jaffé 1955, p.340, note 5; C. van Hasselt in London/Paris/Bern/Brussels 1972, p.97, under no.74.

PAOLO VERONESE

60 · Anonymous Draughtsman after Paolo Veronese (1528–1588), retouched by Rubens

Christ in the House of Simon

COLOUR ILLUSTRATION ON PAGE 3[illegible]

Black chalk with brown wash and white heightening on three vertical strips of paper, retouched with dark brown wash and bodycolour; 52.8 × 91.5 cm. Inscribed *Paolo Calliari da Verona* by Rubens.
The British Museum, London, inv.no.1895-9-15-1053

REFERENCES: Rooses 1886–92, V, p.197, no.1375; Hind 1923, p.20, no.45; Rowlands 1977, p.58, no.54; Vlieghe 1994, p.219; Wood 1994, p.340; B.W. Meijer in Meij 2001, pp.36–7.

This drawing is a large and complete copy of Veronese's *Feast in the House of Simon*, now in Turin, originally commissioned in 1556 by the monks of SS. Nazaro e Celsio in Verona, but not painted until 1559–60. Christ attended a feast in the house of Simon the Pharisee (Matthew 26: 6–13; Mark 14: 3–9; Luke 7: 36–50) where a repentant prostitute (Mary Magdalene) anointed his feet with precious ointment and bathed them with her tears. On the right, the guests attend to her action and Christ's words, but on the left they debate her profligacy and fail to see the point of what is happening. Veronese included a beggar who is being expelled by a servant wearing a red Friulian cap and holding a capuchin monkey on a chain (but retouched by Rubens to look more like a little devil with a hooked nose), perhaps as a reference to the parable of the rich man, Dives, and the beggar, Lazarus (Luke 16: 19–31).

Ridolfi described the work as framed by painted architecture with columns on either side supporting a pediment and swags suspended from animals' skulls.[1] The underlying black chalk copy was made from the original since shaped quadrants at the upper left and right are indicated. These were filled in after the picture reached Turin, but have been uncovered in a recent restoration.

The sheet is constructed from three vertical strips of paper, no doubt because of its size. The head of Christ was cut out and a section stuck on from behind so that it could be redrawn. Rubens's intention was to strengthen a pedestrian copy, as can be seen from the weak draughtsmanship of the balcony, which was left untouched. All the figures in the foreground were redrawn with dark brown wash and heightened with white bodycolour. On some areas this has faint pigmentation, although the overall impression is monochromatic.

The picture was still in Verona at the time of Rubens's visit to Italy, but Ridolfi recorded that in 1628 he had made a full-size copy which was sent to Flanders,[2] so the drawing could have been made there. The retouching has recently been attributed to Erasmus Quellinus II,[3] who may well have owned it at one time,[4] but, in my opinion, the bold and assured reworking is entirely different from his technique, and it should remain attributed to Rubens, as is confirmed by his autograph inscription.

This work has something of the scale and ambition of an oil sketch rather than a drawing. The broad and confident retouching points to a late date, perhaps around the time that Rubens was working on the *Feast of Herod*, now in Edinburgh, dateable to the mid-1630s, and this is supported by the *modello* for Schelte à Bolswert's engraving after that work,[5] which was extensively retouched by Rubens with a similarly broad and encrusted use of wash, bodycolour and white heightening.

1. Ridolfi 1914–24, I, p.307.
2. Ridolfi 1914–24, I, p.308; II, p.298.
3. Vlieghe 1994, p.219.
4. Denucé 1932, p.288.
5. Sold London, Phillips, 7 July 1999, lot 116.

BARTOLOMEO PASSAROTTI

61 · Attributed to Bartolomeo Passarotti (1529–1592), retouched by Rubens *Two Robed Men*

61

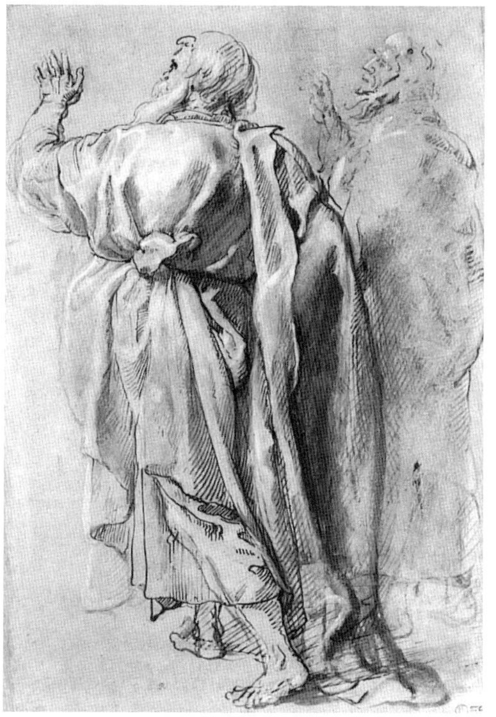

Pen and ink, retouched with brown wash, heightened with grey wash and white bodycolour; 36.2 × 24.4 cm
Lent by the Syndics of the Fitzwilliam Museum, Cambridge, inv.no.3129

REFERENCES: Unpublished

This sheet has an underdrawing with heavy lines and evenly-spaced hatchings in pen and ink, which remains visible in places despite being partly erased. The graphic style has analogies with the work of Passarotti and his school. A comparable figure of a robed man, seen from the back and with his head in profile, appears on a drawing with studies for an *Adoration of the Kings* at Christ Church, Oxford.[1] Even closer is a drawing of *A Standing Robed Man* in the Hessisches Landesmuseum, Darmstadt,[2] made by Passarotti in preparation for his *Presentation of the Virgin in the Temple*, now in the Pinacoteca Nazionale, Bologna.

The reworking of the Fitzwilliam sheet began by erasing the figure to the right, which remains as a ghost image. The retouching added bulk to the main figure who was previously comparatively slender. Outlines were redrawn in brown wash with a brush, and these changes are easy to detect on the man's head (originally clean-shaven but given a thick beard), on his left hand (where the underdrawing is still legible), on his right shoulder, and on his right foot which was much enlarged. Broad grey washes were used to give this figure more three-dimensionality. Lastly, white bodycolour was applied to make the robes shimmer and to appear almost silken, so that the drawing gained a remarkable sense of light and texture.

The fluency and assurance of the retouching is characteristic of Rubens. The drawing is unusual among his reworked sheets because it depicts an isolated figure with an emphasis on draperies (rather than the multi-figured narratives which he generally liked to collect and rework), and this suggests he may have intended using it in one of his own works, perhaps an assumption of the Virgin, although no specific link can be found.

Several sheets after Michelangelo that Rubens owned and retouched are here also attributed to Passarotti or an imitator [see cat.nos.15, 16], and these may have been obtained as a group by Rubens whilst in Italy. Their retouching, however, dates from significantly later in his career, and the same applies in this case. Rubens's bold and vigourous use of the brush on the Fitzwilliam drawing points to a date in the 1630s, and is quite different from the restrained interventions that he made in the 1610s.

1. Inv.no.1393. See Byam Shaw 1976, I, p.238, no.894, repr. pl.543.
2. See Höper 1987, II, p.120, no.Z45.

Italian Artists Working in France

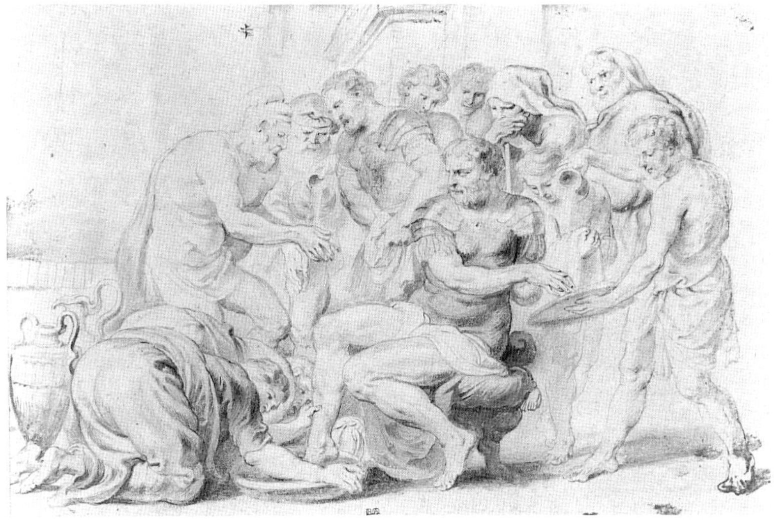

62

FRANCESCO PRIMATICCIO

62 · Rubens after Francesco Primaticcio (1504–1570)

Ulysses, Telemachus, and Two Herdsmen Washing Themselves after Killing the Suitors and Disloyal Serving Women

Brush and coloured wash, heightened with bodycolour; 28.5 × 42.4 cm
National Gallery of Scotland, Edinburgh, inv.no.D 1677

REFERENCES: Burchard/d'Hulst 1956, p.95, no.112; Burchard/d'Hulst 1963, text vol., p.252, under no.163; Rowlands 1977, p.45, no.39; Andrews 1985, I, p.88; Béguin/Guillaume/Roy 1985, pp.294–5; Wood 1990, pp.31–5.

This drawing is based on a fresco, now destroyed, painted by Primaticcio in the Galerie d'Ulysse at Fontainebleau between 1555 and 1560. An etching of this work by Theodoor van Thulden (1606–1669) of 1633 identified the subject as Ulysses cleansing himself after killing the disloyal serving women,[1] but this does not agree exactly with Homer's *Odyssey*, since it was Telemachus, the swineherd Eumaeus, and another herdsman (Mesaulius, the latter's slave), who washed themselves after hanging the women. Ulysses did not cleanse himself until later in the narrative, and this scene was also depicted in the Galerie. Rubens combined these two episodes in a way that Primaticcio did not.

Rubens removed the scene in the background of Primaticcio's composition showing the bodies of the serving women dangling from a rope and the corpse of the goat herd, Melanthius, being sniffed by a dog. It has been said that he did this so as to transform the scene into another episode where the old serving woman, Eurycleia, recognised Ulysses when she bathed his feet and saw the scar he received when hunting boar with the sons of Autolycus.[2] But this identification does not take into account the figure of a man in armour (clearly Telemachus) and the two others wearing phrygian caps (the two herdsmen), who can only be explained as belonging to the later episode.

Rubens gave each figure more space, volume and anatomical articulation. For example, a disembodied hand holding a jug in Primaticcio's composition was 'corrected' by Rubens. Rubens added Telemachus's right arm, so that he could be seen wiping his hands on a cloth,[3] making it obvious that this episode involves several people cleansing themselves, not Ulysses alone having his feet washed by Eurycleia.

This work has been attributed to Van Thulden,[4] but it is not like any of his securely identified drawings, and, in my opinion, is entirely from Rubens's hand. The use of coloured wash links it to his other adaptations after Primaticcio, but the pigment is applied more thinly and transparently (it is also smaller in size), so it may never have been part of that series, although clearly linked by medium, style and date.

Rubens could have studied Primaticcio's fresco during one of his visits to Paris in the 1620s, but variations of detail in this and his other coloured copies [for example, cat.no.63] establish that he worked from a series of chalk copies, now in the Albertina, Vienna, attributed to Abraham van Diepenbeeck (1596–1675). These were made in the early to mid-1630s, and since one of these provides a specific model for the Edinburgh drawing,[5] a dating of *c.*1635 is proposed here.

1. Van Thulden 1633, pl.no.43.
2. Andrews 1985, I, p.88.
3. Wood 1990, p.32.
4. Andrews 1985, I, p.88; Rubens's authorship of the entire group of coloured copies has been doubted by Logan, 1987, p.75.
5. Inv.no.8978. See Béguin/Guillaume/Roy 1985, p.294 (as Van Thulden). A counterproof is in the same collection (Inv.no.8979).

63 · Rubens after Francesco Primaticcio

King Minos Judging the Dead at the Entrance to the Underworld

Brush and coloured washes, heightened with bodycolour and oil; 40.7 × 53.4 cm
Département des Arts graphiques, Musée du Louvre, Paris, inv.no.20262
Exhibited in Edinburgh only

REFERENCES: Rooses 1886–92, V, p.203, no.1387; Lugt 1949, II, p.26, no.1068; Logan 1978, pp.434–5; Sérullaz 1978, p.94, no.95; Béguin/Guillaume/Roy 1985, pp.250–1; Logan 1987, p.75.

This drawing records one of the destroyed frescoes in the Galerie d'Ulysse at Fontainebleau. Earlier descriptions identified Pluto and Mercury in the composition,[1] but none of the figures has Mercury's attributes, and the judge seated with Cerberus at his right hand is King Minos as specified in the *Odyssey*. At this point (Book XI), Ulysses had summoned Teiresias from the dead in order to discover if he would ever return to Ithaca. He had also interrogated his former companion Elpenor and thirteen wives or daughters of princes, among them Ariadne, Minos's daughter, who was shown by Primaticcio seated directly below her father holding a spindle. The remainder of the dead were taken by Primaticcio from Homer's description of a crowd of recent brides, unmarried young men, old men worn out by toil, and numerous warriors with their armour stained with blood.

On the left of the fresco, Primaticcio included Ulysses addressing Hercules with his bow in his hand and a decorated baldric on his chest. The corresponding section of the drawing has been abraded and disguised with a vigorous brown wash. Traces of Hercules's knee and leg appear to the left of Ariadne. If the sheet was always its present size, Hercules would have been squeezed very tightly against

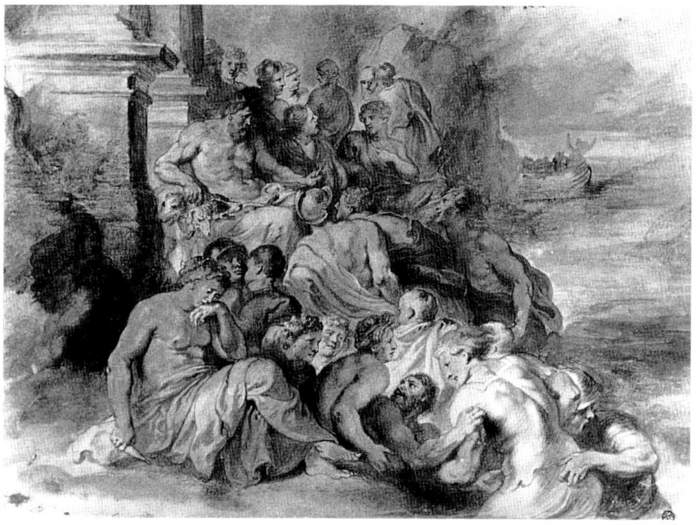

63

the edge so it was probably trimmed. The changes visible are not enough to suggest that Rubens was retouching somebody else's work and are alterations made as work progressed.

As with the other copies in this group a dating to the 1630s has been widely accepted.[2] It is likely that Rubens made use of a detailed black chalk copy in the Albertina,[3] which can be attributed to Abraham van Diepenbeeck. The Louvre drawing was executed with broadly applied coloured wash and fine outlines that were added using the tip of the brush. The figures are drawn in a reddish-pink while the draperies have distinct areas of astringent local colour. Although widely accepted as by Rubens ever since the late-seventeenth century, doubts have been expressed about the unusual use of colour, the flattening of some forms and the indistinctness of detail towards the edges of the composition.[4] But Rubens generally worked from the core of a composition towards its periphery, and the pictorialism of this sheet has parallels with his oil sketches. As with other drawings in this group, it has an unusually thick support made of several sheets of paper laminated together.

To my mind Primaticcio's Ariadne was used by Rubens in his oil sketch of the *Victims of War* in the Liechtenstein collection. Although reversed and with one arm changed, the crossed feet and pensive support of the head make the derivation clear. The oil sketch has been dated *c.*1628 and the adaptation reflected Rubens's recent visits to Fontainebleau.

1. For example, see Dimier 1900, p.477; Lugt 1948, II, p.26, no.1068, amongst others.
2. First proposed by Burchard / d'Hulst 1956, pp.94–5, under no.111.
3. Inv.no.8947.
4. Logan 1978, pp.434–5.

NICOLÒ DELL'ABATE

64 · Nicolò dell'Abate (*c.*1509 / 12–?1571) *The Rape of Helen*

Pen and ink with brown wash, heightened with white bodycolour on brown prepared paper; 47.7 × 41.4 cm
Devonshire Collection, Chatsworth, inv.no.131
Exhibited in Edinburgh only

REFERENCES: Béguin 1962, pp.129–30; McAllister Johnson 1965, pp.295–9; Béguin 1969, pp.111–13, no.53; Jaffé 1994a, p.42, no.437.

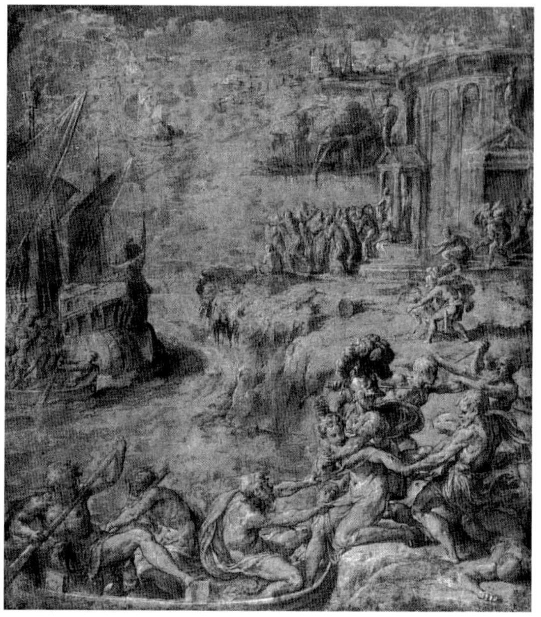

64

The lower part of this drawing, dateable to the early 1550s, is closely related to a sheet that was retouched by Rubens [cat.no.66], and both works are exhibited here for comparison.

The subject concerns Helen, the wife of Meneleus, King of Sparta, who was seized by Paris, the son of Priam, who had fallen in love with her. The composition shows the moment when Paris, wearing a plumed helmet, has forced Helen into a small boat to take her to one of the Trojan vessels. The Greeks have put up a fierce fight on the shore, but the Trojans have gained their prize. The scene of abduction at the temple (at the upper right) and embarkation (at the upper left) can be read as successive events in the story. This composition by Nicolò became more widely accessible when reproduced as a woodcut in a French edition of Dares of Phrygia's *De excidio Trojae*, published in 1572.

Nicolò's drawing at Chatsworth was based on a composition known from two early sixteenth-century engravings of the same subject, one of which is attributed to Marcantonio Raimondi (*c.*1480–1534),[1] and the other to Marco Dente da Ravenna.[2] Marcantonio's print is inscribed as invented by Raphael, but the cluttered composition suggests Giulio Romano's authorship. Nicolò did not copy the model exactly, although the general disposition of figures and their specific actions are similar, with Helen as the object of a tug of war, her body half clinging to the shore and half forced into the boat.

The composition recorded in the Chatsworth drawing has been linked to a lost fresco of the *Rape of Helen* painted in the Chambre du Roi (Chambre de Saint-Louis) on the first floor of the old Donjon at Fontainebleau. The room was decorated in two campaigns, the first carried out by Primaticcio with the assistance of Nicolò Bellin da Modena in 1533–4.[3] The second phase is dateable around 1570, when Nicolò dell'Abate painted eight new frescoes in the room with subjects from the *Iliad*, based on designs by Primaticcio, one of which showed the rape of Helen. These frescoes deteriorated so badly that they were detached from the walls in 1757. However, Nicolò's Chatsworth drawing may have had nothing to do with the fresco, which, it has been suggested, could be known from an entirely different multi-figured drawing by Primaticcio in the Louvre,[4] and an early painted copy in the Bowes Museum, Barnard Castle. The extensive landscape in Nicolò's drawing at Chatsworth certainly makes it look more like a gallery picture than a monumental fresco.

1. Bartsch XIV, pp.170–1, no.209.
2. Bartsch XIV, p.171, no.210.
3. See Béguin 1975, p.202.
4. Inv.no.5870. See S. Béguin in Paris 1972–3, p.135, under no.142.

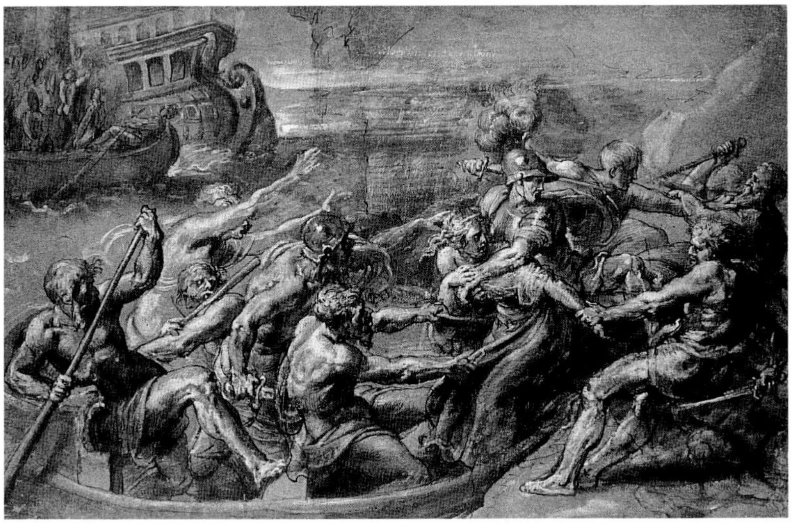

65

65 · Nicolò dell'Abate, retouched by Rubens *The Rape of Helen*

Pen and ink with wash on blue paper, retouched with greenish-brown and dark brown wash with cream bodycolour; 27.5 × 41 cm
Département des Arts graphiques, Musée du Louvre, Paris, inv.no.20268
Exhibited in Edinburgh only

REFERENCES: Rooses 1886–92, V, pp.202–3; Lugt 1949, II, p.28, no.1078; Burchard/d'Hulst 1956, pp.95–6, no.113; J. Foucart in Paris 1972–3, p.195, no.218; Jaffé 1977, p.45; Logan 1978, p.435; Sérullaz 1978, p.95, no.96.

This drawing in the Louvre is closely related to one by Nicolò dell' Abate at Chatsworth [cat.no.64], exhibited here for comparison. The Louvre sheet has a scratchy underdrawing in pen and ink, which, although much more free than the refined and delicate Chatsworth drawing, may well be by Nicolò himself, and fits his drawing style of the 1550s.

A number of details in the underdrawing on the Louvre sheet correspond with the work at Chatsworth. For example, (1) the head of the second man from the left, holding an oar, formerly looked to the left but was pulled round to gaze across at Helen. (2) The helmet of Paris was once ridiculously large but was halved in size by Rubens who masked it with greyish-green pigment. (3) The edge of some cliffs above and behind the main group were disguised by extending the sea and horizon. (4) The legs of the man who seizes Helen's arm (at the bottom right) were redrawn by Rubens so that he leans back using his entire weight as a lever, but his original left leg can still be seen. Lastly, (5) the slumped body of a corpse is still visible at bottom right but was covered over with brown wash. Despite these correspondences, the Louvre drawing was probably always horizontal rather than vertical in format because it has a tighter, more densely-packed composition.

Rubens introduced some entirely new details, including a figure with raised arms behind the two oarsmen, and a man with a sword at the centre of the boat, reaching across to seize Helen by the hair. She was made to look back towards the Spartans rather than demurely down to the ground, and Rubens may have found her pose too passive, making her step – or rather fall – into the boat. At the same time he gave her heavier robes which are grabbed with both hands by one of her assailants. Lastly, one of Rubens's most entertaining changes was made to Paris, who was given a new left leg so as to swing round and kick the groin the man who holds on to Helen's arm for dear life.

The incisive character of Nicolò's penmanship encouraged Rubens to be even more vigorous. In the more delicate and restrained drawing at Chatsworth, the two oarsmen seem about to fall asleep and Helen is oddly quiescent, but Rubens engaged every figure in the narrative. The animation, brilliance and fluency of his retouching points to a late date. The comparison here must be with his drawing of *Hercules and Minerva Fighting Mars* in the Louvre, dateable to 1635–7,[1] both in terms of his use of bodycolour and the urgency with which he responded to the violent subject.

1. Inv.no.20183. See Held 1959, I, p.124, no.66, repr. pl.74; Held 1986, pp.158–9, no.229, repr. col. pl.8.

III · RUBENS'S ITALIAN CONTEMPORARIES

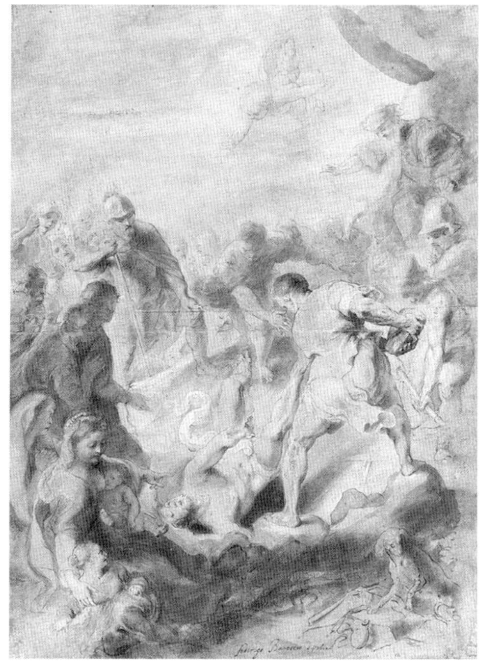

66

FEDERICO BAROCCI

66 · Anonymous Artist after Federico Barocci (*c*.1535–1612), retouched by Rubens

The Martyrdom of Saint Vitalis

COLOUR ILLUSTRATION ON PAGE 31

Pen and ink, retouched with watercolour and white bodycolour; 51.6 × 36.3 cm. Inscribed *federigo Baroccio d'Vrbino* by Rubens.
Collection of the Earl of Pembroke, Wilton House, Salisbury

REFERENCES: Jaffé 1965a, pp.28, 33, note 27; Herbert 1968, p.97, no.31; Jaffé 1977, pp.10, 53; Logan 1978, p.444; Emiliani 1985, I, pp.174–6; Wood 1994, p.340.

This is a copy of an altarpiece, now in Milan, that Barocci was commissioned to paint for San Vitale, the Casentine church in Ravenna, where the saint was the object of local veneration. During the reign of Nero, Vitalis, a Roman soldier, travelled to Ravenna in the company of Paulinus, a magistrate, but after witnessing the execution of a Christian physician he refused to worship pagan gods. Paulinus had Vitalis thrown into a deep pit, upside down, where he was buried alive. Barocci followed the account in the *Legenda Aurea* exactly.

The contract between Barocci and Abate Andrea di Ostiglia was dated 20 June 1580. Barocci provided a *modello* for the patron's approval but was asked to include more figures, which did not please him. The artist did not begin painting the altarpiece in Urbino much before August 1581 and it was not signed and dated until early in 1583 when it was taken to Ravenna in time for the feast of Saint Vitalis in April.

Barocci's altarpiece has been called entertaining rather than horrifying,[1] but although he showed the saint as elegant in death, the work was intended to inspire the spectator. The child feeding a magpie may seem inappropriately charming, but fits the piety of the time which often placed religious events in a domestic or specifically local setting.

It has been said that the drawing was made by Rubens in Ravenna from the original,[2] or from a preparatory drawing or *bozzetto*,[3] but it follows the final work closely, and is more likely to be an anonymous copy that Rubens retouched.[4] The tight and dry pen drawing is easiest to see in the dog and water bottle in the right-hand foreground. More than a third of the surface is given over to the sky, but this occupies only a quarter of the altarpiece, so that the figures in the copy appear smaller and less assertive.

The monochromatic cast of the drawing suggests that the retouching took place at some distance from the original, although a couple of faint indications of colour are similar to Barocci's scheme, and these may have been on the drawing before Rubens added the brown and green washes that make it cohere. He attributed the composition to Barocci at the bottom edge of the sheet, and the only alternative attribution so far proposed – to Cornelis Schut (1597–1655)[5] – is contradicted by the authorship of this inscription and the visual character of the retouching. The use of transparent, lightly tinted wash which clarifies and animates the figures recalls Rubens's coloured drawings after Primaticcio of the 1630s [see cat.no.62 in particular] and suggests the likely date of his intervention.

1. Olsen 1962, p.69.
2. Jaffé 1977, pp.10, 53.
3. Emiliani 1985, I, pp.174–6.
4. Logan 1978, p.444.
5. Vlieghe 1978, p.473.

FEDERICO ZUCCARO

67 · Federico Zuccaro (1540 / 1–1609), with later retouching attributed to Rubens

The Last Supper

Pen and ink with brown wash over black chalk, some late repairs in grey wash, retouched in greenish and yellow bodycolour; 42.5 × 75 cm
Christ Church, Oxford, inv.no.1384

REFERENCES: Jaffé 1965a, pp.21, 30–1, note 5; Byam Shaw 1976, I, pp.153–4, no.541; Jaffé 1977, p.51; B. Cleaver in Oxford / London 1988, p.62, no.17; Acidini Luchinat 1998, II, pp.142, 151, note 131.

This drawing at Christ Church shows the participants at the Last Supper on a small scale and pushed to the back of the multi-figure composition, overwhelmed by a busy crowd of servants and musicians in the foreground. The purpose for which the drawing was made is unknown, but its size and elaboration suggest it was intended as a finished work. It was of sufficient importance to be copied in Federico's studio, as can be seen from a replica of the right-hand side which is in the Museum of Art, Santa Barbara.[1]

The *Last Supper* is typical of Federico's sometimes complex working methods. He constructs a large sheet out of numerous pieces of paper, cutting out and replacing key details, as here, where the servant who carries a wine vessel on his shoulder and the crouching onlooker at the upper right were inserted on separate pieces of paper. In short, although the drawing looks like the polished resolution of the design, it was still a work in progress.

Federico was directly influenced by Veronese's *Marriage Feast at Cana*, painted for

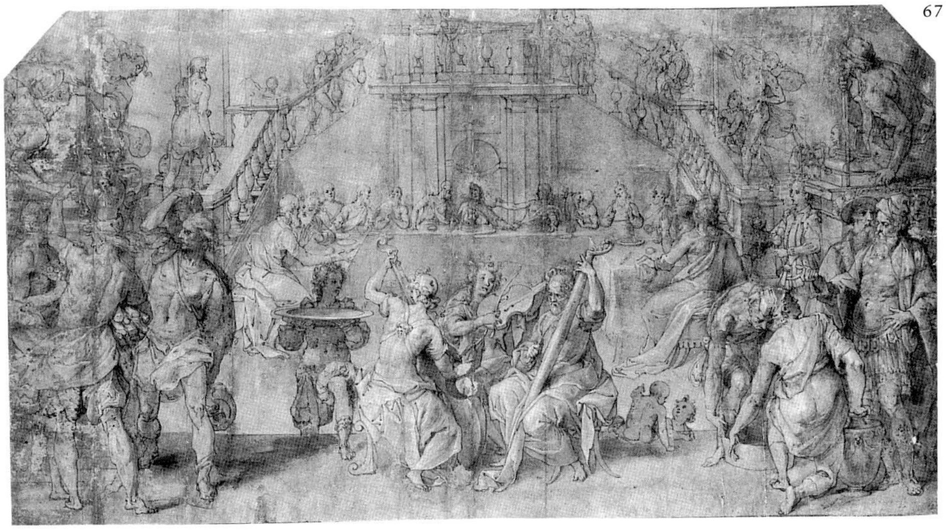
67

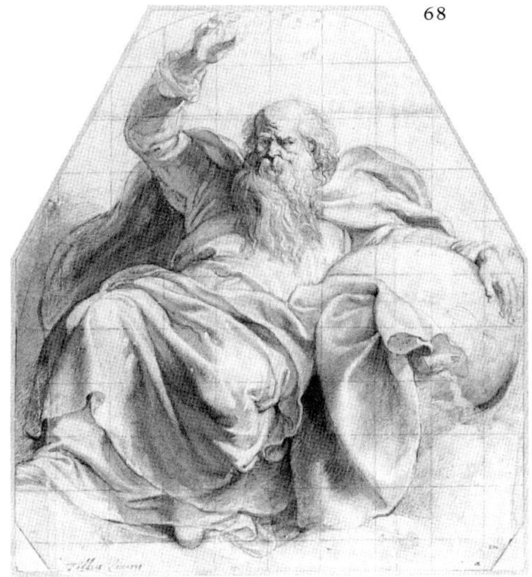
68

the refectory of S. Giorgio Maggiore, Venice, but now in the Louvre, which was completed by 6 October 1563 shortly before Federico's arrival in the city in 1564. He made a rapid pen and ink sketch of this work, now in the Nationalmuseum, Stockholm.[2] But Federico's figures are more balletic than those by Veronese, and his use of vaguely classical dress is very unlike the latter's sumptuous exoticism.

Federico's drawing was made in pen and ink with brown wash on which he added some delicate white heightening. By contrast, the later retouching was applied in broader strokes of brown and yellow bodycolour. This intervention was restricted to the figures in the foreground, and can be most easily seen on the musicians at the centre, the innkeeper at the far right, and the kneeling youth in front of him who is viewed from the back. Dabs of brown and cream bodycolour were applied in Rubens's manner; they increased the solidity of the figures and gave them more of a sense of texture. The retouching of the innkeeper's face shows some skill and adds expression to Federico's mask-like head. On the other hand, these retouchings are cautious and do little to change the design. There is some similarity to Rubens's more limited interventions on drawings in the 1610s, although the use of bodycolour and heightening points to the pictorial effects he favoured in the 1620s. The attribution to Rubens – although uncertain – is worth considering.

1. Inv.no.59–36.
2. Inv.no.H 1522/1863. See Byam Shaw 1976, I, repr. fig.37.

68 · Anonymous Sixteenth-Century Italian Artist, perhaps Federico Zuccaro, retouched by Rubens

God the Father

Black chalk, retouched with brown wash, heightened with white bodycolour and oil. Inscribed *Taddeas* in an early hand and *Zuccarus* perhaps by Rubens; 41 × 36.8 cm

Victoria and Albert Museum, London, inv.no. Dyce 514

REFERENCES: Held 1959, I, p.163, no.170; Burchard/d'Hulst 1963, text vol. pp.217–18, no.140; Logan 1977, p.411; Rowlands 1977, pp.136–7, no.183; Held 1980, I, p.444, under no.319; Held 1986, p.137, no.174; Logan 1987, pp.65, 74–5.

Valerius Röver, a Dutch collector who owned this drawing in the early eighteenth century, had no doubt that it was 'drawn by Zuccaro' and retouched by Rubens.[1] Those scholars who have agreed with Röver have held that Taddeo Zuccaro – whose name was written on the drawing at an early date – is less likely than his brother Federico.

The drawing was evidently made in preparation for a larger work since it was squared for transfer and this squaring, in black chalk, lies underneath Rubens's later retouching. The most widely accepted identification has been with the figure of God the Father in Federico's *The Incarnation as Fulfilment of all Prophecies*,[2] a fresco formerly in Santa Maria Annunciata, Rome, and destroyed in 1626 but known from an engraving by Cornelis Cort of 1571.[3] However, the similarity is not close enough for confidence.

The drawing is made up of several pieces of paper that were pasted together and trimmed at various times. It has been said that the largest section, with its edge running through the head of God the Father, was added by Rubens,[4] but this cannot be so because it contains both the squaring and the right arm in black chalk from the original. Rubens drew very extensively over the surface in brown wash and bodycolour, enlarging draperies and transforming the face of God, as well as extending his patriarchal beard (previously covered by the folds of a billowing cloak) so that it flows down onto his chest. Rubens also added brilliant highlights in white oil paint on the forehead of God and on the globe at his side.

Rubens made use of this drawing in the upper part of an oil sketch of *The Incarnation as Fulfilment of all the Prophecies* in the Barnes Foundation, Merion,[5] dateable around 1628–9. The main difference is that the right hand of God is not raised but falls at his side, holding a sceptre. The drawing has also been linked to Rubens's earlier treatments of *The Trinity*,[6] in particular an oil sketch now in Basle and a large studio version in Munich, dateable to 1615–16. These links are less close, but sufficient to suggest that Rubens may already have owned the drawing. At any rate, it seems likely that the retouching took place at some point after 1615 and before 1628. The later dating is likely because there are similarities between the creamy retouching of the drawing and the succulent technique of the oil sketch, which similarly explores the play of light on luxurious folds of cloth.

1. As listed in Röver's inventory of 1705–39 (Amsterdam University), no.12, see Logan 1987, p.74.
2. Held 1986, p.137.
3. Bierens de Haan 1948, pp.49–51, no.26.
4. Logan 1977, p.411.
5. See Held 1959, I, p.163; Held 1980, I, p.444, under no.319; Held 1986, p.137.
6. Parker 1929, p.19; Rowlands 1977, pp.136–7, under no.183.

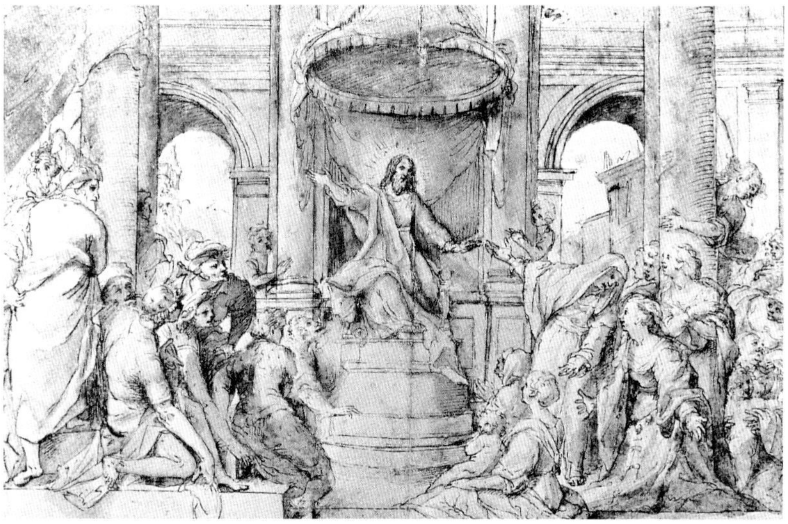

69

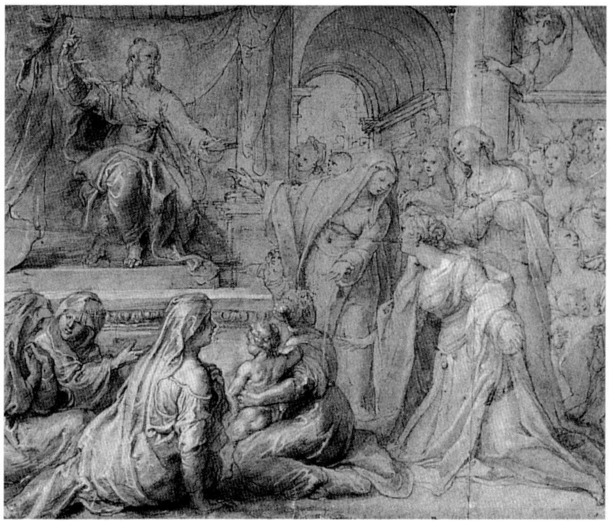

70

69 · Anonymous Draughtsman after Federico Zuccaro
The Conversion of Mary Magdalene

Pen and ink with wash and white heightening; 22.4 × 34.3 cm
Royal Institution of Cornwall, Royal Cornwall Museum, Truro
Not exhibited

REFERENCES: Jaffé 1965a, pp.25, 31, note 11.

Federico arrived in Venice in November 1563, and soon after was at work on the frescoes in the Grimani family chapel at San Francesco della Vigna, which had been begun by Battista Franco (*c*.1510–1561). Federico's *Adoration of the Kings* above the altar is dated 1564. The main scenes on the lateral walls depicted the *Conversion of the Magdalene* (which has no scriptural authority) on the left, and the *Raising of Lazarus* (John 11: 1–44) on the right. These were linked because Mary Magdalene was widely identified as the sister of Lazarus of Bethany, following a tradition that also connected her with the unnamed woman of the Gospels who wept at Christ's feet in the house of Simon the Pharisee and was forgiven her sins. In the early seventeenth century the conversion was often shown as a private event, sometimes with Mary's sister Martha exhorting her to a life of virtue, but, before then, it was occasionally depicted taking place in front of Christ and surrounded by a crowd of witnesses.

The Conversion of Mary Magdalene was painted on the exterior west wall of the church where it decayed, but the composition is known from a detailed drawing in the Uffizi, Florence,[1] and a faithful – though pedestrian – version at Truro, inserted for comparison with cat.no.70. In addition, there is a reversed engraving by Aliprando Caprioli (fl.1574–1599),[2] which dates from the late sixteenth century.

These early copies show that Federico placed Christ at the centre of the fresco seated on a raised throne under a *baldacchino*. The crowd of figures on either side was divided into men on the left and women on the right. The latter included Mary and her sister Martha, who was shown standing between her and Christ, directing her sister's attention to him and encouraging her repentance. This cannot be conflated with the scene in Bethany before the raising of Lazarus when Mary Magdalene reproached Christ for her brother's death, as has recently been proposed.[3] Vasari confidently identified Federico's subject as the conversion of the Magdalene.[4] He was well informed since he had received a drawing of this work from the artist in 1564.[5]

1. Inv.no.11036 F.
2. Sometimes wrongly attributed to Cornelis Cort, see Bierens de Haan 1948, p.88 (wrongly as *Christ and the Woman Taken in Adultery*). Brooke 1998, p.142, under cat.no.79, incorrectly states that both Cort and Caprioli engraved Federico's composition.
3. Brooke 1998, p.142, under cat.no.79.
4. Vasari 1568, III, p.696.
5. Frey 1941, p.201, no.CDLXIII.

70 · Federico Zuccaro, retouched by Rubens
The Conversion of Mary Magdalene Witnessed by a Crowd of Women

Pen and ink with brown wash, repaired and retouched with black chalk, pen and ink with brown wash, and cream bodycolour; 43.1 × 50.8 cm. The lower left-hand portion of the drawing cut off and replaced.
Walker Art Gallery, Liverpool, inv.no.WAG 1995.371

REFERENCES: Jaffé 1965a, pp.25, 31, note 10; Jaffé 1977, pp.38, 51; Brooke 1998, pp.142, 147, note 81, 155–6, no.79; Acidini Luchinat 1998, I, p.260, note 42.

Rubens cut away the lower left of this drawing and inserted a new piece of paper on which he drew some entirely new figures. This resulted in one of the most distinctive of all of his repaired and retouched sheets, directly comparable to his drastic interventions on drawings by Giuseppe Porta, Il Salviati [cat.no.59] and after Annibale Carracci [cat.no.76]. Rubens did not touch the remainder of the Zuccaro drawing, which he clearly respected, even if this meant that the result was not unified visually.

The original appearance of Federico's fresco in San Francesco della Vigna, Venice, to which this drawing relates, is known from several early copies, one of which is illustrated here [cat.no.69] for comparison. Rubens may or may not have known what the complete composition looked like, but by adding four women seated on the ground before Christ, he made it even more obvious that the Magdalene's rejection of worldly vanities could be read as an exhortation to women.

The new piece of paper not only allowed Rubens to add additional figures, already mentioned, but also to redraw Christ's right arm and lower body and reinvent the mother and child in the centre foreground, whose head was retained from Federico's drawing. Rubens began in black chalk, before working over this in pen and brown wash which he strengthened

71

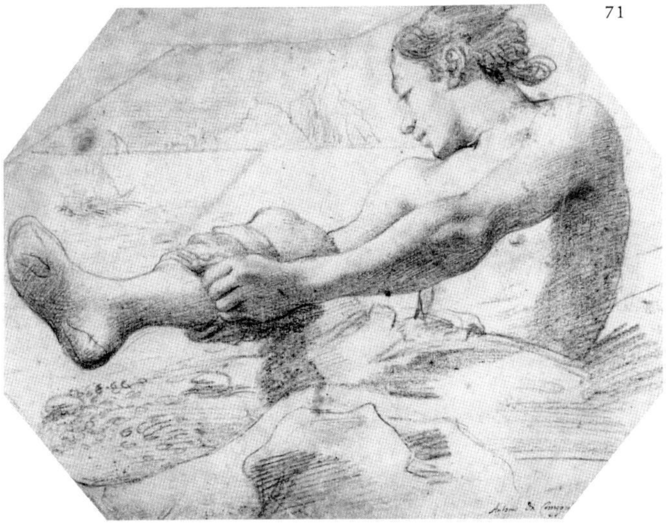

with darker touches that have a purple and pink pigmentation, finally applying cream bodycolour as heightening. As a result, this area in the drawing has an exceptional vibrancy and delicacy of touch, the figures seem to pulsate with life, and both flesh and draperies have a silken sheen.

This intervention has been persuasively placed in the mid-1630s.[1] This late date is justified because of the richness of surface and assurance of Rubens's contribution. Interestingly, Rubens never depicted the conversion of the Magdalene in his own work as taking place in public before Christ. Instead, he preferred the three most popular formats of the early seventeenth century in which the saint is shown as a naked penitent in the wilderness, in ecstasy, or richly dressed and attended by Martha with her discarded jewels lying on the ground.

1. Jaffé 1965a, p.25; Jaffé 1977, p.51; Brooke 1998, p.142, under no.79.

ANNIBALE CARRACCI

71 · Annibale Carracci (1560–1609)
A Young Man Pulling on a Sock

Red chalk; 29.2 × 37.1 cm. Inscribed *Antonio da Correggio* by Rubens.
The British Museum, London, inv.no.1895–9–15–739

REFERENCES: Wood 1994, pp.342, 351, note 53; Robertson/Whistler 1996, p.105, no.57; D. Benati in Washington 1999–2000, p.63, no.6.

This drawing has been dated to the 1580s, the period in which the Carracci established their workshop and academy in Bologna, but it has not been connected with any specific project. It combines a powerful study from the posed model with the playful inclusion of a Roman trireme on the horizon.

The drawing was once owned by Rubens who wrote an attribution to Antonio da Correggio (active 1514–1534) at the lower right. It belongs with several other sheets that were similarly inscribed by him, the most important of which, now in the Louvre,[1] records one of the large Apostles painted by Correggio on the cupola in the Duomo at Parma. This was probably a copy by Annibale,[2] and the remainder of the mis-attributed drawings in this group were certainly by him. They are a red chalk drawing, also in the Louvre, of a young man pulling off his shirt,[3] made in preparation for the *Baptism of Christ* in San Gregorio, Bologna, of 1585, and a black chalk study, exhibited here, of a young man playing a flute [cat.no.73] which Rubens adapted in his *Shepherds and Shepherdesses in a Landscape with an Rainbow* of the mid-1630s, known from versions in Valenciennes and St Petersburg.

From this it seems Rubens could not tell the drawings of Correggio and the Carracci apart, although there was nearly a hundred years between them. This is perhaps understandable since the Carracci were undoubtedly influenced by Correggio in their chalk drawings of the 1580s. In addition, if Rubens obtained a group of Carracci drawings that included the copy of Correggio's Apostle, he may well have been misled into thinking they were all by this artist.

1. Inv.no.20259. Lugt 1949, II, p.32, no.1105, repr. pl.LII; Burchard/d'Hulst 1963, text vol., pp.253–4, no.164, repr. pl.164; Logan 1978, pp.432–3; Sérullaz 1978, p.79, no.76, repr.
2. See Wood 1994, pp.342–3.
3. Inv.no.7320. See Wood 1994, p.342.

72

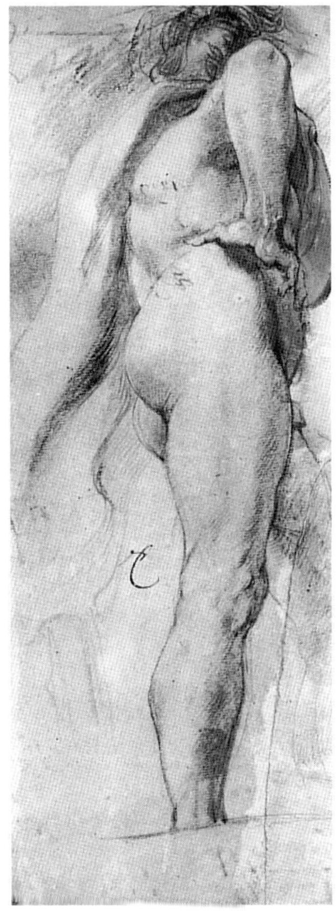

72 · Annibale Carracci, retouched by Rubens
Standing Naked Man, Turned to the Right

Red chalk, retouched with red wash and white heightening; 38.2 × 14.2 cm
Département des Arts graphiques, Musée du Louvre, Paris, inv.no.20255
Exhibited in Edinburgh only

REFERENCES: Glück/Haberditzl 1928, pp.11, 29, no.6; Lugt 1949, II, p.32, no.1106; Burchard/d'Hulst 1956, pp.40–1, no.22; Jaffé 1956, p.317; Burchard/d'Hulst 1963, text vol., pp.254–6, no.165; Jaffé 1977, pp.112–13, note 119; Logan 1978, p.432; Sérullaz 1978, p.79, no.75.

In the nineteenth century this drawing was attributed to Correggio. More recently it was thought to be by Rubens after Correggio's frescoes in the Duomo at Parma,[1] a copy from a drawing by Annibale,[2] or an anonymous Italian drawing retouched by Rubens.[3] In my opinion the drawing is actually by Annibale and related to the figure of Hercules, in reverse, as found in the *Building of the Argo*, one of the frescoes from the story of Jason frieze in the Sala di Giasone at Palazzo Fava, Bologna. This particular scene has been widely attributed to Annibale who collaborated on this commission with his brother Agostino and cousin Ludovico. The palace was built by Filippo Fava around 1580; work on the frieze is thought to have begun around 1583 and its completion is recorded by the date 1584 inscribed below a fictive statue of

73

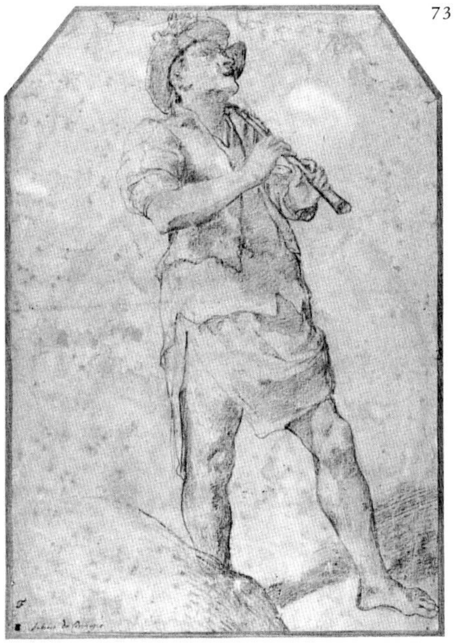

Jupiter. The heavy cloak thrown over this figure's shoulder, in the drawing, suggests that Annibale was already thinking of Hercules's lion skin. A very lightly indicated sketch for Hercules's left hand resting on his knobbly club is visible at lower left.

This drawing is retouched with red wash and yellowish-white heightening in Rubens's characteristic manner. This is evident on the hair, since the head is moved to the right, on the arm and on part of the cloak where touches of wash provide deep accents in the shadows. The aim was not to change the drawing, but to strengthen it.

Rubens used this figure, fully clothed, in his *Esther before Ahasuerus*, one of the destroyed canvases for the ceiling of the Sint-Carolus Borromeuskerk, the Jesuit church in Antwerp, dated 1620–1. The figure was turned into one of the king's attendants, placed at the bottom right, and his elbow was pulled further back than in the Louvre drawing, while his head jutted out more and was easier to see. The second use that Rubens made of this figure was in the *Union of the Crowns* from the Whitehall ceiling, dated 1632–4, which itself recalled the earlier design for *Esther before Ahasuerus* in the relationship of enthroned monarch and foreshortened attendant. It follows that Rubens retouched this drawing at some time between 1620 and 1630 when engaged on these two large ceiling paintings for Antwerp and London, and this provides a key point of reference for dating the reworked drawings.

1. Glück/Haberditzl 1928, p.29, no.6.
2. Jaffé 1956, p.317.
3. Logan 1978, p.432; Logan/Haverkamp-Begemann 1978, p.94; Logan 1983, p.416.

73 · Annibale Carracci
A Man with a Flute

Black chalk; 39.3 × 26.6 cm. Inscribed *Antonio da Correggio* by Rubens.
Devonshire Collection, Chatsworth, inv.no.446

REFERENCES: Hodge 1977, p.268; Jaffé 1994a, p.87, no.492; Wood 1994, p.342.

This drawing by Annibale from the 1580s could have been drawn from a model, but it has not been convincingly related to any particular project. Rubens owned the drawing and mistakenly attributed it to Correggio, as his inscription bears witness. It forms part of a group of similarly misidentified drawings, discussed here under cat.no.71.

The upper part of this figure was used in a very literal way by Rubens in a rapid pen and ink drawing, which is in the Institut Néerlandais, Paris,[1] showing a shepherd and shepherdess seated on the ground. This was a preliminary idea for a larger painting, the *Shepherds and Shepherdesses in a Rainbow Landscape* known from versions in Valenciennes and St Petersburg of the mid-1630s, one of the most Italianate pastorals that he produced, and which can be studied in this exhibition through the reversed engraving by Schelte à Bolswert [cat.no.74].

In this context it is interesting that Mariette recorded the presence of an earlier Italian drawing with a comparable pastoral flautist, Titian's *Shepherd Playing a Flute and Leading his Flock*, now in the Albertina, Vienna,[2] among the drawings from Rubens's collection that passed to Everhard Jabach (1618–1695).[3]

1. Inv.no.2535. See C. Van Hasselt in London/Paris/Bern/Brussels 1972, pp.113–15, no.85, repr. pl.45.
2. Inv.no.1477. See Wethey 1987, pp.161–2, no.46, repr. fig.88; Py 2001, p.168, no.689.
3. Mariette 1851–60, v, p.335.

74

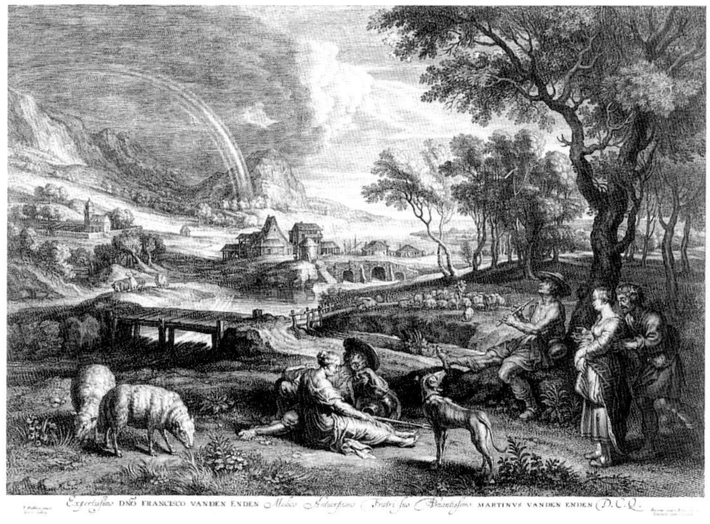

74 · Schelte à Bolswert (*c*.1581–1659) after Rubens
Shepherds and Shepherdesses in a Landscape with an Rainbow

Engraving; 33.5 × 45 cm
The British Museum, London, inv.no.R.5.34

REFERENCES: Voorhelm Schneevoogt 1873, p.234, no.53.10; Van den Wijngaert 1940, p.36, no.98; Bodart 1977, p.55, no.85.

This reversed engraving by Schelte à Bolswert makes it possible to consider the most deliberately Italianate pastoral scene that Rubens ever painted, the *Shepherds and Shepherdesses in a Rainbow Landscape* of the late 1630s, known from versions in Valenciennes (on loan from the Louvre) and St Petersburg, in the context of the present exhibition.[1]

Rubens began by focusing on the figures. A quick pen and ink drawing, in the Institut Néerlandais, Paris, established the pose of the shepherd playing a flute in front of a shepherdess seated on the ground. In doing this, Rubens made literal use of a drawing by Annibale Carracci which he owned [cat.no.73] for the upper part of the shepherd's body, which he turned from a standing to a sitting figure. Rubens made a note to himself on the drawing to enlarge these figures 'with a large flat landscape' (*met een groot slegt lantschap*).

The *Shepherds and Shepherdesses in a Rainbow Landscape* is, in fact, a patchwork of references to north Italian art, in particular, the work by Domenico Campagnola whose tumble-down farms, rustic mills and picturesque bridges were blatantly imitated by Rubens on a number of occasions. Here he took the group of farm buildings near an arched bridge in the middle-distance from a lost drawing, the *Landscape with Pilgrims* by Domenico, which is known from an early seventeenth-century etching.[2]

An even closer relationship exists between

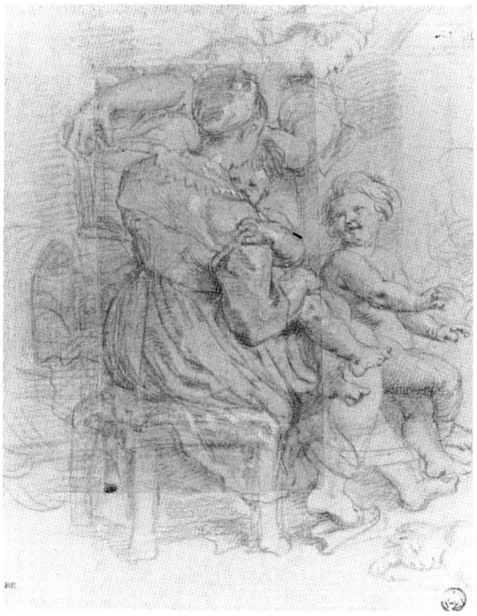
75

Rubens's *Farm at Sunset* in the Louvre, dateable to the mid-1630s, and a drawing by Domenico of a *Landscape with a Mill*, most recently recorded in the collection of Janos Scholz, New York, which is also known from a print.[3] However, since Rubens literally copied these buildings in their unreversed direction, it seems certain he knew the original sheet.

These examples illustrate a contentious point in Rubens's critical fortunes. In 1678, the biographer and theorist Samuel van Hoogstraeten recorded that the artist had been criticised for making excessive borrowings from Italian art. Apparently, Rubens's retort was that others were free to do the same but not everyone was able to do so with advantage.[4]

1. In addition, according to Mariette 1851–60, v, p.337–8, the second in a series of etchings after Titian's Landscapes by Lucas van Uden, inscribed *Titianus invenit*, was reworked by Schelte à Bolswert.
2. See Vergara 1982, p.57, note 96, with further references, and Cafritz 1988, p.121, who reproduces [fig.106] the etching from an impression in the Institut Néerlandais, Paris.
3. See Kieser 1931, p.284.
4. Van Hoogstraeten 1678, book v, p.193.

75 · Annibale Carracci, retouched by Rubens

A Woman with Two Children in Front of the Fire, Accompanied by a Woman Carrying a Basket

COLOUR ILLUSTRATION ON PAGE 18

Red chalk, retouched with additional red chalk, red wash, and cream and white bodycolour; 25.4 × 19.7 cm. A smaller piece of paper (17.7 × 9 cm) inserted into the sheet.
Département des Arts graphiques, Musée du Louvre, Paris, inv.no.20205
Exhibited in Nottingham only

REFERENCES: Lugt 1948, II, p.18, no.1027; Jaffé 1977, p.56; Logan / Haverkamp-Begemann 1978, pp.95–6; Sérullaz 1978, p.26, no.9; Logan 1978, p.430.

The style of the seated woman's dress and the nudity of the children in this drawing sets it apart from contemporary Netherlandish depictions of domestic life. Its origin is suggested by the way it was made, since a small drawing of a seated woman was incorporated into a larger piece of paper in order to extend the design on all four sides. It is, therefore, unlikely to have been drawn from life, as has been suggested,[1] since a quick observational study could not have been made so elaborate. It is probably an earlier work that Rubens enlarged and retouched.[2] The drawing is similar to several others that he expanded [see cat.no.14], and in most cases the nucleus was by another hand.

The core fragment was drawn in dark red chalk. After its enlargement the entire sheet was reworked in a lighter, orange chalk. Touches of cream bodycolour were added on the shoulder and dress of the seated mother and small hatchings in red wash applied to define her waist and sleeve in order to integrate the separate parts of drawing. The child nearest the fire, the woman with a basket, the cradle, and the cat, were all entirely Rubens's invention.

Enough remains visible of the core fragment to show that it fits into a tradition of studies of everyday domestic life found in sixteenth-century Bolognese and Emilian art. The broad and angular handling of chalk points to the Carracci studio as a place of origin.[3] It was during Annibale's early Bolognese years that he made numerous informal studies of people going about their everyday trades – artists at work in the studio, and scenes of domestic life. At the very least, Rubens's enlargement of the present drawing was an exercise in Annibale's manner.

The proposal that this drawing was made in Italy between 1600 and 1608 is unconvincing.[4] Rubens's handling of red chalk in that period shows a more precise and continuous use of outline, crisp description of detail, and relatively smooth internal modelling. The freedom of handling in the drawing, with no real distinction made between outlines and blocks of tone, as well as repeated overdrawing to define form, points to a date of after 1615. In addition, it is close in content and sentiment to Rubens's unfinished panel of *Hélène Fourment with Clara-Johanna and Frans Rubens* in the Louvre, dated to around 1636, although the drawing has an unspecific and Italianate character while the painting contains identifiable likenesses in contemporary Flemish dress.

1. Lugt 1948, II, p.18, no.1027.
2. As noted by Logan / Haverkamp-Begemann 1978, pp.96–7.
3. Logan 1978, p.430.
4. Lugt 1948, II, p.18, under no.1027; Jaffé 1977, caption to pl.167.

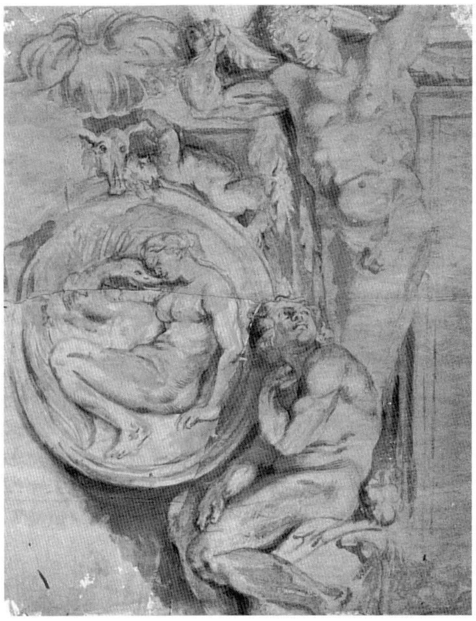

76

76 · Anonymous Artist after Annibale Carracci, retouched by Rubens
A Nude Youth and a Medallion of Leda and the Swan

Black chalk, retouched with brown and yellowish wash, heightened with white; 55.3 × 40.7 cm. A wedge-shaped section removed and replaced at lower left.
Victoria and Albert Museum, London, inv.no.2307

REFERENCES: Burchard/d'Hulst 1956, pp.97–8, no.116; Jaffé 1956, p.317; Jaffé 1957, pp.375–6; Burchard/d'Hulst 1963, text vol., pp.256–8, no.167; Jaffé 1977, pp.55–6; Rowlands 1977, p.57, no.52; A. Balis in Brussels/Rome 1995, pp.305–6, no.171.

Rubens surely enjoyed Annibale Carracci's ability to revitalise the antique while adopting a playful approach to mythology. Among Annibale's greatest achievements in Rome was the decoration of the Galleria at Palazzo Farnese, Rome, the ceiling of which was unveiled shortly before 2 June 1601. This room was intended to display antique sculpture, and Annibale's scheme alluded to this through its many painted statues and reliefs. An illusionistic marble frieze running round the vault is decorated with bronze medallions. Atlas-herms flank the openings in the frieze, and nude youths are seated on marble blocks, as if on the cornice of the gallery, their vivid flesh contrasting with the marmoreal bodies of the herms who, nevertheless, look animated, glancing sideways at each other. This drawing records a section of the frieze that contains a nude youth seated to the right of the *Apollo and Marsyas* medallion.

The work was first drawn in black chalk. What survives of this stage suggests that, before retouching, it was no more than a pedestrian copy after the fresco. A wedge-shaped piece of paper was cut away at the lower left and replaced with a new section containing a medallion depicting Leda and the swan. Brown wash and white heightening was applied vigorously across the entire surface in order to give the drawing visual coherence. The reworking made all the figures appear equally malleable and fleshy, and Annibale's contrast between the softness of the living body and the crispness of carved stone was lost.

The new section with the figure of Leda is confidently handled in Rubens's manner. The retouching was applied with a thick brush, rather than the finer one usually preferred by him, and white heightening was added in broad patches. This fluid and almost deliberately clumsy technique responds to the large scale of the sheet and suggests a date late in his career, since he only started drawing like this with the brush towards the end of the 1620s. The same broad handling can be found in a retouched drawing in the Louvre of *Neptune in his Chariot Pulled by Sea Creatures* after Cornelis Bos.[1] An even more relevant work, for comparison, is a very large sheet in the British Museum which contains a fragment of a hawking party by Barend van Orley (*c.*1488–1541),[2] which Rubens extended and reworked with a boldness and roughness comparable to the *Leda*. In short, although Rubens may have seen the Galleria in 1601, the drawing can only have been reworked in the 1630s.

1. Inv.20275. See Lugt 1949, II, p.26, no.1069; Sérullaz 1978, p.68, no.60.
2. Inv.no.5237–77. See Rowlands 1977, p.56, no.49, repr.

ABBREVIATED REFERENCES

ACIDINI LUCHINAT 1998

C. Acidini Luchinat, *Taddeo e Federico Zuccari fratelli pittori del Cinquecento*, 2 vols., Milan, 1998

ALBERICI 1984

C. Alberici (ed.), *Leonardo e l'incisione. Stampe derivate da Leonardo e Bramante dal XV al XIX secolo*, Castello Sforzesco, Milan, 1984

ALPERS 1995

S. Alpers, *The Making of Rubens*, New Haven and London, 1995

ANDREWS 1985

K. Andrews, *Catalogue of Netherlandish Drawings in the National Gallery of Scotland*, 2 vols., Edinburgh, 1985

ARETINO 1608–9

Il primo [-sesto] libro de le lettere di Pietro Aretino, 6 vols., Paris, 1608–9

ARETINO 1957–60

P. Aretino, *Lettere sull'arte* (*Vite, lettere, testimonianze di artisti italiani*, 3) (eds.) F. Pertile and E. Camesasca, 4 vols., Milan, 1957–60

D'ASTIER 1907

E.R. d'Astier de la Vigerie, *La Belle tapisserye du Roi, 1532–1797, et les tentures de Scipion l'Africain*, Paris, 1907

BACOU 1983

R. Bacou, *Autour de Raphael: dessins et peintures du Musée du Louvre*, Cabinet des Dessins, Musée du Louvre, Paris, 1983

BAGLIONE 1642

Le vite de'pittori, scultori et architetti dal potificato di Gregorio XIII del 1572. In fino a'tempi di Papa Urbano Ottavo nel 1642, Rome, 1642

BALIS 1994

A. Balis, '"Fatto da un mio discepolo": Rubens's Studio Practices Reviewed' in *Rubens and his Workshop: The Flight of Lot and his Family from Sodom* (ed.) T. Nakamura, Tokyo, 1994, pp.97–127

BARTSCH (+ NO.)

A. Bartsch, *Le Peintre-graveur*, 21 vols., Leipzig, 1803–21

BASAN 1775

F. Basan, *Catalogue raisonné des différens objets de curiosités dans les sciences et arts, qui composoient le Cabinet de feu Mr Mariette Controleur général de la Grande Chancellerie de France honoraire Amateur de l'Academie Re de Peinture, et de celle de Florence*, Paris, 1775

BASCHET 1866–7

A. Baschet, 'Pierre-Paul Rubens peintre de Vincent Ier Gonzague, duc de Mantoue (1600–1608). Son séjour en Italie et son premier voyage en Espagne d'après ses lettres et autres documents tous inédits', *Gazette des Beaux-Arts*, XX, 1866, I, pp.401–52; XXII, 1867, II, pp.305–20

BEER 1891

R. Beer, 'Acten, Regesten und Inventare aus dem Archivio General zu Simancas', *Jahrbuch der Kunsthistorischen Sammlungen des Allerhöchsten Kaiserhauses*, XII, part 2, 1891, pp.xci-cciv

BÉGUIN 1962

S. Béguin, 'Niccolò dell'Abbate en France', *Art de France*, II, 1962, pp.113–45

BÉGUIN 1969

S. Béguin, *Mostra di Nicolò dell'Abate*, Palazzo dell'Archiginnasio, Bologna, 1969

BÉGUIN 1975

S. Béguin, 'Remarques sur la Chambre du Roi' in *Actes du Colloque International sur l'Art de Fontainebleau, Fontainebleau et Paris, 18, 19, 20 Octobre 1972*, Paris, 1975, pp.199–230

BÉGUIN / GUILLAUME / ROY 1985

S. Béguin, J. Guillaume, and A. Roy, *La galerie d'Ulysse à Fontainebleau*, Paris, 1985

BELLORI 1672

G.P. Bellori, *Le vite de pittori, scultori et architetti moderni*, Rome, 1672

BENESCH 1954

O. Benesch, Review of F. Lugt, *Musée du Louvre, Inventaire Général des dessins des Écoles du Nord, École flamande*, *Kunstchronik*, VII, 1954, pp.199–203

BERGER 1883

A. Berger, 'Inventar der Kunstsammlung des Erzherzogs Leopold Wilhelm von Österreich, nach der originalhandschrift in fürstlich Schwarzenberg'schen Centralarchive', *Jahrbuch der Kunsthistorischen Sammlungen des Allerhöchsten Kaiserhauses*, I, 1883, pp.lxxix-clxxvii

BIERENS DE HAAN 1948

J.C.J. Bierens de Haan, *L'oeuvre gravé de Cornelis Cort, graveur hollandais, 1533–1578*, The Hague, 1948

BOBER / RUBINSTEIN 1986
P.P. Bober and R. Rubinstein, *Renaissance Artists and Antique Sculpture. A Handbook of Sources*, London and Oxford, 1986

BODART 1977
D. Bodart, *Rubens e l'incisione nelle collezione del Gabinetto Nazionale delle Stampe*, Villa della Farnesina, Rome, 1977

BOON 1978
K.G. Boon, *Netherlandish Drawings of the Fifteenth and Sixteenth Centuries (Catalogus van de Nederlandse Tekeningen in het Rijksmuseum te Amsterdam*, II), 2 vols., The Hague, 1978

BOSTON / TOLEDO 1993–4
P.C. Sutton, *et al*, *The Age of Rubens*, Museum of Fine Arts, Boston, 1993–4 and Toledo Museum of Art, Toledo, Ohio, 1994

BOTTARI / TICOZZI 1822–5
G. Bottari and S. Ticozzi, *Raccolta di lettere sulla pittura, scultura ed architettura scritte da'più celebri personaggi dei secoli XV, XVI, e XVII*, 8 vols., Milan, 1822–5

BRADY 1839
J.H. Brady, *The Visitor's Guide to Knole in the County of Kent, with Catalogues of the Pictures contained in the Mansion, and Biographical Notices of the principal Persons whose Portraits form part of the Collection*, Sevenoaks, 1839

BRIDGMAN 1817
J. Bridgman, *An Historical and Topographical Sketch of Knole, in Kent; with a Brief Genealogy of the Sackville Family*, London, 1817

BRIGSTOCKE 1993
H. Brigstocke, *Italian and Spanish Paintings in the National Gallery of Scotland* (2nd edn.), Edinburgh, 1993

BROOKE 1998–9
X. Brooke, *Mantegna to Rubens. The Weld-Blundell Drawings Collection*, Walker Art Gallery, Liverpool and The British Museum, London, 1998–9

BRUSSELS / ROME 1995
Fiamminghi a Roma, 1508–1608. Artistes des Pays-Bas et de la principauté de Liège a Rome à la Renaissance (ed.) N. Dacos Crifò and B. Meijer, Palais des Beaux-Arts, Brussels and Palazzo delle Esposizioni, Rome, 1995

BURCHARD 1950
L. Burchard, *A Loan Exhibition of Works by Peter Paul Rubens, Kt.*, Wildenstein & Co., London, 1950

BURCHARD 1956
L. Burchard, 'On a Rubens Drawing after Mantegna', *The Burlington Magazine*, XCVIII, 1956, p.415

BURCHARD / D'HULST 1956
L. Burchard and R.-A. d'Hulst, *Tekeningen van P.P. Rubens*, Rubenshuis, Antwerp, 1956

BURCHARD / D'HULST 1963
L. Burchard and R.-A. d'Hulst, *Rubens Drawings (Monographs of the 'Nationaal Centrum voor de Plastische Kunsten van de XVIde en de XVIIde Eeuw'*, II), 2 vols., Brussels, 1963

BYAM SHAW 1976
J. Byam Shaw, *Drawings by Old Masters at Christ Church, Oxford*, 2 vols., Oxford, 1976

BYAM SHAW 1983
J. Byam Shaw, *The Italian Drawings of the Frits Lugt Collection*, 3 vols., Paris, 1983

CAFRITZ 1988
R.C. Cafritz, 'Netherlandish Reflections of the Venetian Landscape Tradition' in *Places of Delight. The Pastoral Landscape* (The National Gallery of Art and The Phillips Collection, Washington, DC, 1988–9), London, 1988, pp.113–29

CANBERRA / MELBOURNE 1992
Rubens and the Italian Renaissance, Australian National Gallery, Canberra and the National Gallery of Victoria, Melbourne, 1992

CARROLL 1987–8
E.A. Carroll, *Rosso Fiorentino. Drawings, Prints and Decorative Arts*, National Gallery of Art, Washington, 1987–8

CHÂTELET-LANGE 1972
L. Châtelet-Lange, 'Michelangelos Herkules in Fontainebleau', *Pantheon*, XXX, 1972, pp.455–68

CHENEY 1963
I.H. Cheney, *Francesco Salviati (1510–1563)*, Ph.D. thesis, New York University, 4 vols., 1963

COHEN 1996
C.E. Cohen, *The Art of Giovanni Antonio da Pordenone. Between Dialect and Language*, 2 vols., Cambridge, 1996

COLOGNE 1977
Peter Paul Rubens, 1577–1640. I, *Rubens in Italien. Gemälde, Ölskizzen, Zeichnungen; Triumph der Eucharistie, Wandteppiche aus dem Kölner Dom*; II, *Maler mit dem Grabstichel, Rubens und die Druckgraphik*, Cologne, 1977

DA COMO 1930
U. da Como, *Girolamo Muziano, 1528–1592. Note e documenti*, Bergamo, 1930

CONDIVI 1553
[A. Condivi], *Vita di Michelagnolo Buonarroti raccolta per Ascanio Condivi de la Ripa Transone*, Rome, 1553

CORDELLIER / PY 1992
D. Cordellier and B. Py, *Raphaël, son atelier, ses copistes, Musée du Louvre, Musée d'Orsay, département des Arts graphiques: Inventaire Général des dessins italiens*, V, Paris, 1992

COX-REARICK 1995
J. Cox-Rearick, *The Collection of Francis I: Royal Treasures*, Antwerp, 1995

CROWE / CAVALCASELLE 1877
J.A. Crowe and G.B. Cavalcaselle, *Titian. His Life and Times with some account of his Family, chiefly from new and unpublished Records*, 2 vols., London, 1877

DAVIDSON 1966
B.F. Davidson, *Mostra di disegni di Perino del Vaga e la sua cerchia, Gabinetto disegni e stampe degli Uffizi*, XXIII, Florence, 1966

DAVIDSON 1985
B.F. Davidson, *Raphael's Bible. A Study of the Vatican Logge, Monographs on the Fine Arts sponsored by the College Art Association of America*, XXXIX, University Park and London, 1985

DENUCÉ 1932
J. Denucé, *De Antwerpsche 'Konstkamers'. Inventarissen van de kunstverzamelingen te Antwerpen in de 16de en 17de eeuwen (Bronnen voor de geschiedenis van de Vlaamsche kunst*, II), Antwerp, 1932

DIMIER 1900
L. Dimier, *Le Primatice, peintre, sculpteur et architecte des rois de France. Essai sur la vie et les ouvrages de cet artiste suivi d'un catalogue raisonné de ses dessins et de ses compositions gravées*, Paris, 1900

DUSSLER 1971
L. Dussler, *Raphael. A Critical Catalogue of his Pictures, Wall Paintings and Tapestries*, London and New York, 1971

EDINBURGH 1999
The Draughtsman's Art: Master Drawings from the National Gallery of Scotland, National Gallery of Scotland, Edinburgh, 1999

EICHE 1981
S. Eiche, 'The return of Baldassare Castiglione', *The Burlington Magazine*, CXXIII, 1981, pp.154–5

EMILIANI 1985
A. Emiliani, *Federico Barocci (Urbino 1535–1612)*, 2 vols., Bologna, 1985

EVERS 1944
H.G. Evers, *Rubens und sein Werk: Neue Forschungen, Arbeiten und Forschungen des Deutschen Instituts in Brüssel*, Brussels, 1944

FLORENCE 1976
Tiziano e il disegno veneziano del suo tempo, Gabinetto disegni e stampe degli Uffizi, XLV, Florence, 1976

FREEDBERG 1978
D. Freedberg, 'L'année Rubens, manifestations et publications en 1977', *Revue de l'art*, no.39, 1978, pp.82–91

FREEDBERG 1984
D. Freedberg, *Rubens. The Life of Christ after the Passion (Corpus Rubenianum Ludwig Burchard,* VII), London, 1984

FREY 1941
K. Frey, *Il Carteggio di Giorgio Vasari dal 1563 al 1565* (ed.) A. del Vita, Arezzo, 1941

FROMMEL 1967–8
C.L. Frommel, 'Baldassare Peruzzi als Maler und Zeichner' *(Römischen Jahrbuch für Kunstgeschichte,* XI), Wien, 1967–8

GARFF / PEDERSEN 1988
J. Garff and E. de la Fuente Pedersen, *Rubens Cantoor. The Drawings of Willem Panneels,* 2 vols., Copenhagen, 1988

GERE 1969
J.A. Gere, *Taddeo Zuccaro. His Development studied in his Drawings,* London, 1969

GERE 1970
J.A. Gere, 'The Lawrence-Phillips-Rosenbach "Zuccaro Album"', *Master Drawings,* VIII, 1970, pp.123–40

GERE / POUNCEY 1983
J.A. Gere and P. Pouncey, *Artists working in Rome, c.1550 to c.1640, Italian Drawings in the Department of Prints and Drawings in the British Museum,* 2 vols., London, 1983

GLÜCK 1937
G. Glück, 'Bildnisse aus dem Hause Habsburg, III: Kaiser Karl V', *Jahrbuch der Kunsthistorischen Sammlungen in Wien,* Neue Folge, XI, 1937, pp.165–78

GLÜCK / HABERDITZL 1928
G. Glück and F.M. Haberditzl, *Die Handzeichnungen von Peter Paul Rubens,* Berlin, 1928

GNANN 1999
A. Gnann, *Roma e lo stile classico di Raffaello* (ed.) K. Oberhuber, Palazzo Te, Mantua and Graphische Sammlung Albertina, Vienna, 1999

GOFFEN 1986
R. Goffen, *Piety and Patronage in Renaissance Venice. Bellini, Titian and the Franciscans,* New Haven and London, 1986

GOLDSCHEIDER 1957
L. Goldscheider, *Michelangelo's Bozzetti for Statues in the Medici Chapel. The Clay and Wax Models in the British Museum, the Pietri Collection, Caracas, and at Florence in the Accademia delle Belle Arti and the Casa Buonarroti,* London, 1957

GOMBRICH 1935
E. Gombrich, 'Zum werke Giulio Romanos: II, Versuch einer deutung', *Jahrbuch der Kunsthistorischen Sammlungen in Wien,* neue folge, IX, 1935, pp.121–50

HARTT 1958
F. Hartt, *Giulio Romano,* 2 vols., New Haven, 1958

HARTT 1991
F. Hartt, with G. Colalucci and F. Mancinelli, *The Sistine Chapel,* 2 vols., London, 1991

HAVERKAMP-BEGEMANN 1978
E. Haverkamp-Begemann, 'Rubens' "Three Caryatids"', *Boymans bijdragen. Opstellen van medewerkers en oud-medewerkers van het Museum Boymans-van Beuningen,* Rotterdam, 1978, pp.44–50

HAVERKAMP-BEGEMANN / LOGAN 1988
E. Haverkamp-Begemann and C. Logan, *Creative Copies. Interpretative Drawings from Michelangelo to Picasso,* London and New York, 1988

HELD 1959
J.S. Held, *Rubens. Selected Drawings, with an Introduction and a Critical Catalogue,* 2 vols., London, 1959

HELD 1980
J.S. Held, *The Oil Sketches of Peter Paul Rubens. A Critical Catalogue,* 2 vols., Princeton, N J, 1980

HELD 1982
J.S. Held, 'Rubens and Titian' in *Titian. His World and his Legacy* (ed.) D. Rosand, New York, 1982, pp.283–339

HELD 1983
J.S. Held, 'Thoughts on Rubens' beginnings', *The Ringling Museum of Art Journal, Papers presented at the International Rubens Symposium, April 14–16, 1982,* 1983, pp.14–35

HELD 1986
J.S. Held, *Rubens. Selected Drawings,* rev. (ed.), Oxford, 1986

HERBERT 1968
Sidney Herbert, 16th Earl of Pembroke, *A Catalogue of the Paintings and Drawings in the Collection at Wilton House, Salisbury, Wiltshire,* London and New York 1968

HIND 1923
A.M. Hind, *Drawings by Rubens, Van Dyck and Other Artists of the Flemish School of the XVII Century, Catalogue of Drawings by Dutch and Flemish Artists Preserved in the Department of Prints and Drawings in the British Museum,* 2 vols., London, 1923

HODGE 1977
R. Hodge, 'A Carracci Drawing in the Studio of Rubens', *Master Drawings,* XV, 1977, pp.268–9

HOOD / HOPE 1977
W. Hood and C. Hope, 'Titian's Vatican Altarpiece and the pictures underneath', *The Art Bulletin,* LIX, 1977, pp.534–52

HOPE 1980
C. Hope, *Titian,* London, 1980

HOPE 1988
C. Hope, 'La produzione pittorica di Tiziano per gli Asburgo' in *Venezia e la Spagna,* Milan, 1988, pp.49–72

HÖPER 1987
C. Höper, *Bartolomeo Passarotti (1529–1592),* 2 vols., Worms, 1987

HUEMER 1977
F. Huemer, 'Rubens and the Mantuan Altar', *Studies in Iconography,* III, 1977, pp.105–44

D'HULST / VANDENVEN 1989
R.-A. d'Hulst and M. Vandenven, *Rubens. The Old Testament (Corpus Rubenianum Ludwig Burchard, III),* London and New York, 1989

HYMANS 1893
H. Hymans, *Lucas Vorsterman. Catalogue raisonné de son oeuvre précédé d'une notice sur la vie et les ouvrages du maître,* Brussels, 1893

JAFFÉ 1955
M. Jaffé, 'Giuseppe Porta, Il Salviati and Peter Paul Rubens', *Art Quarterly,* XVIII, 1955, pp.331–40

JAFFÉ 1956
M. Jaffé, 'Rubens' Drawings at Antwerp', *The Burlington Magazine,* XCVIII, 1956, pp.314–21

JAFFÉ 1957
M. Jaffé, 'The Interest of Rubens in Annibale and Agostino Carracci: Further Notes', *The Burlington Magazine,* XCIX, 1957, pp.375–9

JAFFÉ 1958
M. Jaffé, 'Rubens and Giulio Romano at Mantua', *The Art Bulletin,* XL, 1958, pp.325–9

JAFFÉ, 1964
M. Jaffé, 'Rubens as a Collector of Drawings: Part One', *Master Drawings,* II, 1964, pp.383–97

JAFFÉ 1965A
M. Jaffé, 'Rubens as a Collector of Drawings: Part Two', *Master Drawings,* III, 1965, pp.21–35

JAFFÉ 1965B
M. Jaffé, 'Rubens as a Draughtsman [Review of L. Burchard and R.-A. d'Hulst, *Rubens Drawings* and J.S. Held, *Rubens Drawings*]', *The Burlington Magazine,* CVII, 1965, pp.372–81

JAFFÉ 1966A
M. Jaffé, 'Rubens as a Collector of Drawings: Part Three', *Master Drawings,* IV, 1966, pp.127–48

JAFFÉ 1966B
M. Jaffé, *Van Dyck's Antwerp Sketchbook,* 2 vols., London, 1966

JAFFÉ 1967
M. Jaffé, 'Rubens and Raphael' in *Studies in Renaissance and Baroque Art presented to Anthony Blunt on his 60th birthday,* London and New York, 1967, pp.98–107

JAFFÉ 1968
M. Jaffé, 'Rubens in Italy, part II: some rediscovered works of the first phase', *The Burlington Magazine*, CX, 1968, pp.174–87

JAFFÉ 1971
M. Jaffé, 'Figure Drawings attributed to Rubens, Jordaens, and Cossiers in the Hamburg Kunsthalle', *Jahrbuch der Hamburger Kunstsammlungen*, XVI, 1971, pp.39–50

JAFFÉ 1977
M. Jaffé, *Rubens and Italy*, Oxford, 1977

JAFFÉ 1983
M. Jaffé, 'Rubens and Italy. Two more Drawings', *Master Drawings*, XXI, 1983, pp.397–401

JAFFÉ 1989
M. Jaffé, *Rubens. Catalogo Completo*, Milan, 1989

JAFFÉ 1994A
M. Jaffé, *The Devonshire Collection of Italian Drawings. Bolognese and Emilian Schools*, London, 1994

JAFFÉ 1994B
M. Jaffé, *The Devonshire Collection of Italian Drawings. Venetian and North Italian Schools*, London, 1994

JESTAZ / BACOU 1978
B. Jestaz and R. Bacou, *Jules Romain. L'Histoire de Scipion*, Grand Palais, Paris, 1978

JOANNIDES 1983
P. Joannides, *The Drawings of Raphael with a Complete Catalogue*, Oxford, 1983

KARCHESKI 2001
W.J. Karcheski, 'Rubens's lost Negroli helmet painted by Bartholomeus Breenbergh and others', *Apollo*, CLIII, 2001, pp.28–33

KAUFFMANN 1976
H. Kauffmann, 'Rubens und Mantegna' in *Peter Paul Rubens: Bildegedanke und kunstlerische Form, Aufsätze und Reden*, Berlin, 1976, pp.17–31

KIESER 1931
E. Kieser, 'Tizians und spaniens Einwirkungen auf die späteren Landshaften des Rubens', *Münchner Jahrbuch der bildenden Kunst*, VIII, 1931, pp.281–91

KNAUER 1969
E.R. Knauer, 'Leda', *Jahrbuch der Berliner Museen*, XI, 1969, pp.5–35

KNOWSLEY 1802
Catalogue of Paintings at Knowsley Hall, taken in 1801, Liverpool, 1802

LAWRENCE-INVENTORY
Inventory of the Collection of Drawings by Old Masters Formed by Sir Thomas Lawrence, P.R.A., drawn up while the Collection was still in his House (duplicated typescript; National Art Library, Victoria and Albert Museum, London, 86 W 39)

LIGHTBOWN 1986
R. Lightbown, *Mantegna with a Complete Catalogue of the Paintings, Drawings and Prints*, Oxford, 1986

LIND 1946
L.R. Lind, 'The Latin Life of Peter Paul Rubens by his Nephew Philip. A Translation', *Art Quarterly*, IX, 1946, pp.37–44

LONDON / PARIS / BERN / BRUSSELS 1972
Flemish Drawings of the Seventeenth Century from the Collection of Frits Lugt, Institut Néerlandais, Paris; Victoria and Albert Museum, London; Institut Néerlandais, Paris; Kunstmuseum, Bern and Royal Library of Belgium, Brussels, 1972

LOGAN 1976–8
A.-M. Logan, 'Some Early Drawings by Rubens', *Gentse bijdragen tot de Kunstgeschiedenis*, XXIV, 1976–8, pp.105–12

LOGAN 1977
A.-M. Logan, 'Rubens Exhibitions 1977–78', *Master Drawings*, XV, 1977, pp.403–17

LOGAN 1978
A.-M. Logan, 'Rubens Exhibitions 1978', *Master Drawings*, XVI, 1978, pp.419–50

LOGAN 1983
A.-M. Logan, Review of Julius S. Held, *The Oil Sketches of Peter Paul Rubens. A Critical Catalogue*, *Master Drawings*, XXI, 1983, pp.412–17

LOGAN 1987
A.-M. Logan, 'Review of Julius S. Held, *Rubens. Selected Drawings*', *Master Drawings*, XXV, 1987, pp.63–82

LOGAN 1999
A.-M. Logan, 'Rubens' Design for Pontius' Engraving of the "Assumption of the Virgin"', *Master Drawings*, XXXVII, 1999, pp.231–7

LOGAN / HAVERKAMP-BEGEMANN 1978
A.-M. Logan and E. Haverkamp-Begeman[n], 'Dessins de Rubens', *Revue de l'art*, no.42, 1978, pp.89–99

LUGT 1949
F. Lugt, *École flamande, Musée du Louvre, Inventaire Général des dessins des Écoles du Nord*, 2 vols., Paris, 1949

LUZIO 1913
A. Luzio, *La Galleria dei Gonzaga venduta all'Inghilterra nel 1627–28. Documenti degli archivi di Mantova e Londra raccolta ed illustrati*, Milan, 1913

MADRID 1987
Rubens copista de Tiziano, Museo del Prado, Madrid, 1987

MCALLISTER JOHNSON 1965
W. McAllister Johnson, 'Pictures from the School of Fontainebleau in Seventeenth-Century Guise', *Art Quarterly*, XXVIII, 1965, pp.293–304

MCGRATH 1997
E. McGrath, *Rubens. Subjects from History* (*Corpus Rubenianum Ludwig Burchard*, XIII, 1), 2 vols., London, 1997

MCTAVISH 1981
D. McTavish, *Giuseppe Porta called Giuseppe Salviati*, New York and London, 1981

MANTUA 1977
G. Mulazzani, *et al. Rubens a Mantova*, Palazzo Ducale, Mantua, 1977

MANTUA 1989
Giulio Romano, Palazzo Te; Palazzo Ducale, Mantua, 1989

MANTUA 2001
Perino del Vaga tra Raffaello e Michelangelo, Palazzo Te, Mantua, 2001

MARABOTTINI 1969
A. Marabottini, *Polidoro da Caravaggio*, 2 vols., Rome, 1969

MARIETTE 1741
P.-J. Mariette, *Description sommaire des desseins des grands maistres d'Italie, des Pays-Bas et de France, du Cabinet de feu M. Crozat. Avec des réflexions sur la manière de dessiner des principaux peintres*, Paris, 1741

MARIETTE 1851–60
Abécédario de P.J. Mariette et autres notes inédites de cet amateur sur les arts et les artistes (eds.) P. de Chennevières and A. de Montaiglon (*Archives de l'art français*), 6 vols., Paris, 1851–60

MARIJINISSEN 1959
R.H. Marijnissen, *Het da Vinci-Doek van de Abdij van Tongerlo*, Tongerlo, 1959

MARTIN 1970
G. Martin, *The Flemish School, circa 1600–circa 1900*, National Gallery, London, 1970

MASSARI 1993
S. Massari, *Giulio Romano pinxit et delineavit. Opere grafiche autografe di collaborazione e bottega*, Fruttiere di Palazzo Te, Mantua, 1993

MEIJ 2001
A.W.F.M. Meij, with M. de Haan, *Rubens, Jordaens, Van Dyck and their Circle. Flemish Master Drawings from the Museum Boijmans van Beuningen*, Rotterdam, 2001

MICHEL 1771
J.F.M. Michel, *Histoire de la vie de P.P. Rubens, Chevalier, & Seigneur de Steen, illustrée d'Anecdotes, qui n'ont jamais paru au public, & de ses tableaux étatés dans les palais, eglises & places publiques de l'Europe: & par la démonstration des Estampes existantes & relatives à ses Ouvrages*, Brussels, 1771

MIELKE / WINNER 1977
H. Mielke and M. Winner, *Peter Paul Rubens. Kritischer Katalog der Zeichnungen, Originale, Umkreis, Kopien (Die Zeichnungen Alter Meister im Berliner Kupferstichkabinett)*, Berlin, 1977

MILLAR 1958–60
O. Millar (ed.), 'Abraham van der Doort's Catalogue of the Collections of Charles I', *Walpole Society*, XXXVII, 1958–60

MILLAR 1970–2
O. Millar (ed.), 'The Inventories and Valuations of the King's Goods, 1649–1651', *Walpole Society*, XLIII, 1970–2

MITSCH 1977
[E. Mitsch], *Die Rubenszeichnungen der Albertina zum 400. Geburtstag*, Graphische Sammlung Albertina, Vienna, 1977

MITSCH 1983
E. Mitsch, *Raphael in der Albertina aus anlass des 500. geburtstages des Künstlers*, Graphische Sammlung Albertina, Vienna, 1983

MONBEIG-GOGUEL 1972
C. Monbeig-Goguel, *Maîtres toscans nés après 1500, morts avant 1600: Vasari et son temps, Musée du Louvre, Cabinet des Dessins, Inventaire Général des dessins italiens*, I, Paris, 1972

MONBEIG-GOGUEL 1999
C. Monbeig-Goguel, 'Mantua, Vienna and London: Drawings by Raphael and his Circle', *The Burlington Magazine*, CXLI, 1999, pp.495–9

MORTARI 1992
L. Mortari, *Francesco Salviati*, Rome, 1992

MULLER 1989
J.M. Muller, *Rubens. The Artist as Collector*, Princeton, N.J., 1989

MÜLLER HOFSTEDE 1962
J. Müller Hofstede, 'Opmerkingen bij enige tekeningen van Rubens in het Museum Boymans-van Beuningen', *Bulletin Museum Boymans-van Beuningen*, XIII, 1962, pp.86–118

MÜLLER HOFSTEDE 1964
J. Müller Hofstede, 'An Early Rubens *Conversion of St Paul*. The Beginning of his Preoccupation with Leonardo's *Battle of Anghiari*', *The Burlington Magazine*, CVI, 1964, pp.95–106

MÜLLER HOFSTEDE 1965
J. Müller Hofstede, 'Beiträge zum zeichnerischen Werk von Rubens', *Wallraf-Richartz-Jahrbuch*, XXVII, 1965, pp.259–356

MÜLLER HOFSTEDE 1966
J. Müller Hofstede, Review of L. Burchard and R.-A. d'Hulst, *Rubens Drawings*, *Master Drawings*, IV, 1966, pp.435–54

MÜLLER HOFSTEDE 1967
J. Müller Hofstede, 'Rubens und Tizian: Das Bild Karls V', *Münchner Jahrbuch der bildenden Kunst*, XVIII, 1967, pp.33–96

NANCY 1990
La Transfiguration de Rubens, Musée des Beaux-Arts, Nancy, 1990

NEW YORK 1999
Giulio Romano. Master Designer, An Exhibition of Drawings in Celebration of the Five Hundredth Anniversary of his Birth (ed.) J. Cox-Rearick, The Bertha and Karl Leubsdorf Art Gallery, Hunter College of the City University of New York, New York, 1999

OBERHUBER 1962
K. Oberhuber, 'Vorzeichnungen zu Raffaels 'Transfiguration', *Jahrbuch der Berliner Museen*, IV, 1962, pp.116–49

OBERHUBER 1972
K. Oberhuber, [O. Fischel] *Raphaels Zeichnungen*, IX, *Entwürfe zu werken Raphaels und seiner Schule im Vatikan 1511/12 bis 1520*, Berlin, 1972

OLSEN 1962
H. Olsen, *Federico Barocci*, Copenhagen, 1962

ORSO 1986
S.N. Orso, *Philip IV and the Decoration of the Alcázar of Madrid*, Princeton, N.J., 1986

OXFORD / LONDON 1988
Rubens in Oxford. An Exhibition of Drawings from Christ Church and the Ashmolean Museum, The Picture Gallery, Christ Church, Oxford and P. & D. Colnaghi & Co. Ltd, London, 1988

PACHECO 1649
F. Pacheco, *Arte de la Pintura, su antiguedad, y grandezas*, Seville, 1649

PANOFSKY 1969
E. Panofsky, *Problems in Titian. Mostly Iconographic, The Wrightsman Lectures*, II, London and New York, 1969

PARIS 1972–3
L'École de Fontainebleau, Grand Palais, Paris, 1972–3

PARIS 1977–8
Collections de Louis XIV. Dessins, albums, manuscrits, Orangerie des Tuileries, Paris, 1977–8

PARIS 1983–4
Raphael dans les collections françaises, Galeries nationales du Grand Palais, Paris, 1983–4

PARIS 1993
Le siècle de Titien. L'âge d'or de la peinture à Venise, Grand Palais, Paris, 1993

PARKER 1929
K.T. Parker, 'Unpublished Drawings by Rubens in the Victoria and Albert Museum', *Old Master Drawings*, IV, no.14, 1929, pp.17–20

PARKER 1956
K.T. Parker, *Italian Schools, Catalogue of the Collection of Drawings in the Ashmolean Museum*, II, 2 vols., Oxford, 1956

PERICOLI RIDOLFINI 1960
[C. Pericoli Ridolfini], *Le case romane con facciate graffite e dipinte*, Amici dei musei di Roma; Palazzo Braschi, Rome, 1960

PHILLIPS [1930]
C.J. Phillips, *History of the Sackville Family (Earls and Dukes of Dorset) together with a description of Knole, early owners of Knole and a Catalogue Raisonné of the Pictures and Drawings at Knole*, 2 vols., London, Toronto, Melbourne and Sydney, n.d. [1930]

PILES 1699
R. de Piles, *Abregé de la vie des Peintres, avec des reflexions sur leurs ouvrages, et un Traité du Peintre parfait, de la connoissance des Desseins, & de l'utilité des Estampes*, Paris, 1699

PILO 1988
G.M. Pilo, 'Rubens e il Pordenone. La prova di un soggiorno precoce del pittore fiammingo a Venezia', *Arte Documento. Rivista di Storia e tutela dei Beni Culturali*, no.2, 1988, pp.116–23

POPE HENNESSY [1970]
J. Pope Hennessy, *Raphael* (*The Wrightsman Lectures delivered under the auspices of the New York University, Institute of Fine Arts*, V), London, n.d. [1970]

POPHAM 1927
A.E. Popham, 'An Orley drawing retouched by Rubens', *Old Master Drawings*, I, no.4, March 1927, pp.45–7

POPHAM / POUNCEY 1950
A.E. Popham and P. Pouncey, *The Fourteenth and Fifteenth Centuries, Italian Drawings in the Department of Prints and Drawings in the British Museum*, 2 vols., London, 1950

POPHAM / WILDE 1949
A.E. Popham and J. Wilde, *The Italian Drawings of the XV and XVI Centuries in the Collection of His Majesty the King at Windsor Castle*, London, 1949

POUNCEY / GERE 1962
P. Pouncey and J.A. Gere, *Raphael and his Circle, Italian Drawings in the Department of Prints and Drawings in the British Museum*, 2 vols., London, 1962

PY 2001
B. Py, *Everhard Jabach Collectionneur (1618–1695). Les dessins de l'inventaire de 1695, Notes et Documents des musées de France*, 36, Paris, 2001

RAVELLI 1978
L. Ravelli, *Polidoro Caldara da Caravaggio, Monumenta Bergomensia*, XLVIII, Bergamo, 1978

REISET 1866
F. Reiset, *Notice des dessins, cartons, pastels, miniatures et émaux exposés dans les salles du 1er étage au Musée Impérial du Louvre, Première partie: Écoles d'Italie, Écoles allamande, flamande et hollandaise...*, Paris, 1866

RICHARDSON 1719
J. Richardson, *Two Discourses*, I. *An Essay on the whole Art of Criticism as it relates to Painting* ..., II. *An Argument in behalf of the Science of a Connoisseur*, London, 1719

RICHARDSON 1747
A Catalogue of the Genuine and Entire Collection of Italian and other Drawings, Prints, Models, and Casts, of the late Eminent Mr. Jonathan Richardson, Painter, Deceas'd. Which will be sold by Auction, by Mr. Cock, at his House in the Great Piazza, Covent-Garden, on Thursday the 22d of January, 1746–7, and the Seventeen following Nights, (Sundays excepted), London, 1747

RIDOLFI 1914–24
C. Ridolfi, *Le maraviglie dell'arte ovvero le vite degli illustri pittori veneti e dello stato*, (ed.) D. von Hadeln, 2 vols., Berlin, 1914–24

ROBERTSON / WHISTLER 1996
C. Robertson and C. Whistler, *Drawings by the Carracci from British Collections*, Ashmolean Museum, Oxford, 1996

ROBINSON 1869
J.C. Robinson, *Descriptive Catalogue of the Drawings by the Old Masters, forming the Collection of John Malcolm of Poltalloch, Esq.*, London, 1869

ROOSES 1886–92
M. Rooses, *L'oeuvre de P.P. Rubens: Histoire et description de ses tableaux et dessins*, 5 vols., Antwerp, 1886–92

ROOSES 1904
M. Rooses, *Rubens*, 2 vols., London, 1904

ROOSES 1910
M. Rooses, 'Oeuvre de Rubens: Addenda et Corrigenda', *Bulletin-Rubens (Annales de la Commission officielle instituée par le Conseil communal de la ville d'Anvers pour la publication des documents relatifs à la vie et aux oeuvres de Rubens*, V), 1910, pp.69–102; 172–204; 279–330

ROOSES / RUELENS 1887–1909
Correspondance de Rubens et documents épistolaires concernant sa vie et ses oeuvres, (ed.) C. Ruelens and M. Rooses, 6 vols., Antwerp, 1887–1909

ROWLANDS 1977
J. Rowlands, *Rubens Drawings and Sketches. Catalogue of an Exhibition at the Department of Prints and Drawings in the British Museum, 1977*, London, 1977

SACKVILLE WEST 1906
L. Sackville West, *Knole House: Its State Rooms, Pictures and Antiquities*, Sevenoaks, 1906

SCHARF 1875
Sir G. Scharf, *A Descriptive and Historical Catalogue of the Collection of Pictures at Knowsley Hall*, London, 1875

SCHÉLE 1965
S. Schéle, *Cornelis Bos. A Study of the Origins of the Netherland Grotesque (Acta Universitatis Stockholmiensis, Stockholm Studies in History of Art*, 10), Stockholm, 1965

SCHUCKMAN 1993
C. Schuckman, *Lucas Vorsterman I, Hollstein's Dutch and Flemish Engravings and Woodcuts, 1450–1700*, XLIII (ed.) D. de Hoop Scheffer, Roosendaal, 1993

SEILERN 1955
A. Seilern, *Flemish Paintings and Drawings at 56 Princes Gate, London, SW7*, 2 vols., London, 1955

SEILERN 1969
A. Seilern, *Flemish Paintings and Drawings at 56 Princes Gate, London, SW7*, London, 1969

SEILERN 1971
A. Seilern, *Corrigenda and Addenda to the Catalogue of Paintings at 56 Princes Gate, London, SW7*, London, 1971

SÉRULLAZ 1978
[A. Sérullaz], *Rubens, ses maîtres, ses elévès, dessins du Musée du Louvre*, Cabinet des Dessins, Musée du Louvre, Paris, 1978

SHOEMAKER / BROUN 1981
I.H. Shoemaker and E. Broun, *The Engravings of Marcantonio Raimondi*, The Spencer Museum of Art, University of Kansas, Lawrence; The Ackland Art Museum, University of North Carolina, Chapel Hill; The Wellesley College Art Museum, Wellesley, Massachusetts, 1981–2; Lawrence, Kansas, 1981

SLAVÍČEK 1991
L. Slavíček in *P.P. Rubens (1577–1640)*, Retretti Art Centre, Punkaharju, Finland, 1991

VON SONNENBURG 1979
H. von Sonnenburg, 'Rubens' Bildaufbau und Technik', *Maltechnik-Restauro*, nos.2–3, 1979, I: 'Bildträger, Grundierung und Vorskizzierung', pp.77–100; II: 'Farbe und Auftragstechnik', pp.181–203

STEINBERG 2001
L. Steinberg, *Leonardo's incessant Last Supper*, New York, 2001

TENIERS 1660
D. Teniers, *Le Theatre des Peintures de David Teniers, Natif d'Anvers, Peintre, et Ayde de Chambre des Serenissimes Princes Leopold Guil. Archiduc, & Don Jean d'Austriche: Auquel sont Representez, Les desseins tracés de sa main, & graués en cuiure par ses soins, sur les Originaux Italiens, que le Sere Archiduc à assemblé en son Cabinet de la Cour de Brusselles*, Brussels and Antwerp, 1660

TIETZE / TIETZE-CONRAT 1944
H. Tietze and E. Tietze-Conrat, *The Drawings of the Venetian Painters in the 15th and 16th Centuries*, New York, 1944

TIETZE-CONRAT 1954
E. Tietze-Conrat, 'Un soffitto di Tiziano a Brescia conservato in un disegno del Rubens', *Arte Veneta*, VIII, 1954, pp.209–10

TOLNAY 1964
C. de Tolnay, 'L'Hercule de Michel-Ange à Fontainebleau', *Gazette des Beaux-Arts*, 6ième periode, LXIV, 1964, pp.125–40

TORONTO 1981–2
D. McTavish, K. Corey Keeble, K. Lochnan, and S. Pantazzi, *The Arts of Italy in Toronto Collections, 1300–1800, based on the holdings of the Art Gallery of Ontario, the Royal Ontario Museum and Private Collections in the Ontario Area*, Art Gallery of Ontario, Toronto, 1981–2

VAN GELDER 1965
J.G. van Gelder, 'The Triumph of Scipio by Rubens. P. Crozat Sale (1741) Lot 814', *Duits Quarterly*, no.VIII, 1965, pp.5–20

VAN HOOGSTRATEN 1678
S. van Hoogstraten, *Inleyding tot de Hooge Schoole der Schilderkonst, anders de Zichtbaere Werelt*, Rotterdam, 1678

VAN DER MEULEN 1994
M. van der Meulen, *Rubens. Copies after the Antique (Corpus Rubenianum Ludwig Burchard*, XXIII), 3 vols., London, 1994

VAN THULDEN 1633
T. Van Thulden, *Les Travaux d'Ulysse desseignez par le Sieur de Sainct Martin de la façon qu'ils se voyent dans la maison royale de Fontainebleau. Peints par le sieur Nicolas et gravez en cuivre par Theodore Van Thulden avec le subject et l'explication morale de chaque figure. Dediez à Monseigneur de Liancourt, chevalier des ordres du roi, à Paris, chez Melchior Tavernier. P. Mariette le fils excudit, 1633, cum privilegio*, Paris, 1633

VAN DEN WIJNGAERT 1940
F. van den Wijngaert, *Inventaris der Rubeniaansche Prentkunst*, Antwerp-'s-Gravenhage, 1940

VASARI 1568
G. Vasari, *Le vite de'piu eccellenti pittori, scultori, e architettori*, 3 vols., Florence, 1568

VENICE 1981
Da Tiziano a El Greco. Per la storia del Manierismo a Venezia, 1540–1590, Palazzo Ducale, Venice, 1981

VENICE / WASHINGTON 1990–1
Titian. Prince of Painters, Palazzo Ducale, Venice, 1990 and the National Gallery of Art, Washington, DC, 1990–1

VERGARA 1999
A. Vergara, *Rubens and his Spanish Patrons*, Cambridge, 1999

VERGARA 1982
L. Vergara, *Rubens and the Poetics of Landscape*, New Haven and London, 1982

VEY 1962
H. Vey, *Die Zeichnungen Anton van Dycks (Monographien des 'Nationaal Centrum voor de Plastische Kunsten van de XVIde en XVIIde Eeuw'*, I), 2 vols., Brussels, 1962

VIENNA 1977
Peter Paul Rubens, 1577–1640. Ausstellung zur 400. wiederkehr seines Geburtstages, Kunsthistorisches Museum, Vienna, 1977

VLIEGHE 1972–3
H. Vlieghe, *Saints (Corpus Rubenianum Ludwig Burchard*, VIII), 2 vols., 1972–3

VLIEGHE 1978
H. Vlieghe, Review of M. Jaffé, *Rubens and Italy*, *The Burlington Magazine*, CXX, 1978, pp.471–3

VLIEGHE 1994
H. Vlieghe, 'Erasmus Quellinus der Jüngere und Italien' in *Die Malerei Antwerpens – Gattungen, Meister, Wirkungen. Studien zur flämischen Kunst des 16. und 17. Jahrhunderts, Internationales Kolloquium Wien 1993*, (eds.) E. Mai, K. Schütz, and H. Vlieghe, Cologne, 1994, pp.217–27

VLIEGHE 2000
H. Vlieghe, 'Rubens emulating the Bruegel tradition', *The Burlington Magazine*, CXLII, 2000, pp.681–6

VOLK 1980
M. Crawford Volk, 'Rubens in Madrid and the decoration of the Salón Nuevo in the Palace', *The Burlington Magazine*, CXXII, 1980, pp.168–80

VOLK 1981
M. Crawford Volk, 'Rubens in Madrid and the decoration of the King's summer apartments', *The Burlington Magazine*, CXXIII, 1981, pp.513–29

VOLK 1983
M. Crawford Volk, 'On Rubens and Titian', *The Ringling Museum of Art Journal (Papers presented at the International Rubens Symposium, April 14–16, 1982)*, 1983, pp.140–9

VOORHELM SCHNEEVOOGT 1873
C.G. Voorhelm Schneevoogt, *Catalogue des estampes gravées d'après P.P. Rubens, avec l'indication des collections où se trouvent les tableaux et les gravures*, Haarlem, 1873

WAAGEN 1838
G.F. Waagen, *Works of Art and Artists in England*, 3 vols., London, 1838

WARNKE 1986
M. Warnke, 'Nah und Fern zum Bilde' in *Forma et subtilitas. Festschrift für Wolfgang Schöne zum 75 Geburtstag* (ed.) W. Schlink and M. Sperlich, Berlin and New York, 1986, pp.190–7

WASHINGTON 1983–4
Leonardo's 'Last Supper'. Precedents and Reflections, National Gallery of Art, Washington, 1983–4

WASHINGTON 1999–2000
The Drawings of Annibale Carracci, National Gallery of Art, Washington, 1999–2000

WETHEY 1969–75
H.E. Wethey, *The Paintings of Titian*, 3 vols., London, 1969–75

WETHEY 1987
H.E. Wethey, *Titian and his Drawings, with reference to Giorgione and some close Contemporaries (National Gallery of Art/Kress Foundation Studies in the History of European Art*, VIII), Princeton, N.J., 1987

WILDE 1957
J. Wilde, 'Notes on the Genesis of Michelangelo's Leda' in *Fritz Saxl, 1890–1948. A Volume of Memorial Essays from his Friends in England* (ed.) D.J. Gordon, London and New York, 1957, pp.270–80

WOOD 1990
J. Wood, 'Padre Resta's Flemish Drawings. Van Diepenbeeck, Van Thulden, Rubens, and the School of Fontainebleau', *Master Drawings*, XXVIII, 1990, pp.3–53

WOOD 1994
J. Wood, 'Rubens's Collection of Drawings: His Attributions and Inscriptions', *Wallraf-Richartz-Jahrbuch*, LV, 1994, pp.333–51

WOOD 1995
J. Wood, ''Damaged by Time and Rubens'. Rubens's restorations and retouchings', *Apollo*, CXLII, no.406 (new series), 1995, pp.16–23

WOOD 2000
J. Wood, 'Rubens as Thief. His use of Past Art and some Adaptations from Primaticcio' in *Concept, Design and Execution in Flemish Painting (1550–1700)* (eds.) H. Vlieghe, A. Balis, and C. Van de Velde, Turnhout, 2000, pp.153–70

ZAMBONI 1778
B.C. Zamboni, *Memorie intorno alle pubbliche fabbriche più insigni della città di Brescia*, Brescia, 1778

ZÖLLNER 1991
F. Zöllner, 'Rubens reworks Leonardo. The Fight for the Standard', *Achademia Leonardi Vinci: Journal of Leonardo Studies and Bibliography of Vinciana* (ed.) C. Pedretti, IV, 1991, pp.177–90

ZÖLLNER 1998
F. Zöllner, *La Battaglia di Anghiari di Leonardo da Vinci fra mitologia e politica (Lettura Vinciana*, XXXVII), Vinci and Florence, 1998

PETER PAUL RUBENS · A BRIEF CHRONOLOGY

28 JUNE 1577
Peter Paul Rubens was born in Seigen, Westphalia. His parents originated from Antwerp

1578
The family settled in Cologne

1587
Rubens's father died, his mother later returning to Antwerp

1591
Rubens trained in the studio of Tobias Verhaecht

1592
Studied under Adam van Noort

*c.*1594–5
Moved to studio of Otto van Veen

1598
Became a Master in the Painters' Guild of St Luke, Antwerp

9 MAY 1600
Travelled from Antwerp to Italy, first visiting Venice

*c.*1601
Engaged as court painter to the Duke of Mantua, Vincenzo I Gonzaga, perhaps through the recommendation of Archduke Albert, Regent of the Netherlands

5 OCTOBER 1600
Perhaps went to Florence with Vincenzo and his entourage to attend the marriage by proxy of Maria de' Medici (a future patron of Rubens) to Henry IV of France

LATE SUMMER 1601
Sent by Vincenzo to Rome, via Bologna, to the household of Cardinal Alessandro Montalto, nephew of Pope Sixtus V

EASTER 1602
Returned to Mantua

MARCH 1603
First diplomatic mission – sent as Vincenzo's envoy to Spain to deliver gifts to the court of Philip III at Valladolid, via Florence, Pisa and Alicante

AUTUMN 1603
Painted the equestrian portrait of the Duke of Lerma

EARLY 1604
Returned to Mantua via Genoa

AUGUST 1604–25 MAY 1605
Commissions for the Jesuit Church, Mantua

1606
Lived and worked in Rome, remaining in the service of the Gonzaga

1606–8
Worked on the high altarpiece of Santa Maria in Vallicella, the 'Chiesa Nuova' in Rome

28 OCTOBER 1608
Left Italy upon news of his mother's ill health to return home

11 NOVEMBER 1608
Arrived back in Antwerp, shortly after his mother's death

1609
Became court painter to the Regents of the Netherlands, Archduke Albert of Austria and his wife, the Infanta Isabella.
Set up his workshop in Antwerp

3 OCTOBER 1609
Married Isabella Brandt

1609–21
Rubens bought a house on the Wapper, Antwerp (now the Rubenshuis museum), finishing renovations in 1615, and added a large studio in 1618. Prolific period of artistic production such as the paintings for Antwerp Cathedral, the tapestry designs for the cycle of *Decius Mus* and series of *History of Constantine*, as well as altarpieces and sketches for ceiling paintings for Antwerp's new Jesuit church. Anthony van Dyck began to work in Rubens's studio from about 1616 and Rubens collaborated with Frans Snyders and Jan Brueghel the Elder between 1615–20

1622
Published *I Palazzi di Genova*
Was active as a diplomat from 1622/3, continuing until 1633 as a political agent for Infanta Isabella

1622–5
Worked on the large series of paintings depicting the *Life of Marie de' Medici* for the Palais de Luxembourg, Paris (now in the Louvre)

1626
Painted the *Assumption* altarpiece for Antwerp Cathedral
Death of Isabella Brandt on 20 June

1627
Diplomatic mission to the northern Netherlands

1628–29
Diplomatic mission to Spain
Made copies of works by Titian in the collection of Philip IV
Met the Spanish artist Diego Velázquez

1629–30
Diplomatic mission to England
Knighted by Charles I
Worked on ceiling of the Banqueting Hall at Whitehall

1630
Returned to Antwerp
Married 16 year-old Helena Fourment on 9 December

1631
Diplomatic mission to the Northern Netherlands

1634
Oversaw the production of decorations for the *Pompa Introitus Ferdinandii*, the triumphal entry of Cardinal-Infante Ferdinand into Antwerp, supervising the designs worked on by many colleagues and assistants

1635
Purchased the Castle of Steen, Elewijt, outside Antwerp

1636
From this year, directed the production of works for large commission for the Torre de la Parada for Philip IV of Spain

1639
Rubens became gravely ill, making his will on 16 December. Work in progress in his studio was finished by Jacob Jordaens and others

30 MAY 1640
Rubens died in Antwerp

2 JUNE 1640
Buried in the St Jacobuskerk in Antwerp

PHOTOGRAPHIC CREDITS

Photo: Artothek, fig.9

© Ashmolean Museum, Oxford, cat.no.28

Prudence Cuming Associates, London, fig.4

Reproduced by permission of the Duke of Devonshire and the Chatsworth Settlement Trustees. Photo: Photographic Survey, Courtauld Institute of Art, cat.nos.7, 58, 64, 73

Photo: © Ursula Edelmann, fig.17

© Fitzwilliam Museum, University of Cambridge, cat.no.61

Fellows of Harvard College, cat.no.8

Louvre, D.A.G. Photo: RMN, Michèle Bellot, cat.nos.1, 20, 21, 23, 46, and figs.12, 13

Louvre, D.A.G. Photo: RMN, J. G. Berizzi, cat.nos.15, 16, 25, 42, 75 and fig.6

© The National Gallery, London, fig.11

Board of Trustees of the National Museums and Galleries on Merseyside (Walker Art Gallery), cat.nos.11, 70

© National Gallery of Scotland, cat.nos.19, 52, 62

Collection of the Earl of Pembroke, Wilton House, Wiltshire / Bridgeman Art Library, fig.19

National Trust Photographic Library. Photo: John Hammond, cat.no.54

Antonia Reeve, fig.8

© V&A Picture Library, cat.nos.68, 76